Losing
our Religion?

Changing Patterns of Believing
and Belonging in Secular Western Societies

Kevin R. Ward

WIPF & STOCK · Eugene, Oregon

LOSING OUR RELIGION?
Changing Patterns of Believing and Belonging in Secular Western Societies

Copyright © 2013 Kevin R. Ward. All rights reserved. Except for brief quotations in critical publications or reviews, no part of this book may be reproduced in any manner without prior written permission from the publisher. Write: Permissions, Wipf and Stock Publishers, 199 W. 8th Ave., Suite 3, Eugene, OR 97401.

Wipf & Stock
An Imprint of Wipf and Stock Publishers
199 W. 8th Ave., Suite 3
Eugene, OR 97401

www.wipfandstock.com

ISBN 13: 978-1-62032-411-0

Manufactured in the U.S.A.

Losing our Religion?

To Simon, Scott, and Kirsten, whose journeys in life and faith have kept me thinking about how religion continues to adapt to the changing societies we inhabit.

Contents

Preface | ix

1. Are we Losing our Religion? | 1
2. Religion in a Post-Aquarian Age | 12
3. Changing Patterns of Church Life | 32
4. A Terminus Quo for the Mainline? | 53
5. The Charismatic Movement and the Churches | 70
6. Emerging from the Shadow of Christendom | 88
7. Is the Future Churchless? | 109
8. Being the Church in a Fragmented World | 138
9. It Might be Emerging but is it Church? | 161
10. Migration and the Future of Christianity | 184
11. Sport and Religion: Lens or Threat? | 204
12. Religion Beyond the Boundaries | 225

Bibliography | 251

Preface

FOR MUCH OF THE twentieth century secularization theorists asserted that religion must inevitably decline in the modern world. Some predicted its ultimate demise as the sure and certain findings of reason and science put an end to the superstition and myth that constituted religion. Some were slightly more generous, and rather than forecasting religion's complete disappearance expected it to continue, but only in the lives of a small and beleaguered minority. As we moved into the current century, however, it became increasingly clear that much of the world was as religious as ever, and that religion was making a comeback in the most unlikely of places, such as post-communist Russia and China and, most surprisingly, in many secularized Western countries.

This book is not primarily about the secularization thesis and its shortcomings, but it does provide the backdrop to the story it seeks to tell, as it looks at the changing location and forms of religion in contemporary Western societies. In particular, it does so using the concepts of believing and belonging, and examining the relationship between these. In most Western societies there is no doubt that religious belonging has declined in recent decades, by whatever measure is used. It was mainly through investigating this data that support was given for secularization theorists. However, over the last decade of the twentieth century researchers began to focus increasingly on collecting and analyzing data on religious believing as a separate variable. They found that it remained at surprisingly high levels, and even showed some indications of increasing. Previously it was largely assumed that the two (believing and belonging) went together, and that believing depended on belonging. Can believing be sustained without belonging? If it can, does it remain the same? If it is not maintained and passed on by institutions (through belonging), what other forms might be mediating it? If, in fact, "believing without belonging" is increasing, what does this mean for the future of churches? These are some of the themes this book explores.

The book analyzes comparative data and studies on the changing patterns of religious belonging and believing over the past five decades, in five Western countries—the United Kingdom, the United States, Canada, Australia, and New Zealand. It is argued that, while there are various particularities in each case, the general trends demonstrate considerable similarity. The major focus is New Zealand and most of the examples are taken from there, primarily because that is where I live and do my research. At the same time, in my travels in all of these countries, meeting and being generously hosted by academics while presenting papers at various conferences, or spending time on study leave in some of their institutions, I have come to see that New Zealand provides a helpful window through which to view some of the general trends. I have discovered that academics in northern hemisphere countries tend to know a great deal about what is happening religiously in their own continent, but not so much about the other side of the Atlantic, and I have been at times a conduit in bringing the two together in conversation.

One of the advantages of being a small country like New Zealand, distant from where the "real" action is yet influenced by what happens there, is that we tend to have an internationalist outlook. Settled by colonists from the U.K. but without an established church, and heavily influenced by the U.S. since World War II, we have been shaped by trends coming from both societies, and so share similarities and differences with each.

I was an interested listener to a paper presented by the German sociologist Christof Wolf at a Sociology of Religion conference in Leipzig in 2006.[1] He had been researching the degree of secularization in Germany, and presented comparative data from other countries to do so. Unlike many studies in this area, he split his data into two categories—those indicating religious believing on the one hand, and religious belonging on the other. In his framework New Zealand sat approximately in the middle of the scale measuring degree of secularization, with the U.S. less so and the U.K. more so. Whereas the U.S. connected religious believing strongly with religious believing, and in the U.K. believing was relatively disconnected from belonging, New Zealand sat somewhere near the

1. See Wolf, "How Secularised is Germany?"

preface xi

middle. This suggested another reason why the New Zealand case may provide some helpful windows into trends in other Western societies.

The book begins by examining comparative data from these five countries which indicate how church-going patterns have changed. It looks at reasons for declining church attendance, how churches have responded to these changes, and why some churches have shown resiliency in this changing context. The findings from the research on which this section is based indicate that the most significant factor accounting for decline is the impact on church life of the cultural and social changes that have occurred since the 1960s, rather than being the result of loss of religious believing itself. Church decline, however, has not been universal or even, and the way in which particular churches have responded to these changes has been a major factor in determining the degree of resilience they have shown in this period of overall decline. The factors that have contributed to decline or vitality are explored through particular congregational examples.

Chapters 4 to 7 explore some of the challenges and possible outcomes which these changes might suggest for churches. The churches that have suffered the most dramatic decline are the historic mainline Protestant churches. Do the trends, and in particular the dramatic aging of these churches, suggest that while other churches might continue, their future seems to include a "full stop" which is coming ever closer? During this time of the decline of mainline churches, the charismatic movement seemed to bring growth and vitality to other churches. Does this suggest a way ahead, or is it a movement that is now also ebbing away and, like the mainline, is still tied to forms of belonging and practice that are increasingly outmoded?

This work suggests that the forms of church found in both of these expressions are still largely those which were formed in Christendom, and while these served the church well for some centuries they are no longer doing so, and churches need to be freed from those constraints. Finally, given these trends of declining levels of belonging for most forms of church, yet continuing high levels of believing, does this indicate that while religion may well continue in the essential meaning of the word, its future may in fact be churchless?

Several different ways of forming church in response to these changes are examined in chapters 8 to 10. If the comprehensive parish church model of Christendom is indeed largely obsolete, how do we form churches in the fragmented pluralized world which most of us now inhabit? Many argue for developing churches which gather together people in a particular socio-cultural fragment of society. We investigate some of the pragmatic and social science factors arguing for this, and explore some of the ways in which these might be worked out.

The Emerging Church movement, which can be seen as one particular expression of this trend, is then examined. At the heart of the questions raised by this understanding of church is that of the relationship between church and culture. To what extent should our expressions of church be shaped by our cultural context, and to what extent are there theological constants that should override or constrain some of those expressions? The next chapter looks at the impact which the high levels of immigration into Western countries is having on religious life, and in particular on Christianity. Most of the recent growth of churches in countries like New Zealand has been among immigrants, resulting in new immigrant churches. What is the long-term future for these churches and, as with the Emerging Church, how should they be engaged with from a theological or gospel perspective?

The final two chapters explore how religion, despite this institutional decline, still continues to play a significant and ongoing role in society, and how it is sustained and mediated in a multiplicity of diffuse cultural forms. The first looks at the relationship of sport and religion, suggesting that sport itself has undergone similar changes to religion, and that these changes might offer some indications of the directions in which changes in the forms of religious belonging might go.

The final chapter looks at a variety of other ways in which religion is expressed and carried in our societies. In the first instance, these provide ongoing evidence that religion is indeed alive and well in most secularized Western societies, often outside of those institutions where it was formerly located. At the same time, at least in New Zealand, religion is not completely institutionally disconnected, with religious institutions playing at least occasional roles in the lives of individuals and in community occasions. This raises a question regarding how churches respond to these trends in order to make stronger connections between the religious believing that exists and the belonging they wish to offer.

I have written this book with various people in mind. Broadly it is intended for anyone concerned about the place and future of Christianity and the Christian Church in Western societies, such as New Zealand. This includes church leaders, teachers and students of theology, those working in mission agencies, and religious researchers. The risk is that I end up pleasing no one: academics may find it a bit too broad and even colloquial in language at times, while the general reader may find the language a bit too technical at other times. My hope is that there is something for everyone: a combination of solid sociological research, cultural analysis, theological reflection, and practical missiological and ecclesiological concerns. There is a great need to bring the academic and practical together in ways that are helpful to church leaders, and it is in the service of this goal that I have aimed most of my more recent work. Above all, I have written for those concerned for the future of the Christian faith, in which I believe the church will continue to have a critical role.

The earliest part of the book draws on my own doctoral research, which changed my perception and understanding of the challenges facing Christianity in Western societies, as I sought answers as to why my generation (baby boomers) had deserted the church in droves. It was only the beginning of a journey that has continued in the years since. Some of the material here has been presented at academic conferences in various countries, and I am grateful for discussions with many colleagues who have helped to develop and sharpen my thinking over the years. Other insights have come out of material I have developed for teaching my students, who are increasingly two generations removed from me, and I am indebted to their ongoing questions, challenges, and insights. Still other material has initially been developed in preparation for presentations in seminars or papers for church leaders, and I am grateful for the practical concerns and insights they have raised in the journey. If this book helps any of those groups in their ongoing work I will be satisfied that it has fulfilled a worthwhile purpose.

1

Are We Losing Our Religion?

IN 1966, SHORTLY BEFORE the Beatles began a tour of the United States, an interview with John Lennon was published in a popular music magazine in which he stated: "Christianity will go. It will vanish and shrink. I needn't argue about that; I'm right and I'll be proved right. We're more popular than Jesus now."[1] The Beatles, and Lennon in particular, had by this stage become virtual spokespersons for the post-war generation and the comment caused an outcry across the country. Lennon survived the acrimony which erupted, and after the break-up of the band had an enormous solo hit with the song *Imagine*, which pictured a world from which religion had indeed vanished. About twenty years later REM, speaking for the generation which followed, also had a huge hit with their song *Losing my Religion*. It seems that "losing our religion" was a theme which resonated with young people in the later decades of the twentieth century.

In contrast to the attention given to popular music, the media in New Zealand has paid scant regard to the topic of religion over the past thirty or so years. When it has, it has by and large followed the lead of these songs. Baby Boomers and GenerationXers have indeed been "losing my religion," and seem to believe that the world will be a better place,

---

1. The remark caused a storm of protests and Beatles record burning events in the U.S. It had some months earlier been published in a two-page article in the UK. There it was not even highlighted and caused little comment, whereas in the U.S. it became the headline for the article. Both this treatment by the publishers and the different responses illustrate the divergent religious contexts of the two countries in the post-war world. A good account of this issue can be found in Turner, *Gospel According to the Beatles*, 18–36.

2 losing our religion?

as Lennon suggested, when there is indeed "no religion." New Zealand's most prominent weekly magazine, *The Listener*, has in recent years, in a nod to the religious dimension of Christmas, featured in its festive copy each year some reflection on the state of religion and the churches in New Zealand. In its final edition of the twentieth century its lead article was entitled "Faith in the Future: Searching for Jesus Christ at Christmas."

> Over 50 years, the expression may have grown sharper, the message more urgent, but the conclusion is inescapable: you can see the end of Christianity from here, 2000 years after the birth of Christ . . . Consult all the statistics and all the data—falling church attendance figures, the growing absence of 'Christian' on census returns—and the news is bad and worsening for the Christian mainstream.
>
> What are we witnessing? Not the death of spirituality, not the death of belief, not the death of meaning, but the death of religious institutions, the death of organised religion, the erosion of Christianity's historical core, its hold on the heart of the West . . . It is the death of Christendom, says theologian Lloyd Geering.[2]

Lloyd Geering[3] has probably commanded more media attention in New Zealand over this period than all the other religious commentators combined. He has consistently espoused this line, and for most of the period the available data seemed to provide support for it. More recently, when the most recent New Zealand census data were published in 2007,[4] headlines in leading newspaper ran such lines as "Christian Church Withering," "Pakeha[5] Quit Traditional Churches 'in Big Numbers,'" and "Churches on Slippery Slope." One ran an editorial under the title "Withering Belief," stating that "the nation is undergoing what amounts to a revolution in belief . . . symbolised by Christianity's fast decline into what may soon be minority status."[6] The editorial went on to suggest that when

---

2. Matthews, "The Afterlife," 17.

3. Geering will be referred to a number of times in this work. In the 1960s he was the Principal of the Theological Hall for the Presbyterian Church. In 1969 he was tried for heresy by the Presbyterian Church. He was found not guilty but left to take up a position in religious studies at Victoria University. Rather than furthering the cause of Christianity in New Zealand he is seen by evangelicals and other conservatives as the individual most responsible for its decline in New Zealand.

4. *Census of Population and Dwellings*, 2006.

5. The term the indigenous Maori population uses for European New Zealanders.

6. "Withering Belief," A-8.

that occurs New Zealand will have lost a "defining characteristic that has prevailed since the arrival of the missionaries in the early 19th century." Over those 200 years Christianity "moulded culture and the institutions" so that we became, at least nominally, a Christian country.

Easter is also a time when the media chooses to focus on religion in society and in 2013, anticipating the results of census data currently being analyzed,[7] the *Christchurch Press* ran such an article, under the heading "Are we Losing our Religion to Modern Life?" Picking up the theme that has dominated the city's story for the past two years—the destruction caused by the 2010 and 2011 earthquakes—it began: "Christchurch's churches have taken a bit of a battering over the past few years, with many lying broken and in pieces. And it seems the state of faith in the city has taken a hit too. The number of Christians in Christchurch is dropping, while those identifying as non-religious is steadily on the rise."[8]

The story of Christianity's 200 years in New Zealand is of course a relatively brief one, and one might make a case that it was never deeply embedded here. This kind of speculation, however, has not been limited to New Zealand. In almost all Western countries the influence and significance of the Christian church has been in decline since the beginning of the modern period; in many of those societies it has been present for over well over a thousand years. In England, for example (the country from which Christianity arrived in New Zealand), the number of people attending church has dropped steadily over the past one hundred and fifty years, from a time when 40 percent of the population attended church weekly in 1871 to the point where, by 2005, it was under 7 per cent.[9]

In Canada weekly church attendance of 60 percent in 1945 had dropped to 40 percent by 1970, 23 percent by 1990,[10] and 17 percent by 2006, with suggestions it may reach close to 10 percent by 2015.[11] In Australia 44 percent of the population in 1950 claimed to attend church at least monthly. This was still 41 percent in 1961, but by 1980 had declined to 24 per cent. Attendance stabilized in the 1980s but continued to

---

7. In New Zealand a census is carried out every five years. Normally this would have been done in 2011 but the data was lost because one of the buildings destroyed in the 2011 earthquake was that of the Department of Statistics.

8. "Are we Losing our Religion to Modern Life," 24.

9. Brierley, *Pulling out of the Nose Dive*, 227.

10. Bibby, "Religion in the Canadian 1990s," 279.

11. Coggins, "The State of the Canadian Church."

decline in the 1990s,[12] and by 2006 it was estimated that weekly church attendance amounted to only 7.5 percent of the population,[13] with monthly attendance estimated to be about 15 per cent.

The United States has shown some degree of exception. Finke and Stark have shown that whereas in 1860 37 percent of the population belonged to a church, by 1952 this had reached 59 percent.[14] However, there also been decline in the U.S. since the mid-1960s. Robert Putnam, after analyzing five independent survey archives, concludes that they show "a decline in church attendance of roughly one-third between the late 1950s and the late 1990s, with more than half of the total decline occurring in the 1960s."[15] Weekly church attendance in 1958 was indicated by 49 percent of the population, but by 1972 this had declined to 40 per cent,[16] and by 2000 to 30 per cent,[17] although the real figure of actual attendance may be somewhat lower than that indicated by polls.[18]

In short, figures indicate continuing overall decline in Christian identity and church attendance, and Dianne Butler Bass, surveying a range of data, concludes that "religious patterns in the United States are beginning to resemble those of other Western industrialized countries and no longer indicate the American sort of exceptionalism boasted about by previous generations."[19] Indeed, in 2009 *Newsweek* based its cover article on recent survey data and headlined it "The End of Christian America."[20] And in 2011 sociologist Mark Chaves claimed that "The evidence for a decades-long decline in American religiosity is now incontrovertible."[21]

In New Zealand, long-term patterns are much more difficult to pinpoint because of inconsistent and variable patterns of surveying. Church attendance has never been particularly high. The 1881 census indicated that approximately 20 percent of the population attended church weekly,

---

12. Kaldor, et al., *Build My Church*.
13. Powell and Jacka, "Moving Beyond Forty Years."
14. Finke and Stark, *The Churching of America*, 9.
15. Putnam, *Bowling Alone*, 71.
16. Gallup and Castelli, *The People's Religion*, 24–31.
17. Wuthnow, *All in Sync*, 3.
18. Methods using head counts have consistently arrived at a figure of 22–24 per cent. See Hadaway, Marler, and Chaves, "What the Polls Don't Show," 741–52; Marler and Hadaway, "Testing the Attendance Gap," 175–86.
19. Bass, *Christianity after Religion*, 16.
20. *Newsweek*, April 4, 2009.
21. Chaves, "The Decline of American Religion,"

and in the 1896 census 29 per cent, the highest recorded figure.[22] There are indications of some decline in the first decades of the twentieth century, and Hugh Jackson suggests that by 1926 church attendance was around 20 percent again,[23] a figure sustained until 1960. By the end of the 1970s this appears to have declined to about 16 per cent,[24] by 1990 to about 13 per cent,[25] and by 2000 to about 10 per cent.[26]

The 1991, 1999, and 2008 ISSP Surveys in New Zealand[27] revealed that the 20 percent who attended weekly for the first six decades of the century now did so monthly. In the census returns in 1926,[28] only 7 percent of the population did not indicate a religious affiliation that could be defined as Christian. In 1961 the figure had shown only a slight increase to 10.9 per cent, but by 2006 this had risen dramatically to 44 per cent. In 1960 there were 169,000 children on the rolls of Sunday Schools in New Zealand Protestant churches, which was 40 percent of the primary school roll. By 1975 this had fallen to 93,200 and by 1985 to 52,800, a mere 11.4 percent of primary school rolls.[29] These figures indicate some erosion of Christian profession and membership prior to the 1960s, but since then it has been much more marked.

What is common across most Western countries, regardless of patterns of decline or otherwise from the mid–eighteenth to mid–nineteenth centuries, is that since the middle of the 1960s church-going has declined. In a concluding essay in a collection of studies on establishment religion in ten different Western countries, Roof, Carroll, and Roozen write: "Religious establishments—whether legal or cultural—have substantially weakened if not collapsed in most of the nations we have considered . . . the declines have been especially pronounced among the post-war generation, and accelerated dramatically during the late 1970s."[30]

---

22. In New Zealand, between 1874 and 1926, at every census of population and housing there was also a census of religious practice.

23. Jackson, *Churches and People*, 117.

24. Perry and Webster, *The Religious Factor in New Zealand Society*, 13.

25. "Heartland Survey," *Sunday Star*, 1990.

26. "Age of Rockers Sustains Mega-Church," 5.

27. *International Social Survey Programme*, 1991, 1998, 2008.

28. *Census of Population and Dwellings*, 1926, 1961, 1996.

29. Dickey, *What's Happening to the Children?* In 1950, 50 percent of children were enrolled.

30. Roof, Carroll and Roozen, *The Post-War Generation*, 244. The countries studied were England, Australia, United States, the Nordic countries, Germany, The Netherlands, France, Belgium, Italy, and Greece.

Indeed, it does seem that globally the church has been increasingly challenged over this period. In 2010 the estimated number of Christians around the world was 2 billion, 32 percent of the total population. This appears to show a significant increase over the 1960 figure of 920 million. However, this constituted 34 per cent, of the world's population, so in percentage terms, despite the dramatic and well documented growth in numbers in Asia, Africa and Latin America, the church worldwide has not continued to see a significantly growing proportion of the population numbered within its ranks, as it had in the previous one hundred years. The gains in these areas have been more than negated by losses in the West.[31]

One important point that Peter Brierley makes is that if the churches are broken up into two groups, institutional and non-institutional, very different patterns are found. Institutional churches, which he defines as those which are the state church in at least one country, made up 87 percent of the numbers in 1960, but had declined to 77 percent in 1995. Non-institutional churches made up only 13 percent of the total in 1960, but by 1995 had increased to 23 per cent. Thus the pattern of decline may not be evenly distributed within the Christian church at large.

Returning to Western societies, it is what might be called institutional churches that have certainly caused the most significant proportion of the decline, especially Protestant churches. It is these mainline Protestant churches that will be the focus of these reflections, although they will embrace other churches as well. There will also be a particular focus on New Zealand, as that is my context and therefore the one I know best, but the endeavor throughout will be to find what may be common strands there that might help to inform a wider understanding of trends and future possibilities for the church in all Western societies.

Examining religion in Britain since 1945, Grace Davie observes: "Statistically there can be little doubt about the trends; they go downward, whichever indicator is selected."[32] The decline, however, occurs at varying rates. Church attendance, which was 18 percent of the population weekly in 1960, had declined to 11.7 percent in 1979, 9.9 percent in 1989, 7.5 percent in 1998 and 6.3 percent in 2005.[33] The dominant church in England has been the Anglican Church, but "It is not exaggerated to conclude that between 1960 and 1985 the Church of England as a going

---

31. *Global Christianity*, December 19, 2011.
32. Davie, *Religion in Britain*, 52.
33. Brierley, ed., *UK Christian Handbook*, 2, 46.

concern was effectively reduced to not much more than half its previous size."[34] The Presbyterian and Methodist churches have experienced similar rates of decline.[35] Consequently, Steve Bruce points out that when we speak of the decline of British churches we should more properly talk about the decline of liberal and mainstream Christianity, as we find a general pattern of resilience as we move from "left" to "right" across the Protestant spectrum. Conservative elements have generally survived the best, and a number of groups have shown marked growth.[36] However, these churches are relatively small in total numbers so have made little impression on membership and attendance statistics as a whole.

In Canada, once again the losses are unevenly distributed. The four major mainline denominations[37] in 1961 had 15.2 percent of the Canadian population as members, but by 1985 this had declined to 8.3 per cent. Over this period of time all of the Conservative Protestant denominations had maintained 7 percent of the population as members.[38] Since the mid-1990s, mainline decline has continued, and by 2006 the approximately 750,000 attending these churches weekly was considerably fewer than the more than 1.1 million attending conservative Protestant or Evangelical churches:[39] "By around 2015 the previously dominant mainline denominations will have less local church members than the conservative Protestants. Even more important, their combined weekly attenders will be about one-third of the conservative total."[40] Similarly, in Australia research indicates the following:

> These declines have been partly counterbalanced by growth in the Pentecostal and large Protestant denominations. Rather than seeing the church as a single institution, it is important to recognise that it is a collection of organisations representing a diversity of traditions. While sections of the church are in decline there are many denominations and congregations that are growing significantly. However, the gains in some sectors of the church . . . have not outweighed the losses in others.[41]

34. Hastings, *A History of English Christianity*, 603.
35. See Davie, *Religion in Britain*, 46–49.
36. Bruce, *Religion in Modern Britain*, 67.
37. United Church, Anglican, Lutheran, and Presbyterian.
38. Bibby, *Fragmented Gods*, 15, 28.
39. Coggins, "Canadian Church."
40. Bibby, "Religion in the Canadian 1990s," 284.
41. Kaldor, Bellamy and Hughes, "A Time of Opportunity," 18.

In the period from 1991 to 2001, for example, Anglican Church weekly attendance in Australia declined by 7 per cent, the Uniting Church by 22 per cent, and the Lutheran Church by 18 per cent. On the other hand, the Assemblies of God experienced an increase in weekly attendance of 30 per cent, the Apostolic Church 32 per cent, and Baptists 9 per cent.[42] Census returns indicate a similar pattern, with the 2011 census revealing that these groups had all shown decline in the percentage of the population identifying with them from the 2006 figures. The National Church Life Survey researchers suggest that "Theological orientation is perhaps the most important factor behind these denominational differences," with the Traditional and Liberal Protestant sectors of the church "less likely to be growing."[43]

Despite showing greater religiously vitality and slower rates of decline, the pattern has been similar in the United States:

> Before the sixties there was little reason to question the vitality of American religion . . . the years between 1950 and 1960 saw a church-membership surge . . . However, in the mid-sixties, an unexpected and massive change began. Many of this country's culture-affirming 'mainline' denominations began to experience membership *declines* for the first time. The declines were sudden, dramatic, and persistent. Between 1965 and 1985, for example, the Presbyterian Church declined 24 per cent, the Episcopal Church declined 20 per cent, the United Methodist Church declined 16 percent . . .
>
> Meanwhile, conservative churches and religious movements grew. Between 1965 and 1985, the Assemblies of God more than tripled, the Church of God . . . increased nearly two and a half times . . . Conservative denominations closer to the mainstream also grew, generally at a slower rate: the Church of the Nazarene grew by 50 percent and the Southern Baptist Convention grew by 34 per cent.[44]

This pattern continues. A report in 2002 comments that "by and large the growing churches are those that we ordinarily call conservative . . . (of) those that are declining, most were moderate or liberal

---

42. Bellamy and Castle, "Church Attendance Estimates."

43. Kaldor, *Build My Church*, 68. The other theological positions they identified were Catholic/Anglo Catholic, Evangelical and Pentecostal/Charismatic.

44. Parrott and Perrin, "The New Denominations," 29–33.

churches."⁴⁵ While the claim is often made that liberal churches are declining and conservative churches are growing, with many of the latter now also experiencing decline, it is true as elsewhere that more conservative forms are showing greater resilience.

When we come to New Zealand, a similar pattern emerges. In the 1926 census, 73.3 percent of the population indicated affiliation with one of the three main Protestant denominations—Anglican, Presbyterian, or Methodist. By 1961 there had been a slight decline, to 64.1 per cent. However, the next three decades saw a dramatic decline, so that by 2006 the figure was 27.6 per cent. If we take another grouping of churches which we may define as conservative—Baptist, Brethren, Salvation Army, Churches of Christ, and Pentecostal—the 1926 census indicated affiliation by 4 percent of the population. This figure has remained relatively constant over the century, at 3.9 percent in 1961 and a moderate increase to 4.3 percent by 2006.

The Presbyterian Church provides a good example of the mainline church in New Zealand. In 1920 attendance was about 80,000 a week, increasing to 119,000 by 1960, but dropping to 34,000 in 2005 and seeming to stabilize somewhat since. Denominational figures show a pattern of steady increase for the first half of the century, rapid increase in the 1950s, and equally rapid decline in the four decades since 1960. This is true not only for attendance but for almost all dimensions of measuring church life: numbers under pastoral care, church membership, Sunday School enrollments, and numbers in Bible Classes.⁴⁶ In the 1926 census 575,000 people indicated affiliation with the Anglican Church, and by the 1966 census this had risen to 901,000. By 2006, at 555,000 this had fallen below the 1926 figure, despite a population increase of 2.7 million. An average weekly attendance of 47,500 in 1986 had declined to 39,000 by 1999 and further to about 32,000 by 2006. In 1960 there were 58,007 on the roll of Anglican Sunday Schools. Over the next fifteen years this figure more than halved, to 24,341 in 1975, and had fallen further to 10,840 by 1985.

Baptist profession in census returns has remained remarkably constant throughout the century at about 1.6 per cent. Church membership of 10,456 in 1951 rose rapidly to 17,237 in 1966. This was followed by a period of modest increase to 23,855 in 1991, but since then has fallen slightly to be 22,898 in 2010. Church attendance figures have only been

---

45. "Conservative Churches Grew Fastest in 1990's." "Religious Congregations and Membership: 2000."

46. Veitch, "1961–1990: Towards the Church for a New Era," 145.

kept since 1990, but for Baptist churches these tend to be slightly higher than membership figures. Estimates have been made of about 18,500 in 1976 and 26,500 in 1986. During the 1990s attendance figures again indicate a relatively static situation, with a weekly average of around 32,000. There was a slight increase to about 36,000 in 2006 but since then this has declined slowly.[47] These figures suggest that the Baptist church in general has shown some degree of resilience in this period, especially in comparison with the mainline churches. It experienced overall growth in the period up to 1990, although only keeping up with population growth, but since then has in percentage terms tended to plateau overall.

As has been the case in all of these countries, the most dramatic growth has been experienced by the Pentecostal sector of the church. In census returns these churches do not figure until 1961, when they accounted for 0.1 percent of religious professions. By the 1996 census 2 percent of the population indicated a Pentecostal affiliation, a figure repeated in 2006. It is obvious from these percentages that we are still dealing with relatively small numbers, and their growth has done little to offset the very large decline experienced by mainline churches. Gordon Miller estimates that they account for about 18 percent of those in church on an average Sunday. Most of these churches do not keep records, but the Apostolic Church records indicate weekly attendance of 3,500 in 1981, 8,300 in 1991, and 12,000 in 1999. The last figure is the same as for 1996, indicating that the rapid growth experienced in the 1970s and 1980s is slowing. This seems to be true for all Pentecostal churches in New Zealand, as indicated by census returns taken as a percentage of the population, and reflects the pattern that Brierley has found in Britain and elsewhere.

One other indicator of church patterns is the age profile of church attenders. Obviously a church consisting largely of an elderly congregation indicates that it has failed to draw into its ranks continuing numbers of younger age cohorts, who are subsequently missing from its profile. In 1997 the first New Zealand Church Life Survey was carried out. The report on the findings began with the age issue:

> The New Zealand population is ageing—and it looks as if the church is leading the way. Compared to 20% in the community, some 41% of church attenders are over 60 years of age. A further . . . 34% are in their 40s and 50s, while 21% are between 20 and 40 years and 5% between 15 and 19 years of age: 'The low

---

47. Figures from *Baptist Union and Missionary Society* Year Books.

levels of young attenders is a huge issue for the churches—the implications of which will only magnify in time."[48]

The prediction of the researchers has proved correct. By the 2007 survey,[49] those over 60 made up almost 63 percent of attenders, those in their 40s and 50s had dropped to 31 per cent, with only 16 percent between 20 and 40, and a mere 4 percent between 15 and 19. In the mainstream churches, in 1997 53 percent of Methodist attenders and 49 percent of both Anglican and Presbyterian attenders were over 60 years. These figures have increased to 66 per cent[50] and 62 percent respectively. Only 17 percent of Anglicans, 18 percent of Methodists, and 20 percent of Presbyterians were aged between 15 and 40 years, dropping to 10 per cent, 8 per cent, and 12 percent for the respective groups in 2007.[51] This compared dramatically with the 50 percent or so of New Zealand population as a whole. In comparison, those in this age group made up 41 percent of the total in Brethren churches, 43 percent in Baptist churches, and 48 percent in Elim churches in 1997. Only figures for the Baptists were available in 2007, but this had dropped to 30 per cent, while the percentage of those over 60 had increased from 19 percent to 29 per cent, indicating that an aging profile was affecting most churches and not just those classified as mainline.

These figures indicate that it is the generations that reached adulthood during and after the decade of the 1960s—the baby boomers, their children, and increasingly their grandchildren—who are largely missing from the ranks of the church and consequently account for most of the loss. Understanding what has happened with the religious beliefs and behavior of these age groups is therefore of considerable interest in endeavouring to see if we are indeed "losing our religion" and, if we are, why. A further question worth exploring, if that is the case, is "with what it is being replaced?"

---

48. Brooks and Currow, "Lifting the Lid," A–1. This was published a year after the survey.

49. Figures from the 2007 survey have not been published but were supplied by Church Life Survey New Zealand.

50. The Methodist Church did not take part in the 2007 figure, but this is the figure for Union and Cooperating Churches, whose figures have been very similar to Methodist Churches, who make up the largest group in these parishes.

51. This is a dramatically different picture of these churches from that which Hans Mol found in the 1960s. His survey showed that 63 percent of Presbyterian and 76 percent of Anglican attenders (including children) were under 20 years. Mol, "Church Attendance Survey," 7.

2

Religion in a Post-Aquarian Age

Secularization

IN ENDEAVORING TO EXPLAIN the almost universal decline of church-going in Western societies, especially since the 1960s, the most widely held explanation has been the secularization thesis. The word "secular" has had a long and complex history and so might be placed in that category of slippery terms that must be used with much caution. In the Middle Ages secular clergy lived "in the world," in contrast to religious clergy who belonged to monasteries or orders. Later, secularization implied the state taking away property from the church. The understanding that the secular indicates an absence of the religious emerged strongly during the Enlightenment, when control of religious institutions and concepts began to be removed from science, medicine, philosophy, art, law, and so on, and placed in the hands of secular authorities.

The term *secular* then simply refers to those areas of life that are not under the control of religious institutions, beliefs, or symbols. Secularization is the process whereby this occurs, as the control of the religious is rejected. When it has totally rejected such characteristics, a state of secularity may be said to exist. In this sense almost all Western countries, including the U.S, may be described as secular. In contrast, secularism refers to a consciously held ideology whereby adherents deliberately attempt to bring about a state of secularity.

The "secularization thesis," as used here, is somewhat more specific. Under the influence of Max Weber, it proclaims an ongoing rationalization of society, eventually leading to the disappearance of religion altogether.[1] For most of this century, among sociologists and historians, secularization in this sense has been simply accepted.[2] Perhaps the most famous expression of this view was that of the cover of *Time Magazine* on April 8, 1966, which set the question "Is God Dead?" in large grey letters against a solid funereal black background. The article surmised that for modern individuals traditional religion, Christian or otherwise, was no longer accessible.

Secularization interpreted in this way has been vigorously attacked. Some sociologists of religion, such as David Martin,[3] have challenged the very notion of secularization as being inaccurate and ideological. The development of the Pentecostal and charismatic movements in the West, the rapid growth of conservative evangelical churches in the United States, the emergence of "new religious groups," and the quasi-magical world of the New Age have all been listed as evidence falsifying the theory.[4] Closer to New Zealand, Bouma and Dixon made this claim in *The Religious Factor in Australian Life*: "The facts indicate that the myth of Australia the secular society needs to be put aside. Australians are far from secularists according to the data provided by this study."[5]

In a similar vein, Peter Berger made this assertion regarding secularization theory:

> By the late 1970's it had been falsified with a vengeance. As it turned out, the theory never had much empirical substance to begin with. It was valid, and continues to be valid, for one region of the world, Europe, a few scattered territories, such as Quebec which underwent an amazing process of secularization after the Second World War, and a fairly thin stratum of Western-educated intellectuals everywhere. The rest of the world is as

1. For many early sociologists this certainty was eagerly welcomed.

2. Stark and Iannaccone claim that "perhaps no other single social scientific proposition has been so widely accepted." Stark and Iannaccone, "A Supply-side Reinterpretation," 230–52.

3. Martin, "Towards Eliminating the Concept of Secularisation," 169–82.

4. The growth of Evangelicalism and Pentecostalism in Latin America, growing religious interest in Eastern Europe since 1989, Islamic Fundamentalism, and Catholicism in Poland are also discussed as indicators of the strength of religion in the modern world.

5. Bouma and Dixon, *The Religious Factor in Australian Life*, 167.

fervently religious as it ever was, and arguably more so than it was earlier this century.[6]

He was later to write that sharing this perspective—that modernity necessarily leads to decline in religion—was the "one big mistake" he made in his career as a sociologist.[7]

Robert Warner, in arguing the need for a new paradigm in studying religion, reports that now "it is the anti-secularization thesis that has become the accepted wisdom."[8] There is increasing evidence that even in Western Europe the theory may not stand up.[9] The proponents of secularization have responded by calling for a re-examination of what is meant by the term secularization. Mark Chaves states that secularization is "best understood not as a decline of religion (as in the old paradigm) but as the declining scope of religious authority,"[10] which he sees occurring at societal, organizational, and individual levels.

This involves a significant redefinition of the concept of secularization, from the decline of religious belief in society to a changing role for religion in society. Davie links this change to the shift in postmodern society. "Religious life—like so many other features of post-industrial or postmodern society—is not so much disappearing as mutating, for the sacred undoubtedly persists and will continue to do so, but in forms that may be very different from those which have gone before."[11]

Thus a use of the term secularization that implies a decline of faith, an abandonment of the religious dimension to life, is of little help in explaining changing patterns of church involvement. The emphasis of more recent writers, with their focus on religious change rather than decline, may be more helpful. Of particular significance is their focus on declining religious authority and privatization of religion. However, in light of the confusion and ambiguity surrounding the meaning of the term itself, it does not seem a helpful way of describing this change.

---

6. Berger, "Sociology: A Disinvitation," 15.
7. Berger, "Protestantism and the Quest for Certainty," 782.
8. Warner, "Work in Progress toward a New Paradigm," 1044–93.
9. See, for example, Davie, *Religion in Britain Since 1945*. Also her *Religion in Modern Europe*.
10. Chaves, "Secularization as Declining Religious Authority," 750.
11. Davie, *Religion in Britain since 1945*, 198.

Patterns of Religious Change

What is central in the complexity of the trends in a variety of data that might be taken to indicate what is happening to religion in the West are the findings of many researchers that, while church involvement has declined over the past four decades in almost all Western countries, the population of those countries has continued to remain overwhelmingly religious. Writing from the perspective of the United States, Leonard Sweet states:

> We are only now realizing how dead wrong scientists like Carl Sagan or secularization theorists like Max Weber or science fiction writers like Isaac Asimov and Gene Rodenberry actually were. Far from the future being religion-free, the future is more filled with soulprints than ever before . . . U.S. America is one of the most religious nations in the developed world. It is also one of the most secular . . . We are living in a secular society but a spiritual culture. Postmoderns prefer a nonreligious spirituality—a spirituality that is not associated with organized religion . . . On the same day on the same page of the same journal, one headline read "Spiritual Renewal Flourishes," and the companion headline bannered "Religion's Influence May Be Fading."[12]

Even in the U.S., while the decade of the 1990s saw declining levels of church involvement, the indicators were that increasing percentages of people were holding to religious or spiritual beliefs. Americans overwhelmingly affirm their faith in God and claim to pray to God often. The 1998 Princeton Religious Research Center index found that 61 percent stated that religion was "very important" in their lives, an increase of 7 percent from the 1988 figure. A 1997 survey from the Pew Research Center found that 71 percent of Americans said they "never doubt the existence of God," up 11 percent from 1987. The Barna Research Organization found that religious beliefs had remained stable over the 1990s. What is important in these surveys is not their precise accuracy in determining real levels of religious commitment, but the trends they indicate. An article in *American Demographics* on religious trends concluded that "Amid the crumbling foundations of organized religion, the spiritual

---

12. Sweet, *SoulTsunami*, 408. In 1998 Peter Berger wrote: "In the course of my career as a sociologist I made one big mistake . . . which I shared with almost everyone who worked in the area in the 1950s and '60s, was to believe that modernity necessarily leads to decline in religion."

supermarket is on the rise . . . Numerous surveys show that Americans are as religious as ever—perhaps more than ever."[13]

Sociologist Reginald Bibby has been researching life in Canada since the beginning of the 1970s. He argues that "Belief in a supernatural dimension of reality is widespread in Canada, and shows no sign of abating.[14]" A 1993 poll found that 23 percent of Canadians reported an increase in their spirituality over the previous five years, and Bibby goes on to claim that central to the search for an explanation for the patterns of declining church involvement is the paradox "that at a time when organized religion is facing very serious problems, the interest in spirituality, whether verbalized as such or not, appears to be extremely pervasive."[15]

The same picture emerges in Britain. Davie, in her study of religion in post-war Britain, expressed her findings in the subtitle she gave the book, "Believing Without Belonging":

> Within this book, one particular theme predominates. It concerns the increasingly evident mismatch between statistics relating to religious practice and those which indicate levels of religious belief . . . On the one hand, variables concerned with feelings, experience and the more numinous aspects of religious belief demonstrate considerable persistence in contemporary Britain (as they do throughout Western Europe); on the other, those which measure religious orthodoxy, ritual participation and institutional attachment display an undeniable degree of secularisation.[16]

She goes on to add that, as indices of religious belief have not dropped in the way that was predicted a generation ago, an approach to the study of religion based on the concept of secularization is becoming more and more difficult to sustain. "It seems to me more accurate to describe late-twentieth-century Britain—together with most of Western Europe—as unchurched rather than simply secular."[17] More recent research confirms that while there has been considerable change in religious beliefs, the kind of decline postulated by the secularization thesis has not eventuated.[18]

13. Climmo and Lattin, "Choosing My Religion."
14. Bibby, "Religion in the Canadian 1990s," 288.
15. Ibid.
16. Davie, *Religion in Britain since 1945*, 4.
17. Ibid., 13.
18. Gill, Hadaway and Marler, "Is Religious Belief Declining in Britain," 507–16.

It is more difficult to gain an objective picture of what the trends have been in New Zealand. There have been few attempts to analyze longitudinal quantitative data about religious belief. In part this is because of the lack of availability and accessibility of relevant survey data. National social survey questions on religious beliefs in New Zealand have been, until the late 1980s, irregular and unsystematic. However, the results of those surveys that have been conducted indicate a similar conclusion to the other Western countries examined. The ISSP Survey carried out in 1991, 1998, and 2008 indicate some small variations, but overall that religious believing remains reasonably constant, with perhaps an increase in the 1990s before falling back in the first years of the next decade. Certain belief in God was indicated by 29 percent in 1991, 31 percent in 1998 and 27 percent in 2008; belief in life after death went from 57 percent to 60 percent and back to 57 per cent; 22 percent of people indicated they prayed several times a week, increasing to 30 percent in 1998, and then falling to 25 per cent. There is no identical survey going back further than this, but Perry and Webster's study in 1989[19] would seem to support the view that religious believing had at least held its own. Different questions were asked so it is difficult to make exact comparisons, but there seems to have been little if any decline. If we take together all the three questions which, in both the 1985 and 1998 surveys, indicate people either do not believe in God or do not know what to believe, they total 28 percent in each case. In 1985 43 percent believed in life after death and 37 percent in heaven, compared with 57 percent and 51 percent in 2008. The figures, rather than indicating any significant decline in a religious view of life, point to some kind of stability at least, if not a small increase from the 1980s.

New Zealand, like Western countries in general, does not appear to have seen the gradual extinction of religious believing as the twentieth century moved out of the 1960s toward its conclusion. Instead, many of the generation who left the churches in the 1960s and 1970s, rather than becoming "secular atheists," have been conducting a renewed search for the spiritual. In all of these Western countries, the pattern seems to be consistent. People have continued to express an interest in things spiritual, and religious beliefs have continued to be held by the great majority. Indeed, over the past two decades interest in these dimensions appears, if anything, to have increased. On the other hand, the pattern has been

---

19. Perry and Webster, *The Religious Factor in New Zealand Society*.

consistent in Western countries as regards attendance at church services and involvement in institutional forms of Christianity—the figures point downward. How are we to explain this apparent paradox?

A Post-Aquarian Age

As the picture of declining involvement began to emerge in the late 1970s, researchers were unanimous in pointing to the baby boom generation[20] as the major source of the downturn: "[The] losses can be explained to a significant degree as the result of young people being thrust together by a variety of historical events into a countercultural generation unit whose values and lifestyles did not include, and were often in active opposition to participation in organised religion."[21]

The speed of change is demonstrated in Gallup figures indicating how Americans have viewed the importance of religion. In 1957, 69 percent believed it was increasing its influence, and only 14 percent saw it as losing its influence. By the end of the next decade, in 1970, these figures were almost reversed. Only 14 percent believed religion was increasing in influence, and 75 percent that it was losing its influence.[22] This was a staggering change in so short a period. Why did it occur?

It is now universally accepted that the 1960s saw the beginnings of a significant change in the cultural values of most Western societies, and the impact of these changes, sometimes referred to as the Age of Aquarius, hit the churches from the outside in significant ways. These changes came about as a result of the environment of an affluent security that emerged in the post-war years and in which the baby boom generation came of age.[23] The value changes that developed with them were in the direction of individualism, personal freedom as self-fulfillment, and tolerance of diversity.

At the center was a rebellion by the young against the values, conventions, and authorities of the older generation, and the emergence of a new cultural style—the "expressive revolution"—based on individual self-exploration and self-transformation, informality, spontaneity, and

---

20. The name given to the generation born in the post-war period, 1946–1964.
21. Wuthnow, *Experimentation in American Religion*, 143.
22. Lindsay and Gallup, *Surveying the Religious Landscape*, 11.
23. The best study of the development of these changes in Western societies and culture can be found in Inglehart, *Modernization and Postmodernization*, 33–34.

immediate experience.[24] There appear to be five main values that have had a significant impact on the life of the church and its place in society. These are *individualism, privatism, pluralism, relativism,* and *anti-institutionalism.*

(a) *Individualism.* In their influential study, *Habits of the Heart,*[25] Robert Bellah and his associates argue that the rise of modern self-centred individualism, with its obsession with our personal interests, our feelings, and the advancement of our own ambitions, is undermining the vital bonds of community that have sustained society in the past. In the sphere of religion, this emphasis on the self can result in faith without community. As the level of individualism has risen, increasing numbers have come to believe that church-going and church authority are optional and no longer necessary to sustain spirituality and faith, or to be a good Christian. A common theme in literature on the religiosity of the baby boom generation is a distinction between personal spirituality and organized religion. Many do not make a direct connection between their personal religiosity and participation in religious institutions.

Perhaps the most significant study has been that of Philip Hammond in *Religion and Personal Autonomy.*[26] He makes the case that, since the 1960s, religion has been far less a matter of traditional kinds of denominationalism and parish activity, and much more one of "personal autonomy," in which external religious authority is widely rejected. This has resulted in a "loose-bonding" of individuals to religious institutions and the growth of forms that find cohesion not in the system but in the person, not in the institution itself but in the people who draw on its resources to illuminate their daily lives."[27] These findings have been supported by Roof's study of baby boomers,[28] where he notes a radical shift from an ethic of self-denial to an ethic of self-fulfillment—to the notion that it is important to "find meaning," to "grow," and to find "self-expression."[29] The result is a religion functionally and spatially located in the self; individuals are free to create their own religious faith and consecrate their own sacred space. This kind

24. Hillard, "Religious Crisis of the 1960s," 210.
25. Bellah, et al., *Habits of the Heart.*
26. Hammond, *Religion and Personal Autonomy.*
27. Cox, *Fire from Heaven,* 305.
28. Roof, *A Generation of Seekers.*
29. This ties in with Inglehart's findings of a move to post-materialist values, where rather than self-denial in order to ensure that economic security is maintained, the emphasis is on personal fulfillment in order to satisfy inner needs.

of religious individualist neither wants nor feels the need for formal religious institutions.[30] These trends have continued, and indeed been heightened by the following generations.

(b) *Privatism*. This is a term used to describe the way in which people live their lives less in public and more in private or within the family. Again, it is a phenomenon affecting more than just the religious sphere and is seen, for example, in the trend in residential patterns toward "lifestyle enclaves," which act as retreats from public involvement. Where religion is concerned, a number of sociologists[31] argue that individuals in the modern world, with its increased segmentation, are forced to move among a plurality of institutions that no longer form parts of an integrated whole. Integration can be achieved only on the individual level. Because modern society allows for a plurality of structures, religion is therefore banished to the private sphere. It is more to do with private prayer and privately held beliefs than acts of corporate worship or public action, such that religion today is "more internal than external, more individual than institutional . . . more private than public."[32]

This stance has encouraged the growth of a utilitarian perspective on faith and church involvement. These are seen to have importance for a person to the extent to which they contribute to personal success and fulfillment. Hence it is argued that goals of personal advancement and success have displaced the collective purposes that have traditionally undergirded the organized church. Certainly this is a complaint that one hears increasingly from local church ministers and pastors. Rather than being committed to the church for the sake of the organization or wider social functions, people are increasingly involved to the extent that it benefits their own private lives.

(c) *Pluralism*. If one message rang loud and clear for the church from the 1960s, it was that "pluralism in religious and cultural styles was here, and here to stay."[33] Members of the post-war generation were ex-

---

30. Roozen and Hadaway, *Church and Denominational Growth*, 265.

31. See, for example, Berger, *The Heretical Imperative*; and Luckmann, *The Invisible Religion*.

32. Roof, "God is in the Details," 153. He cites as evidence of this a national poll reported by *U.S. News and World Report* in April, 1994, in which 65 percent of Americans said thought that religion was losing its influence on American life, yet so far as their own personal lives are concerned, 62 percent said that religion was increasing in importance.

33. Roof and McKinney, *American Mainline Religion*, 15.

religion in a post-aquarian age

posed to pluralism of all kinds. It is important to see this as much more than just the arrival of a few more religious options from which people could choose, such as Pentecostalism, Buddhism, Hare Krishna or New Age spiritualities. What is even more important is the changing mix of peoples and cultures in most Western countries, including New Zealand, that began to emerge in the 1960s and has accelerated in the past two decades. In the U.S. in the 1960s, changes in immigration laws saw increasing number of Hispanics and Asians immigrating, and civil rights legislation gradually broke down the segregation of American society. In Britain, West Indians and Asians began to arrive in massive numbers. In New Zealand, the 1960s saw the beginnings of large numbers of immigrant workers from the Pacific Islands, rapid migration of much of the Maori population from rural areas to the cities, and in the 1980s and 1990s considerable Asian immigration.

What has appeared is a new ethnic and religious landscape. The rapid globalization of this period has brought many differing peoples, cultures, and lifestyles into the same space, particularly in the cities where people have increasingly chosen to live.[34] Rather than living in small communities where similar values, beliefs and ethics are held by the vast majority, people now live next to, work alongside, and play with people who may hold a wide diversity of differing viewpoints.

Hoge, Johnson and Luidens see this as a very important factor. "Pluralism assaults traditional plausibility structures. We believe that it is an important historical factor explaining the problems of mainline churches."[35] Plausibility structures are the networks of persons in constant contact who hold to a common worldview and set of moral commitments and thus help to maintain beliefs.[36] Obviously the more varied or plural the beliefs held in a community or society, the weaker the plausibility structures are for any one particular set of beliefs. When a basically Christian set of values and beliefs are held by the great majority, then people are more likely to continue holding to those beliefs and values. It is almost the only voice heard. As alternative worldviews sit alongside these beliefs and values, the structures reinforcing previous beliefs and

---

34. In New Zealand, for example, 87 percent of the population now live in cities, despite the continuing myth of a "rural identity," or "people close to the land." We are an urban people.

35. Hoge, Johnson, and Luidens, *Vanishing Boundaries*, 201.

36. The theory was developed in Berger, *A Rumour of Angels*.

values are undermined.[37] Thus when individuals are faced with making choices in life about all kinds of things, they are confronted with a multiplicity of options that simply were not available to previous generations. In addition, the social cost that was previously associated with choosing an alternative set of beliefs or values is now greatly diminished, if not removed completely, because of the fourth factor closely associated with pluralism—relativism.

(d) *Relativism.* If pluralism describes a social and cultural reality, relativism is an attitude that allows one to live comfortably and at peace in such a diverse setting. The popular form of relativism is expressed in the attitude, "You can believe (do, be) whatever you like, so long as it doesn't hurt me." It is an attitude that casts doubt on the whole concept of truth and falsehood, right and wrong, good and bad. In pre-modern societies there was a coherent and binding sense of truth and goodness. People simply accepted those beliefs and values. There were not really any competing options. In an increasingly pluralistic society, however, how does one live alongside those who hold different religious beliefs, moral standards, or gender and sexual preferences? A belief that you are right and they are wrong becomes increasingly difficult to hold. It is easy to hold that Buddhists are "ignorant pagans destined for eternal damnation"[38] when they live on the other side of the world, but much more difficult when they are your pleasant, well educated, friendly neighbors or co-workers.

This increasingly common fact of life over the past five decades has combined with an understanding of culture and beliefs as being local rather than universal. Here tolerance becomes the great virtue of contemporary society, as it is the only way in which a diverse mix of often diametrically opposed cultures, lifestyles, and beliefs can coexist together. The trouble, as Hoge, Johnson and Luidens point out, is that while "tolerance of diversity . . . makes civility and cooperation possible in a pluralistic society . . . (it) also makes for weak churches."[39] Relativism, which sees other beliefs as equally valid, lessens the impulse to be engaged in

---

37. While regarding religious decline in the modern world as his big mistake, Berger asserts that his one big insight was "that pluralism undermines the taken-for-grantedness of beliefs and values." Berger, "Protestantism and the Quest for Certainty," 782.

38. This statement is intended to sum up the kind of attitude held toward other religions by most church-going Westerners before the 1960s. It provided the motivation for much of the missionary endeavors of the church in the previous 150 years.

39. Hoge, Johnson and Luidens, *Vanishing Boundaries*, 185.

evangelistic activities. Why seek to change people's beliefs and behaviors if they are all of equal value?

(e) *Anti-institutionalism.* In the previous era, church-going was an expression of belonging and civic loyalty. In contrast,

> In the 1960s and 1970s, a much different cultural milieu prevailed. In the early phases of this period particularly, young people . . . experienced widespread alienation from many institutions of the society. This was not a climate in which religious belonging flourished . . . To many in the anti-establishment climate of the 1970s, these churches and synagogues seemed deeply implicated in a culture that itself had gone awry . . . Hence the mood of 'rejecting' organized religion reached unusually high levels in those years.[40]

Many developed a deep cynicism in this period toward public institutions, as well as an inclination to make autonomous decisions irrespective of conventional mores or traditions. One legacy of the 1960s and 1970s has been a heightened sense of the view that institutions should serve individuals and not vice versa. When an institution no longer appears to be serving individual needs, then people no longer feel a need to belong to or to contribute to the institution. It is important to realize that, while this has had a major impact on the church as an institution, it has also affected a wide range of institutions in society at large. The effect is seen in all kinds of voluntary organizations which are now finding it difficult to recruit members. In New Zealand, for example, sport has become increasingly important as a value in our culture, yet across the board sports clubs and organizations are finding it difficult to recruit and retain members, and many are being forced to close or merge. Robert Putnam points out that in the United States more people than ever are bowling, but numbers in organized bowling leagues have plummeted.[41]

The important observation that religious believing seems to have become detached from religious belonging should be understood, then, in relation to the parallel observation that virtually all voluntary associations have been finding it difficult in the last few decades to attract and retain members. In other words, "belonging" has been simultaneously losing its popularity in religion *and* in other fields as well. The split between believing and belonging is therefore part of a broader pattern of

40. Roof and McKinney, *American Mainline Religion*, 46.

41. Quoted in Roof, "God is in the Details," 155. Putnam documents the decline in involvement in a whole host of organizations.

change which happens to affect religious organizations amongst others. It is not a problem unique to religion and does not necessarily arise from the inner dynamics of religious organizations alone.[42]

It appears, then, that this has been a significant factor in the increasing gap that has occurred between believing and belonging, between people's pursuit of the spiritual and their involvement in institutional religion. It is not that the post-war generations have been less interested in the religious dimension of life, but their distrust of institutions means that increasing numbers of them believe that religious organizations are more likely to hinder than help them in their search for a satisfying spirituality. Alongside these value changes in the culture, there appear to be at least three other important social changes that have had a significant impact on religious patterns. First has been a weakening of local community ties; second, changing patterns of marriage and family life; and third, the changing nature of the workplace.

(i) On the loss of local community, Hoge, Johnson and Luidens write, "We find it plausible that there was a decline, since people today travel more, move residences more readily, and enjoy more personal freedom in decision-making. Extended families are less important today. Probably this has been important for church life since churches depend so strongly on community ties . . . [these] have weakened over the decades and that has cut down on church involvement."[43]

Prior to the 1960s a substantial part of life took place in local communities. The mainstays of local community life were married women, most of whom spent much of their week within its confines. They shared the local community with their husbands during weekends, involved in local and church sporting and social clubs, as well as local churches. Married women began entering the workforce in large numbers in the 1960s, and increasingly shopping was done at regional centers. With men and women both regularly out of the local community, it became less significant.

Research has consistently shown that, for baby boomers, the highest correlation of all factors affecting whether or not a person remained in the church tradition in which they were raised is the distance they had moved from the community where they received their religious upbringing.[44] Roof and McKinney claim that this happens because such

---

42. Quoted in Davies, *Religion in Britain since 1945*, 19.

43. Hoge, Johnson and Luidens, *Vanishing Boundaries*, 202.

44. See, for example, Hoge, Johnson and Luidens, *Vanishing Boundaries*, 46. Bibby concludes that in Canada, "residential mobility frequently contributes to a decrease

mobility "results in weakened ties—to family and kin, to neighborhood and community . . . and erode social infrastructures undergirding corporate faith."[45] Bruce points out that religious beliefs are most readily maintained when they are unexamined and simply accepted as the way things are, part of the "taken for granted world," a condition most easily achieved when the same view is shared by the entire social group in which a person lives and where it is reinforced by all elements of social interaction.[46] One of the key social trends of this period has been the increasing mobility of the population. In the 1960s many baby boomers left home to pursue higher education, and since then they have been a very mobile generation.[47] With the fragmentation of this kind of cohesive local community, the social expectation of both relatively uniform religious believing, and church-going as part of that, has been diminished, if not removed completely.

(ii) In looking at changing patterns of marriage and family life, Roof speaks of the "massive changes" that have occurred since mid-century:

> In the older, white bourgeois Protestant family that came to be the normative nuclear family, religious and family symbolism were closely intertwined—indeed, one might say families created religious space. The family was an extension of the church, the place where faith and practice were lived out . . . The mainline churches relied heavily on intact families with children to replenish them. Penny Long Marler's research shows that, among other demographic changes, declines in nuclear family units have contributed most to the decline in Protestant church membership since 1950, leading her to conclude that 'as the family goes so goes the church.'[48]

---

in religious participation, especially among younger people." Bibby, "Going, Going, Gone," 303.

45. Roof and McKinney, *American Mainline Religion*, 66. Wuthnow points out that "There appears to be a relationship between the loss of family or community ties and a propensity toward eclecticism in one's attitudes and activities." *After Heaven*, 67.

46. Bruce, *Religion in Modern Britain*, 130.

47. My own extended family is one example. I grew up as one of 12 cousins, children of 3 brothers, in the South Island of New Zealand. We all left home to gain tertiary education. Of the 12 only one has returned to our home town. 3 others have returned to live in the South Island after considerable time in the North Island. Another lives in the North Island, and the remaining 7 are all overseas.

48. Roof, "Toward the Year 2000," 161. While Roof speaks about the nuclear family, it is also important to recognize the role of the extended family, particularly in the more stable local communities, with members of the wider kin network living in close

Again, we need to be aware that because of the higher levels of church involvement in the United States the relationship between church and family has undoubtedly been stronger there. However, the relationship in New Zealand has also been significant, as seen, for example, in the number of parents who sent their children to Sunday School before the 1960s. It is interesting how much church literature, from all sectors of the church, stressed the link between church and family life in New Zealand.

It has always been true that a significant number of people drop out of church, at least for a time, in their young adult years. In the past, however, churches could count on them returning to the fold in their early twenties when they sought marriage for themselves and a religious upbringing for their children. "The establishment of a family brought a return to church."[49] This has not happened with baby boomers, despite hopes in the 1980s that it would. Changes in family life, including the postponement of marriage and family formation and relatedly low birth rates, "cut deeply into the historically strong connection between church and family."[50] Wuthnow points out the enormous impact of the contraceptive pill alone.

During the 1950s the average time between confirmation class and birth of the first child for U.S. young people had been only seven years; by the end of the 1960s, in large part due to the impact of new contraceptive technologies, this period had more than doubled to fifteen years. Since the time between confirmation and parenthood has always been one in which young people could drop out of established religion and turn their attention to other things, the doubling of this period was of enormous significance.[51]

Research seems to indicate that the motivation for adults to go to church is weaker when there are no children present.[52] Accompanying the delay in having children has been the increasingly high divorce rate, the increasing percentage of married couples deciding to have no children, the increasing numbers of adults remaining single, and those living

---

proximity and attending the same church, a pattern that used to be much more common. Many older and more conservative New Zealand churches still have significant familial ties of this kind.

49. Hoge, Johnson and Luidens, *Vanishing Boundaries*, 15.
50. Roozen and Hadaway, *Church and Denominational Growth*, 242.
51. Withnow, *After Heaven*, 67.
52. See Hoge, Johnson and Luidens, *Vanishing Boundaries*, 74. Also Hoge and Roozen, *Understanding Church Growth and Decline*, 42–68.

in one-parent families.[53] All of these factors fragment the dominance of the two-parent nuclear family in society.[54] With so much focus in church life on marriage and raising children in two-parent families, as well as the stigma still often attached to divorce and sex outside of marriage, the increasing numbers of adults who do not fit into this pattern often find church life problematical at best and alienating at worst.

Related to these trends, and in some ways parallel to them, have been changes in women's roles. As more and more women become part of the workforce, fewer are available for the voluntary activities on which churches have relied to maintain their programs. In addition, even weekend involvement becomes more difficult, as the work week leaves little time for domestic matters and these become focused over the weekend—whenever work does not intrude there. Further, with the rise of the feminist movement in the 1970s, the teachings and practices of the church have been widely criticized for being patriarchal. This has led to many women feeling alienated from the church. With these changes becoming stronger in the younger generations, it could be expected that these trends will increasingly have a significant impact on church life and involvement.

(iii) Work looms larger for a growing proportion of the population. Many now derive much of their purpose and achievement from their job, make friends at work, and gain a sense of belonging, or community, from the workplace. In the 1970s most sitcoms were based around home and family, but by the 1990s workplace was a much more common locale. For many years interesting and stimulating full-time jobs with many

---

53. Hugh McKay presents figures that indicate that for most of this century 75 percent of Australians married—so 25 percent did not. The figures now seem to be moving toward a 50–50 ratio. McKay, *Turning Point*, 144.

54. New Zealand Census figures indicate that the divorce rate has moved from 4 persons per 1000 experiencing divorce in 1961 to 15 per 1000 in 2001 (an increase in the rate from 7 percent to 38 percent of marriages ending in divorce). In 1971, 45 people in 1000 were getting married; by 2001 this had dropped to 16 in 1000. 20 years ago the birth rate was 2.6 babies per woman; now it is 1.8. Between 1986 and 1996 there was a 30 percent increase in single person households, and by 2001 they made up 27 percent of households. Two-person households made up 30 per cent; together nearly 60 percent of households. A couple and children made up only 32 percent of New Zealand households (if only married couples were counted, it would be doubtless less than 25 per cent). A single parent and children accounted for 11 per cent. These figures clearly show the nuclear family, consisting of married parents and their own children, is no longer the normative New Zealand household, but only one pattern among a number.

opportunities for relationships were the privilege of a small minority, but that has begun to change. Automation and technology now take care of many routine tasks, and this makes possible more complicated tasks for workers, requiring greater skills and collaboration.

As jobs become more challenging, more people find and seek fulfillment through their work. A recent University of Auckland survey found that almost 90 percent of New Zealanders were satisfied with their work and found it enjoyable. Not only is it more enjoyable, but people are working longer and longer days, and longer weeks. The sacred weekend is now very much a thing of the past. In short, work is more and more at the center of an expanding number of people's lives. Their social and relational networks are connected around the workplace rather than the home or local community. Sports events and social activities are increasingly based around work communities.

The recent flood of women into paid employment has reinforced this trend enormously. The families where both parents work increased from 30 percent in 1986 to 37 percent in 2001, and those where the father works and the mother does not dropped from 49 percent to 28 per cent. The percentage of women in the workforce increased from just over 30 percent in 1995 to 50 percent in 2001.[55] Not only do men now spend much of their time physically absent from the home and local community but women also, sharply reducing women's involvement in local communities.

Bibby points out that it is a commonly held view that women are more "devout" than men and that because of traditional sex-role expectations, women in the past provided much of the spiritual leadership in the home. However, the Canadian research indicates a different picture as the twentieth century ended, one in which women "only marginally exhibit greater religious tendencies than men."[56] David de Vaus, in an Australian study, found that workforce participation was an important factor in accounting for religious differences between men and women, and that "as the workforce participation of women increases, the religious orientation of women will become more like that of men."[57] Nancy Ammermann and Wade Clark Roof, in an introductory essay to a collection of papers on *Work, Family and Religion in Contemporary Society*, noted the following:

55. *New Zealand Families Today.*
56. Bibby, *Fragmented Gods*, 100.
57. de Vaus, "Work, Sex and Religion." This is supported by a number of studies in the United States that indicate that "gender differences in religiosity are due at least in part to differences in workforce participation." Hertel, "Work, Family and Faith," 83.

Younger generations' . . . experience of individualism and feminism continue to place barriers between them and much of organised religion. It seems likely that some of this survey evidence hints at a kind of mutual exclusion going on between conservative religionists and people committed to new patterns of family and work. It may be that many congregations have already promulgated family values that have pushed non-traditional members out.[58]

Conclusion

In seeking to summarize these changes, a number of phrases recur:

(a) *From public to private:* This argument has long been pursued by Wuthnow: "The character of spirituality appears to be changing in response to changes in the culture . . . Their beliefs are becoming more eclectic, and their commitments are often becoming more private. Growing numbers of Americans say they are spiritual but not religious, or their spirituality is growing but the impact of religion on their lives is diminishing. Most Americans say their spirituality is private —that it must develop without the guidance of religious institutions."[59]

Many argue that a distinctive characteristic of contemporary religion is its fondness for privacy. The authors of a 1993 poll on religion in Canada, which indicated that 73 percent of adults disagreed with the statement "I am not a Christian," conclude: "It is not that (people) have forsaken God—many just do not feel compelled to worship in an establishment church anymore. Whatever beliefs they hold tend to be private ones—their lives clearly divided between the public secular world . . . and the personal, reflective realm of God . . . Christianity in Canada has undergone a profound metamorphosis outside—and sometimes alienated from—the mainstream churches."[60]

Religious belief and practice in industrialized Western countries around the world today is increasingly individualized and contained within the private domain. This is producing an intensifying disjunction of the traditional links between believing and belonging. It is this change that has had the most significant impact on church life over this

---

58. Ammerman and Roof, eds., *Work, Family and Religion*, 11.
59. Wuthnow, *After Heaven*, 1–2.
60. "God is Alive," 32.

period. It is not, as postulated by the secularization thesis, that people are increasingly becoming irreligious, but that religious believing no longer necessarily leads to belonging to a religious institution.

(b) *From religious commitment to religious consumption:* Marler and Roozen claim that "the increasing dominance of religious consumerism as a form of cultural individualism is the most important change in the religious marketplace of the late eighties."[61] As ascriptive social ties have eroded and social differences become blurred, so religious preference has become more a matter of individual choice than an expression of belonging to a particular social group or community. Institutions exist primarily to serve the individual, not vice versa, and individuals choose religious involvement or not based on the degree to which they find self-fulfillment in belonging to a church. In other words, instead of being a system of belief and practice to which one is committed and that addresses and shapes the whole of life, the gods have been reshaped so that religion has "become a neatly packaged consumer item—taking its place among other commodities that can be bought or bypassed according to one's consumption whims."[62]

Roof describes this as "pastiche styles of belief and practice," and Bibby as "religion a la carte." In *Fragmented Gods* he argues that the gods of old have been broken into pieces and offered to religious consumers in piecemeal form. This seems to be a helpful description of what has happened not only in Canada but also much of the contemporary Western world. It has happened because of the kind of societies that the process of modernization has created. Durkheim observed that as societies become more advanced they come to be fragmented into many smaller and more specialized units, each with their own set of values and controls. Individuals also tend to become more specialists as they are called on to play a variety of often diverse roles. As a consequence, we tend to relate more and more to each other in very specialized ways, in diverse roles that are often not connected together, such that we deal with entirely different groups of people in each of them. In this kind of society it is sometimes difficult to be the same person in all of these different roles.

In this light, it is not surprising that many people in Western countries find that Christian commitment, particularly with the pressure to conform that has been present in most of the major traditions during the

---

61. Marler and Roozen, "From Church Tradition to Consumer Choice," 266–67.
62. Roof, "Toward the Year 2000," 165. David Bryant uses the term "smorgasborditis."

modern era, creates problems. It calls for a level of role consistency that is very difficult to achieve. Business ethics are frequently incompatible with Christian ethics. Sexual inclinations, particularly for the increasing percentages of unmarried and previously married, commonly conflict with church expectations. Increasing numbers of frustrated people have protested that religion is simply not relevant to life as they know it. The use of religious fragments, on the other hand, permits one to retain some central elements of belief and practice without requiring a high level of role consistency.

Consequently, in responding to the highly complex, specialized kind of society that emerged in the second half of the twentieth century and has carried over into the twenty-first, people seem to be trying to find integration and meaning in the self rather than in existence as a whole. This is a radical change from the way in which Christianity, or religion in broader terms, has been historically viewed, and this shift has had, and will continue to have, a significant impact on the life of the church. Roof asks:

> What if these are signs of a new mode of the religious? What if we are witnessing the emergence of a world where individuals are less rooted in traditions and are becoming, as Zygmunt Bauman says, more like tourists exploring the religious terrain in search of fragments of truth and insight? What if we are in the early stage of a shift in religious-identity construction in which, as Daniélle Hervieu-Leger says, religion has become like a "toolbox" of assorted beliefs and practices available to individuals for their selective use.[63]

If these are not just temporary trends in a time of change, but rather, as postulated by Bauman, the beginning of a very different world, then the impact and implications are of great significance. Regardless of what the future may hold, it is in a context shaped by these kinds of changes that the church has sought to live out its existence over this period.

---

63. Roof, "God is in the Details," 155.

3

Changing Patterns of Church Life

Introduction

THE CONGREGATIONAL STUDIES SUMMARIZED here are based on a research project examining how social and cultural changes in New Zealand since 1960 have impacted on Protestant churches in New Zealand, and how they have responded to these changes.[1] Research on the patterns of church involvement over this period had established, as we have seen, that New Zealand fit into the pattern of overall decline seen in other Western societies. However, this research also demonstrated that within this decline there have also been cases of churches experiencing significant growth.

My reflections on the research and on my own journey as a church leader over this period[2] suggested that a church's ability to adapt to these changes was critical to its success. Donald Miller, in a study of churches such as Vineyard and Calvary Chapel in the U.S.—"new paradigm" churches which thrived while mainline Protestant churches declined—made this claim: "If Christianity is going to survive, it must continually reinvent itself, adapting its message to the members of each generation, along with their culture and the geographical setting . . . Church-

---

1. Ward, "Losing My Religion?"

2. I had been a church minister from the mid-1970s through to the late 1980s; then, while mainly working as a theological teacher, I spent four years as a part-time pastoral staff member in the late 1990s and early 2000s.

es . . . that do not constantly 'resymbolize' their message eventually die; in contrast groups that have the foresight to encapsulate their message in contemporary symbols and form not only have the potential to survive, but sometimes grow at remarkable rates."[3]

As the research developed, it became clear that an equally important factor, alongside social and cultural adaptation, was commitment to a strongly "orthodox" theological foundation, providing some support for the commonly heard argument that conservative churches grow and liberal churches decline.[4] Miller claims that those attending new paradigm churches "want to anchor their understanding in an authoritative framework of meaning and the Bible provides a center for doing this."[5] In developing a basis for assessing commitment to the historic orthodox beliefs of the Christian faith, four indicators were used: the uniqueness of Christ, both as a being and in mediating salvation; the authority of Scripture; belief in a personal God who acts; and the need for conversion in the sense of life change.

These two parameters, then, of strong commitment to the historic orthodox beliefs of the Christian faith, and the ability to adapt their life and message to a changing social and cultural context, enabled four different kinds of congregations to be identified for the study. The congregation that exhibited both of them would in all likelihood illustrate the case being made.

Congregational Studies

The material for the case studies was obtained from two main sources: the first written, and the second oral. For the written material all of the congregations gave access to a wide range of archival material. This consisted of church histories and annual reports, minutes of vestry, session, board or deacons meetings, as well as church meeting reports and in some cases

---

3. Miller, *Reinventing American Protestantism*, 18.

4. Dean Kelly, in *Why Conservative Churches are Growing*, demonstrated that the further one moved to liberal end of spectrum the more rapid the rate of decline for churches became, and the further one moved to the conservative end of the spectrum the more rapid the rate of growth was. He argued that people are attracted to religious groups because they want compelling, clear-cut answers to questions about the meaning of human existence. His argument was picked up by conservative churches and the church growth movement

5. Miller, *Reinventing American Protestantism*.

letters. Church magazines were provided where those had been produced and kept. Strategic planning reports and individual church surveys were also provided, as well as, in three cases, the Church Life Survey New Zealand data was provided. Finally, there was material which the churches had produced, setting out their vision or mission, as well as describing their ministries and programmes.

The oral sources consisted in the first instance of personal interviews. In each case the senior minister of the church was interviewed first. The nature of the research was explained, including the framework that was being used. The ministers' permission and cooperation were secured and a general picture of their perception of the church was recorded. An outline was provided as to why their particular church was chosen for study, and where it was felt the church fit on the four sector framework. They were asked if they thought that was a fair assessment. Their help was solicited to select and set up a group of between six and twelve current members for a focus group, from whom a general timeline for the church over the period could be constructed and some of the key changes and perspectives identified.

From this meeting other individuals whom it would be helpful to interview were also identified. Formal interviews were carried out with between ten and twenty individuals[6] from each of the congregations. These were "unstructured, ethnographic interviews" of between one and a half and two hours in length, although they occasionally ran over that. Besides the formal interviews, there were of course countless conversations in hallways, before and after meetings, or over cups of coffee. Because the nature of the research elicited widespread interest, conversations with people about both the wider findings and also the specific congregations involved also provided valuable insights.

After each case study was completed it was given to two members of the church to read, one a lay person and the other someone who had been on the pastoral staff of the church, to provide feedback on its accuracy of both details and perceptions.

---

6. Ammermann uses between 10 and 15 for congregational studies in *Congregation and Community*, 42. Thumma suggests that between 5 and 10 is sufficient for small congregations and up to 30 for very large congregations. Thumma, "Methods for Congregational Study," 205. Spreydon is large but not a very large congregation, so I felt 20 was adequate there. The others are in the small to medium category.

Four Congregations: An Overview

The four congregations studied were all located in the city of Christchurch.[7] They are:

- Spreydon Baptist Church, an evangelical/charismatic church which has constantly changed to adapt to contemporary culture;
- Opawa Baptist Church, a conservative and traditional evangelical church;
- St. Ninian's Presbyterian Church, a self-identified liberal mainline church which has constantly changed to relate to contemporary culture;
- St. Nicholas' Anglican Church, a middle of the road mainline church which has kept to fairly traditional forms of life.

Spreydon Baptist Church—Orthodox and Contemporary

In 1960 Spreydon Baptist had a weekly attendance of 92, membership of 60, and saw 3 people baptized. It remained in much the same state until a new minister arrived in 1968—Murray Robertson, who remains the minister of the church. Beginning slowly at first, from the mid-1970s to the mid-1980s Spreydon saw fairly spectacular growth, so that by 1985 it had about 1,215 in attendance weekly, a membership of 654, and in most years saw between 60 and 80 people baptized. From then growth slowed and was more spasmodic, so that by 1999 it had 1,387 in attendance, 809 members, and between 30 and 40 baptisms.

---

7. Christchurch is New Zealand's second largest city, with a population of about 350,000. Since this study was carried out it has become reasonably well known globally because of the significant earthquake it experienced, devastating most of the CBD and many of its churches.

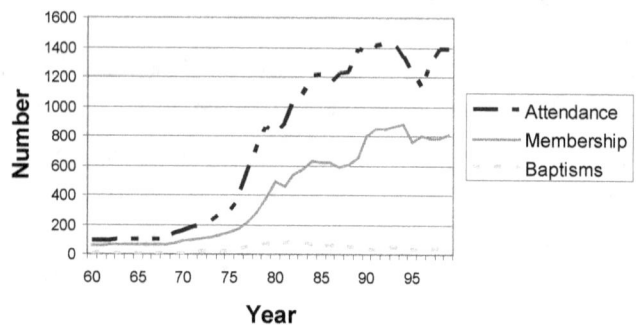

Membership Statistics, Spreydon Baptist Church, 1960–1999
[Statistics from Spreydon Baptist Church records and from the *Baptist Union and Missionary Society of New Zealand Year Books*, 1960 to 1999]

Opawa Baptist Church—Orthodox and Traditional

In 1960 Opawa Baptist had 265 in attendance weekly, 190 members, and 17 baptisms. Between then and 1975 it saw steady and, for a period, rapid growth, so that by 1975 it had 650 in attendance, 425 members, and almost 50 people baptized. Since then it has suffered steady attrition, such that by 1999 attendance was down to 245, membership to 228, and usually less than 10 baptized annually.

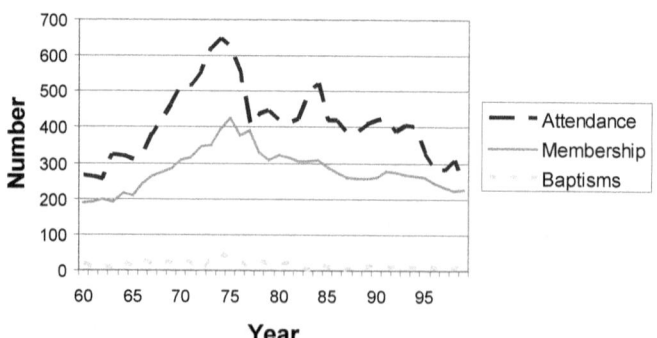

Membership Statistics, Opawa Baptist Churh, 1960–1999
[Statistics from Opawa Baptist Church Annual Reports and *Baptist Union and Missionary Society of New Zealand Yearbooks*, 1960 to 1999]

St. Ninian's Presbyterian Church—Non-Orthodox and Contemporary

In 1960 Sunday attendance at St. Ninian's Presbyterian was 636, with 477 members, 26 baptisms, and 246 in the Sunday School. By 1980 this had declined to 250 in attendance, 345 members, 11 baptisms, and 88 in the Sunday School. Further erosion meant that by 1999 there were only 69 in attendance, membership was down to 166, there was 1 baptism, and the Sunday School no longer existed.

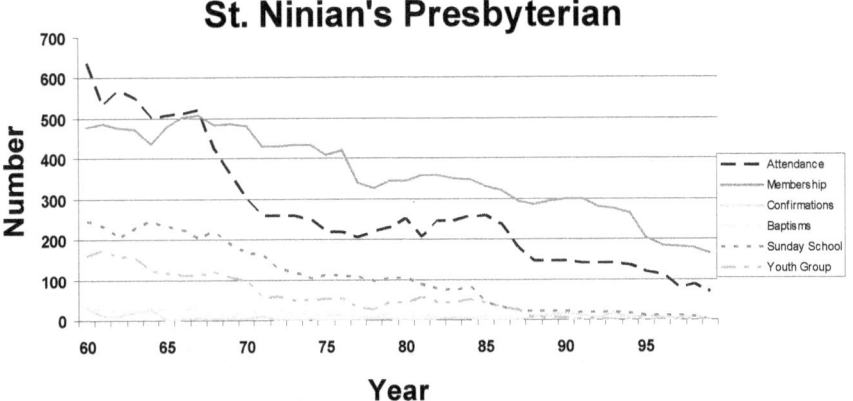

Membership Statistics, St. Ninian's Presbyterian Church, 1960–1999
[Statistics from the *Year Book and Proceedings of the General Assembly of the Presbyterian Church of New Zealand*, 1960 to 1999.]

St. Nicholas' Anglican Church—Non-Orthodox and Traditional

St. Nicholas' Anglican peaked in 1963, with an average of 133 in attendance weekly (on special days over 300), 280 in the Sunday School, and over 50 baptisms. By 1980 attendance was down to 54, there were only 20 in Sunday School, and 13 baptisms. Since then the church has shown some improvement in several areas (partly as a result of amalgamation with another parish), so that by 1999 there were 82 in attendance, but only 2 baptisms, and still 20 in the Sunday School. [Chart.04]

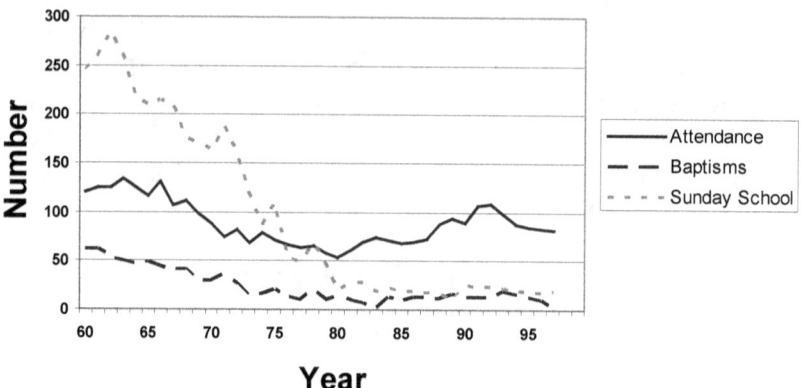

Membership Statistics, St. Nicholas' Anglican Church, 1960–1999
[Statistics from St. Nicholas' Church records and from the *Christchurch Diocesan Year Books*, 1960 to 1999]

What are Effective Congregations?

To analyze these studies I utilized international research on effective and/or growing churches. It was necessary in the first instance to define what is meant by effective churches. Obviously numerical growth is often an indicator, but it is not the sole factor. I found the most helpful material on this was the National Church Life Survey material, from Australia. The authors helpfully summarize the purpose of a congregation or local church as being "to assist people from within and beyond the congregation to worship God, respond to the Christian faith and to explore its implications in everyday life. Christians understand themselves to be called into a relationship with God, with others in the congregation and with those in the wider community. They are called to be bearers of the Good News, to be signposts to God's kingdom in word and deed."[8]

On the basis of this view of the church, they defined three fundamental dimensions of congregational life: an *attractional* dimension, drawing people into congregational life; an *incarnational* dimension, encouraging engagement in the wider community; and a *faith exploration* dimension, encouraging attenders in their faith. A number of

---

8. Kaldor, et al., *Shaping a Future*.

indicators were then developed to measure effectiveness in these dimensions, and a range of questions developed to assess each. I used these indicators as a base for developing my own measures. I also utilized material from the Institute for Church Development by Christian Schwarz,[9] and research by sociologist Kirk Hadaway[10] on separating fact from fiction in church growth material. I refined these to produce the following criteria for my analysis.

1. *An outward focus* among leaders and members expressed in *both* a concern for evangelism and for wider social engagement in the community.
2. *High levels of participation*, as shown by worship attendance, small group commitment, and involvement in leadership and ministry.
3. *A strong sense of belonging*, as shown by high levels of satisfaction among members, a growing sense of commitment, healthy relationships, and low levels of conflict.
4. *A clear sense of direction*, whereby members regard their congregation as having a sense of purpose. Leadership here has a strong vision for the growth of the congregation, both numerically and in other dimensions, to which the members are committed and willing to make changes in order to accomplish.
5. *Effective leadership* which is inspiring and directive, but listens to members and empowers them to use their gifts and skills.
6. *A lively faith* with individuals growing in faith, experiencing moments of conversion or commitment, and demonstrating high levels of devotional activity.
7. *Inspiring and engaging worship services* which provide a sense of transcendence for those who attend and which are expressed in appropriate cultural forms that enable personal engagement.
8. *A younger age profile* as a result of successful retention of young adults and attraction of newcomers.

Of course it was important to ask where the two major parameters I was testing—orthodox beliefs, and social and cultural relevance—fit within this framework. Looking at the first, orthodox beliefs, a number

9. Schwarz, *Natural Church Development*; also *Paradigm Shift in the Church*.
10. Hadaway, *Church Growth Principles*.

of the characteristics identified would be difficult to achieve in a church that was not marked by strongly held orthodox beliefs. The most obvious is a concern for mission or evangelism. Without strong and certain convictions, the motivation for evangelism diminishes. In addition, a lively or passionate faith, high levels of involvement, and inspiring worship are much less likely where there is no clear set of strongly held beliefs. In line with this, the NCLS researchers note that "Every aspect of congregational vitality, except for involvement in the wider community, is positively related to a conservative orientation to the Bible . . . apart from providing a more clear-cut message, conservative beliefs may tend to generate vitality by encouraging an outward focus and higher levels of commitment among attenders."[11]

Regarding the second parameter, social and cultural relevance, again a number of these factors would be difficult without a strong commitment to achieving this. An outward focus, if it is to connect with people outside of the church, needs to be relevant to the context in which they live. In order for worship to engage with and be meaningful for those attending, it needs to be expressed in forms that are relevant to people, especially if people from outside the existing church community are going to be attracted. Effective leadership and a sense of direction often come out of seeking to make the faith relevant to a changing culture. Schwarz finds in his research "an extremely negative relationship between traditionalism and both growth and quality within the church."[12] Likewise, more traditional church structures and forms tend to mitigate against high participation in church life and keep ministry contained within closely maintained bounds.

Further support for these two key parameters, as well as some of the eight factors identified, is provided by a widely reported research project in Canada.[13] This found that effective churches were identified primarily by four basic strengths:

1. *Orthodoxy*—in touch with truth.

2. *Relevance*—in touch with the times.

3. *Community*—in touch with personal needs.

4. *Outreach*—in touch with the needs of others.

---

11. Kaldor, *Shaping a Future*, 209, 233.

12. Schwarz, *Natural Church Development*, 28. He speaks of churches which are described by members as "tradition bound."

13. Posterski and Baker, *Where's a Good Church?*

As well as identifying the two key parameters of orthodoxy and relevance, the Canadian study confirms the importance of an outward focus, or concern for outreach, as well as a strong sense of community, or of belonging, identified as important in all of the research we have examined.

Analyzing the Congregational Studies

Spreydon Baptist Church

Spreydon Baptist clearly met both dimensions of the central proposition argued, for orthodoxy and relevance. It is a church that has maintained a very strong commitment to the core tenets of orthodox Christian belief over this period, and this has been particularly expressed through the biblical preaching that is so central to the church's life. In the 1997 CLSNZ, 90.6 percent viewed scripture as the "Word of God," compared with 64.3 percent for all congregations; 83 percent saw the most important aspect of communion as recalling "that Jesus died for us," compared with 48 percent nationally.

Alongside this commitment to orthodoxy, Spreydon has shown a considerable ability to adapt its message and life into forms that many New Zealanders, in the rapidly changing social and cultural environment of this period, have been able to identify with. This has meant significant change at several points in its story. In particular, Spreydon early on embraced the charismatic movement, and I will argue in a later chapter that the significant strength of this in New Zealand church life over this period can be explained, at least partially, as an adaptation to the more "expressive" culture that emerged out of the 1960s counter-culture and was embraced by so many of the baby boom generation.[14]

For most of the period under study, Spreydon scored strongly on all of the other indicators identified:

1. *An outward focus* was a consistent theme that emerged in the study of the church, and Robertson constantly put a strong emphasis on involvement in both evangelism to the local community and a wider social engagement. Both of these emphases also featured in a strong emphasis on mission overseas.

---

14. Ward, "Losing My Religion?"

2. *High levels of participation.* The church has always had figures of attendance at worship considerably higher than its membership, and a significant proportion have been involved in small groups since the mid-1970s. It has a high percentage involved in its many ministries and the style of worship has encouraged high levels of participation and involvement.

3. *A strong sense of belonging.* It was clear from the interviews, as well as observing involvement in services and ministries, that people had a very strong sense of belonging. One factor that helps develop a sense of belonging is low levels of conflict, and while there were some periods of conflict it usually involved only a small percentage of the congregation and was for limited periods of time, usually when significant change was taking place.

4. *A clear sense of direction.* Robertson has provided a visionary style of leadership and never allowed the church to merely drift along, but has been always ready to point in new directions. The church membership has also been highly committed to the focus on mission he has provided.

5. *Effective leadership.* By any criteria Robertson has provided effective leadership over a long period. Not only has it been inspiring and directive, but he has been able to provide encouragement to many others to develop their own leadership and put into action their gifts and skills.

6. *A lively faith.* There were many indications of this: the high number of baptisms, the biblical preaching that many spoke of as being important in their spiritual growth, and for many in their faith journey the importance of involvement in house groups. High numbers of church attenders have become involved in ministry and mission.

7. *Inspiring and engaging worship.* An important dimension of the Spreydon story has been the changing styles of worship in order to keep it fresh and engaged with the changes in its cultural context. This dimension has been indicated by the continued high attendance at worship.

8. *A younger age profile.* From the beginning of his ministry, Robertson attracted a younger age group to the church and this has continued. In the CLSNZ, 31 percent of attenders were age 15 to 29, considerably higher than the average for all churches of 12 per cent, or of the

population at 26 per cent. Likewise, those 30 to 49 were 45 per cent, compared with 29 percent for all churches, and 39 percent of the population. 45 percent of the congregation had come to the church in the past 5 years, compared with 29 percent for all churches.

As a case study, then, Spreydon illustrates the profile of effective churches we have suggested, with a strong commitment to orthodox beliefs and adapting its life to contemporary culture. It also scored highly on the eight criteria we identified as being characteristic of these churches.

Opawa Baptist Church

Opawa was identified as a church that combined a strong commitment to orthodox beliefs with a traditional approach to church life and was, therefore, unlikely to have experienced and maintained growth over this period. Its commitment to a conservative evangelical outlook has been maintained through the nature of its preaching, the influence of American evangelicalism in the church, as well as input from a variety of conservative evangelical para-church organizations, such as Navigators and overseas mission agencies. It was well contextualized into the largely conservative churched culture that still existed in New Zealand throughout the 1960s, and it thrived under the strong leadership of a leading evangelical pastor throughout that decade and into the 1970s. However, unlike Spreydon, since that time it has failed to adapt its beliefs and practices into the rapidly changing culture that emerged, and has instead endeavored to stay within traditional forms and styles of church life and ministry. In particular, it failed to embrace the charismatic movement; indeed, there was a conscious decision to reject it in 1975, and the ministers from that time into the early 2000s indicated that the church was making a commitment to traditional forms and styles of ministry.

Analyzing the church in terms of the indicators suggest that it scores well on many of them in the early period, but does not do so well from the mid-1970s on:

1. *An outward focus.* The church has had a strong commitment to evangelism over all of this period; however, through keeping to traditional forms this has become increasingly less effective. It has not had a high commitment to social engagement.

2. *High levels of participation.* In early years there was a considerable involvement of high numbers of key people with excellent leadership gifts, as well as high participation in worship. In the second half of the period these levels declined markedly, and considerable concern over this is repeatedly expressed in its documents.

3. *A strong sense of belonging.* Again, this was a characteristic of the church in the early years, but from the mid-70s it became greatly diminished. People did not speak of a sense of being loved and cared for, which has led to many leaving. There were high levels of mistrust and a reluctance to talk about the past, indicating dysfunctional rather than healthy relationships. Since then there have been high levels of conflict in the church around a number of different issues.

4. *A clear sense of direction.* In the early years there was a common consensus about this, and their minister, Coombs, was able to promote this. When the charismatic split arose, Coombs failed to provide a sense of direction, feeling obligated to be neutral and follow the direction which the congregation chose. After he left, the ministers who followed have not been able to provide a sense of direction and were at times heavily criticized for having no real vision or direction. Increasingly it has become a church which harked back to a glorious past rather than anticipating a positive future.

5. *Effective leadership.* Clearly Coombs provided this in the early years, especially with his ability to inspire people, but when it came to the critical point in the congregation's journey he abdicated leadership, and those who followed have been quite unable to inspire people by their leadership.

6. *A lively faith.* The early story of the church provided ample evidence of a lively faith and passionate spirituality. Many were coming to faith, being baptized, and becoming involved in ministry and mission. However, later there is a clear sense that people's faith was ossifying. They kept looking back to the way things were rather than growing in their faith and finding new commitments. Numbers being baptized were small.

7. *Inspiring and engaging worship.* Again, this was clearly evident in the stories of the early period. It appears that by refusing to embrace the charismatic dimension that enabled a more expressive

and culturally relevant style, the church's traditional format become uninspiring to many and has failed to attract newcomers.

8. *A younger age profile.* In the early years it attracted large numbers of young people and young families. It was many of these who left over the charismatic issue, and since then it has been marked by an increasingly aging profile. Although not participating in the CLSNZ survey, the church directory indicated that 60 percent were above 50, higher than the average for New Zealand congregations.

The argument that conservative churches grow certainly has some merit, although on its own is an insufficient explanation, but this has been found to be truer of the 1960s and 1970s than later. Thus Opawa's conservative beliefs may account to a significant extent for its growth over the first period of this research, but as the period went on this became insufficient to sustain vitality, and its failure to adapt to the emerging culture lead to slow and steady decline.

St Ninian's Presbyterian Church

St. Ninian's was identified as a church that had moved to a position of non-orthodox or weak beliefs and had endeavored to express these in contemporary forms. While at the commencement of the period it was solidly orthodox in its beliefs, from the end of the 1960s it gradually drifted away into what those in the church were happy to define as a liberal position. More than just being a non-orthodox position, by the 1990s the stance the church took at times denigrated those who still held to orthodoxy as being out of touch with contemporary thought and social realities. While not explaining everything about St. Ninian's decline over the period, it does seem difficult to find churches which have maintained a healthy vitality and been effective in a broad sense that have not held a strong commitment to orthodox beliefs. As the NCLS research shows, an orthodox faith stance impacts positively on every measure of vitality.

At the same time, St. Ninian's has attempted to express its faith in forms that are contemporary. It has demonstrated a willingness to embrace change in its forms and structures and to engage with contemporary social issues. There was a strong commitment from the 1970s to be relevant to the kind of society people saw as emerging. Indeed, the departure from orthodoxy was part of the attempt to be contemporary, because orthodox beliefs were thought to be unacceptable to "modern" people.

Unfortunately, however, hindsight has shown that, rather than pointing in the direction of the future, the culture this kind of liberalism embraced was in fact the last period of dominance for Enlightenment rationalism, or what is often termed "modern" culture. It was itself rendered increasingly less influential by the emergence of the new and different social and cultural realities that have emerged since.

Analyzed in terms of the eight indicators, it was found the St. Ninian's did not score very well:

1. *An outward focus.* In the early 1960s it had a strong commitment to evangelism, but even by the end of the 1960s this was significantly diminished, and consequently it has seen few younger people coming into its life. It has had a very strong focus on social concern and justice issues.

2. *High levels of participation.* There were very high levels of participation in worship services and the traditional church organizations through the first part of the 1960s, but the story since then has been one of declining participation in every area. Financial giving of members is a form and indicator of participation, and since the mid-1980s a lack of income has been an ongoing problem.

3. *A strong sense of belonging.* From the mid-1960s the church has recorded a steady and consistent loss of people, indicating low levels of satisfaction and belonging. While there was no open conflict there was an undercurrent of dissatisfaction, first with the academic liberalism of the ministry and, in the later period, over the affirmative stance of the leadership on homosexuality, particularly as concerns the issue of ordination of gay and lesbian persons for ministry,[15] In the 1990s this turned very personal for the church as the current minister came out as being lesbian and in a same-sex relationship.

4. *A clear sense of direction.* The church scored very well on this and the church has always been willing to make changes to move in the agreed upon direction. However, the direction desired did not at any point give priority to evangelism or numerical growth, illustrating the necessity of a church to have some concern for these issues in order to remain effective.

---

15. This has been a very divisive and hotly debated issue in the Presbyterian Church of Aotearoa New Zealand since 1986.

5. *Effective leadership.* The ministers of St. Ninian's all appear to be competent leaders, and were generally well liked and respected. In much church growth literature the role of the pastor as leader is rated the number one factor for effective churches. The St. Ninian's story would indicate this can be overrated, and does not lead to growth if other important factors are not also in place.

6. *A lively faith.* There are not strong indications of this. People did not speak easily of their faith or spirituality, and when asked about it usually spoke about values. In the CLSNZ material only 3.9 percent could identify a decisive moment of faith commitment during the past 5 years, compared with a national figure of 16.4 per cent. Numbers of baptisms and confirmations steadily declined to very low levels. Only 11 percent were involved in small groups, compared with 21 percent nationally.

7. *Inspiring and engaging worship.* The church had made strong efforts to adapt its forms of worship to cultural changes. However, while there was an attempt to be relevant it does not appear that the worship inspired people and provided a sense of transcendence. This seems related to a context where a loss of orthodoxy has weakened the sense of transcendence in favor of immanence. Only 30 percent indicate they had a strong sense of God's closeness in services, compared with 55 percent nationally.

8. *A younger age profile.* It has become an aging congregation. 54 percent were over 60, compared with 38 percent for all congregations, and only 6 percent were between 15 and 29, compared with 12 percent nationally. The CLSNZ data also shows that only 8 percent had arrived in the past 5 years, compared with 29 percent nationally.

With a strong orthodox faith being significantly linked to a number of these indicators, it would appear that its movement to a weak or non-orthodox faith is a significant explanatory factor in accounting for its decline. It has been a church that has attempted to evolve in response to the changing cultural and social context in order to make itself more relevant. However, because the church regarded the nature of their beliefs themselves as part of what needed to be changed, it has led to accommodation rather than adaptation, and seems to confirm the argument that, without a strong commitment to orthodoxy, it is difficult for churches to remain effective or to grow. St. Ninian's seems a clear illustration of the problem that a strongly liberal stance created for many churches.

St. Nicholas' Anglican Church

St. Nicholas' was identified as a church that combined a weak commitment to orthodox beliefs with a traditional approach to church life. While beginning the period broadly orthodox in its beliefs, it had soon drifted away from a strong commitment to these beliefs and, at times, embraced clearly non-orthodox views This was clearly a factor at some points in people looking to other churches that were strongly committed to orthodox beliefs, in order to have their faith strengthened and to be spiritually nurtured.

At the same time a constant theme in reading the case study documents was a desire to stick to traditional forms and styles of church life and a reluctance to change these to make the church more relevant to contemporary culture. This was particularly clear during the critical decade of the 1970s. There was a strong concern to ensure that things were done in an "Anglican way." By the end of the 1980s it appeared as a small and aging remnant of a style of Christianity and church (the current minister described it as "Christendom churchianity") that had lost touch in significant ways with the culture around it, and whose faith had become so weak that it had little to offer the wider community.

When evaluated in the light of the eight factors, this church fared probably the most poorly of any of the churches:

1. *An outward focus.* This is a dimension that seemed to be completely lacking in all of the reading of documents and did not feature as an important issue in interviews, either in terms of evangelism or social concern until the 1990s.

2. *High levels of participation.* In the most obvious dimension of worship attendance, the constant decline from the mid-1960s indicates a lack of participation by increasing numbers. Both ongoing financial problems and low levels of involvement in small groups were further indicators. In fact, there was strong resistance for long periods to even the idea of small groups. It appeared to be increasingly difficult to find people willing to participate in leadership.

3. *A strong sense of belonging.* When I first met with a group from the church it struck me that they did not have a strong sense of relational connection. People did not have high levels of satisfaction as they talked about their experience of the church, and there was a constant complaint about a lack of pastoral care. In the CLSNZ

data only 41 percent felt a strong sense of belonging, compared with 50 percent nationally. For much of the period there was underlying conflict in the church.

4. *A clear sense of direction.* In the 1960s there was a widespread consensus about the place and role the church should have, but it was a "chaplaincy" understanding of the place of the church in society. There was no vision about growth or mission, and as the older understanding broke down there was no new direction that developed.

5. *Effective leadership.* The first vicar in this period provided inspiring and visionary leadership but since then none of the vicars were able to provide the needed leadership. They either simply fulfilled a maintenance role or, if they did want to move in new directions, did not have the skills or personality to take others with them or empower them for leadership.

6. *A lively faith.* I was struck by a reticence to talk about faith or spirituality. The CLSNZ data indicated that 33 percent found it hard to express their faith, compared with 20 percent nationally; only 9 percent could name a specific moment of faith commitment, compared with 16.4 percent nationally, and none of these were in the past 5 years. The low number of baptisms and confirmations mirror the aging congregation.

7. *Inspiring and engaging worship.* Once again, declining levels of worship attendance indicate that people did not find worship inspiring or engaging. In interviews people did not talk appreciatively of the services or of how they had found them inspiring or helpful. Because of their commitment to worship in a traditional Anglican way, they have found it difficult to adapt to the changing culture. There has been continued and strong opposition to the presence of children in worship.

8. *A younger age profile.* The church's records indicate a realization that by the end of the 1980s they were faced with the problem of an aging congregation. Since the mid-1960s it has failed to retain the children of members as they became young adults. Only 15 percent had joined the church in the past 5 years, compared with 29 percent nationally. Even after a merger with a younger parish, 51 percent were over 60, compared with a national average of 38 per cent, and only 7 percent between the ages of 15 and 29 compared with 12 percent nationally.

50 losing our religion?

St. Nicholas' scores rather poorly on all of our indicators of an effective congregation. Again, as with St. Ninian's, the weakening of its commitment to orthodox beliefs can be seen to be a significant factor, as strongly held orthodox beliefs are clearly tied to a number of these. In addition to being what we have described as non-orthodox in its beliefs, St. Nicholas' has been determined to retain traditional forms and styles of church life and has resisted, often quite strongly, attempts to bring about change that would help it relate more effectively to the contemporary social and cultural context. It thus provides a good illustration of the issues that have confronted many mainline Protestant churches which have moved down a somewhat liberal approach to belief, while simply continuing to organize their life and worship in traditional forms and styles.

Conclusion

The studies of these four congregations clearly illustrate, in the first instance, the basic argument that has been presented—that the churches which have thrived over this period are more likely to have combined a strong adherence to the basic tenets of orthodox Christian belief with an ability to adapt their life and message to forms that relate effectively to the rapidly changing social and cultural context in which they have found themselves. This is also the conclusion of the NCLS researchers. "The NCLS results . . . suggest the importance of maintaining strength in commitment and meaning systems, yet expressing them in non-alienating cultural forms."[16] In addition, the studies of these churches also serve to illustrate the significance of those indicators we have found identified in wider research as features of effective churches. In a number of cases these indicators are significantly related to the two primary factors.

When we place the findings of these studies into the wider church scene in New Zealand over this period, this same pattern is demonstrated. If one moves across the theological spectrum from the "conservative" (or strongly orthodox) to the "liberal" (or weakly orthodox), those at the more liberal end—the mainline Anglican, Presbyterian and Methodist—showed considerable decline. Of these the Methodists, as the most liberal, showed the greatest decline. Baptists, perhaps described as moderately conservative, showed steady growth until the early 1990s and then plateaued, while Pentecostals, very conservative, showed strong growth

16. Kaldor, *Shaping a Future*, 216.

until the late 1990s, when they also plateaued. That this is not a complete explanation is indicated by the fact that the Salvation Army, Brethren, and Church of Christ, all of which sit at the conservative end of the spectrum, showed rates of decline similar to the mainline churches.

This brings us to the other major factor: cultural and social adaptation. Here, as was indicated in the case studies, the charismatic/Pentecostal movement seemed to have been a major factor in helping churches adapt to the significant cultural change that began in New Zealand in the mid-1960—the "expressive" revolution. The widespread embrace of this by Baptist churches enabled them to adapt to these changes, and the Pentecostal churches also emerged out of that culture in 1960s New Zealand.[17] Of the conservative churches, the Salvation Army, Brethren and Church of Christ on the whole resisted the charismatic movement, and this made it more difficult for them to adapt.

When we look at the mainline churches, there was some significant degree of acceptance by a considerable number of Anglican and Presbyterian churches, and comparative studies within those denominations suggest that congregations which embraced it were more likely to have experienced growth. The Methodist church showed significantly less influence and this also is likely to have increased their rate of decline.[18] A related factor is that the more independent and autonomous nature of congregational life in Baptist and Pentecostal churches may have made it easier for them to adapt to new forms than churches which were much more nationally controlled, such as the Anglicans, Presbyterians, Methodists, and the Salvation Army.

There is, however, one significant qualification to this finding. As Spreydon Baptist was the case study used to illustrate churches that had thrived and grown over this period, I felt it necessary to do additional research to discover the sources of its growth. This was done by surveying the Sunday worshipping congregation, asking attenders about their church background before coming to Spreydon. This identified a surprisingly low percentage of attenders (3.9 per cent) who had no previous church background, with the majority coming from mainline Protestant churches. When the same survey was done in three other similar churches which had also experienced growth, the pattern was confirmed, with less than 4 percent coming from non-churched backgrounds and the majority being from mainline Protestant church backgrounds.

17. Pentecostalism arrived in New Zealand in 1926, but by 1961 only numbered 3000. By 1976 this had increased to 13,000.

18. The significant role of the charismatic movement in New Zealand churches is examined in more detail in chapter 5.

This pattern clearly suggests that the growth of evangelical, charismatic, and Pentecostal churches has largely occurred through people moving to them from mainline Protestant churches. The decline of one group has fostered the growth of the other. Another significant source of growth was from older conservative churches which have also declined. This pattern was supported by the CLSNZ 1997 data. Again, this pattern is found in the research in most Western countries, rather than being a uniquely New Zealand phenomenon. Given these sources of growth, we would expect to see a slowing down of the growth of these kinds of churches as the pool of New Zealanders raised in mainline Protestant churches, and to a lesser degree in older conservative evangelical churches, began to age and diminish. Trends in the wider church scene in the 1990s and into the 2000s confirm this. Many leaders of these churches talk about the heyday of the 1970s and 1980s, the years of easy growth.

This research, then, on both local congregations and wider church trends in New Zealand, demonstrates the general validity of the argument developed. It is a combination of a strong adherence to the basic tenets of orthodox Christian belief, along with an ability to adapt their life and message to forms that relate effectively to their social and cultural context, which has enabled some churches, such as Spreydon Baptist Church, to be effective over this period. This is likely to continue to be the case.

However, while these churches made this adaptation in relation to the kind of society and culture that emerged from the mid-1960s to the late 1980s, especially with baby boomers, the changes that have developed so rapidly since the 1990s, with the growing dominance of a post-traditional or postmodern society and the increasingly post-Christian culture of post-boomer generations, mean that the adaptive forms and styles which they developed earlier have become increasingly less effective. Since these churches have largely drawn in those socialized in other churches and in the Christian faith,[19] the increasingly smaller percentage of succeeding generations in that category indicates a progressively shrinking market. In other words, they are attracting a larger slice of a continuingly diminishing pie. The challenge confronting them is once again to make the changes needed to adapt their life and message to a changing social and cultural context, one much more distant from the heritage of faith they represent. This, it seems, is an even more demanding task than that which they faced in the late 1960s and 1970.

---

19. See chapter 6 for a development of this argument.

4

A Terminus Quo for the Mainline?

Introduction

THE CHAPTERS IN THIS book examine the changing patterns of church involvement and religious participation in Western societies since the 1960s. Most of the illustrative material is drawn from New Zealand. Here, as in most of these societies, church participation has declined significantly, with attendance in terms of the percentage of the population dropping to approximately half of what it was in 1960. Echoing the situation found in most other Western societies, the sector most affected by that loss has been the mainline Protestant churches.

For much of New Zealand's history, mainline Protestant churches have accounted for the majority of people's religious commitments. This reflects the history of New Zealand's pattern of immigration for its first 120 years, since planned settlement began in the 1840s. It was a British colony and the vast majority of settlers came from England and Scotland, with a relatively small percentage migrating from Ireland, compared with other colonies.[1] In the 1926 Census, 73.3 percent of the population indicated affiliation with one of the three main Protestant denominations, Anglican, Presbyterian, or Methodist.

---

1. One of the features of New Zealand colonization was that it had the highest percentage of Scots settlers of any of the colonies, explaining the strength of Presbyterianism here and significantly influencing its culture.

There appears to have been some decline in church-going overall during the next couple of decades, but concern eased in the 1950s when churches thrived and membership grew. In New Zealand it was a time when many existing suburban churches grew and a host of new churches were established in the expanding suburbs. For Anglicans, the numbers attending Easter communion increased from 46,219 in 1940/41 to 93,513 in 1963/64. Membership in the Presbyterian Church increased from 55,317 in 1940 to 91,982 in 1966. Methodist membership increased from 25,393 in 1940 to 32,496 in 1965.[2] For Anglicans and Presbyterians this represented a rate of growth greater than that of the population. The Presbyterians opened 66 new churches in these "years of confidence and expansion."[3] In 1960, 119,041 adults attended church on an average Sunday, 76,030 children were on the Sunday School rolls, and 20,507 young people in Bible Classes,[4] as "baby boomers of the late 1940s and 1950s attended Sunday School in large numbers, straining resources."[5] In 1961 the mainline Protestant churches still accounted for 64.1 percent of the population on census returns. Jim Veitch argues that

> The influence of Christianity on New Zealand life until the mid-sixties was extensive. It was a rare family who did not have some connection with the church. Women and children in particular used the church and its extensive social activities. It was in the Sunday School that children received moral education, and most parents . . . went to church in support of this . . .
>
> Christian influence still dominated Sundays and holidays, shaped attitudes to books and entertainment, and even controlled the language people used . . . The moral principles of Christianity . . . were sufficiently well known in the community to provide business, industrial and community leaders with a broad ethical framework.[6]

This mood of mainline buoyancy and optimism continued into the 1960s. Combined membership figures in 1965 for Anglicans, Presbyterians, and Methodists came to about 220,000. In contrast, conservative churches[7] made up only 3.6 percent of census affiliation and membership

---

2. Davidson, *Christianity in Aotearoa*, 161.
3. Veitch, "1961–1990: Toward the Church for a New Era," 144.
4. *Proceedings of the General Assembly of the Presbyterian Church, 1960.*
5. Veitch, "1961–1990: Toward the Church for a New Era," 144.
6. Veitch, "Christianity: Protestants since the 1960s," 90.
7. Baptists, Brethren, Salvation Army, Congregational, and Churches of Christ.

was probably a bit over 50,000, about 25 percent of the "big three." The optimism with which the mainline churches entered the decade did not last long, however. From the early years of that decade numbers at youth activities began to drop sharply, followed later in the decade by declining adult attendance. In the early 1970s, Sunday School numbers began to fall. By 2006 census affiliation had been more than halved to 26.7 percent of the population and combined attendance had fallen to about 90,000, considerably less than that for Presbyterians alone in 1960. In contrast, census affiliation for conservative churches had risen slightly to 4 percent and combined attendance figures had doubled to about 100,000, slightly more than for mainline Protestants.

In seeking to explain this decline in mainline Protestant churches, their current age profile yields a significant number of clues. The data for this from which this chapter was developed was initially taken from the Church Life Survey New Zealand (CLSNZ) in 2001. Where churches were found to have a significantly older age profile, this indicates that decline in attendance was caused by losses in those younger age groups who were now absent in significant numbers. The data showed that the loss of numbers began with the baby boomer generation (those then aged 40 to 59), and continued with the generations following. The CLSNZ 2007 figures demonstrate that the trend identified then has continued as the population has aged.

A Picture of an Aging Church

The CLSNZ 2001 data represented responses from considerable samples of Anglican, Presbyterian, Methodist, Catholic, and Baptist churches, as well as some smaller groups, including Cooperating Parishes. Cooperating Parishes are parishes in which Presbyterians, Methodists, Anglicans, and Churches of Christ work together in a single congregation. Presbyterians and Methodists are the most significant partners. These cooperating churches developed during the heyday of the church union movement of the 1960s and 1970s. When the Anglican Church withdrew from these union discussions, the Presbyterian also chose not to commit to union, unlike in Australia and Canada where these two became the main contributors to the new Uniting and United Churches respectively.

Because, with one or two exceptions, Pentecostal and independent charismatic churches chose not to participate in this survey, they were not represented sufficiently for the data to be useful in making generalizations about the total church community in New Zealand. The data does, however, provide a reliable picture of mainline Protestantism, since churches from this sector make up the great bulk of the material collected. The Baptist Church, which in New Zealand stands perhaps midway between mainline Protestant churches and Pentecostal/charismatic churches in most of the statistical counts (as well as in other ways), provides a good comparison with which to measure the mainline trends.

Included in the data were figures specifying the age profile of church attenders. Comparative data from the religion question in the 2001 New Zealand Census was also used. Since the initial research was carried out, the figures from CLSNZ 2007 and the 2006 New Zealand Census have been used to bring the material closer to the present. Analysis is made of the age distribution figures for the mainline Protestant churches, and this is compared with the figures for the Roman Catholic and Baptist churches and with the general population of New Zealand. In the New Zealand Census there are two forms to be filled in. The first is filled in by the head of the household, and the second is an individual form for those aged 15 and over. The religion question is included in this second form so, since only results for those aged over 15 are included, the results are likely to represent the individual's religious response rather than that of his or her parents. It is acknowledged though that some degree of parental influence may be found in the 15 to 19 age group.

As can be seen in Figure 1, plotting the age profile of the mainline Protestant churches from the CLSNZ data over against the population age profile from the census provides a graphic illustration of the basic issue. The church is heavily over-represented in the older age groups and under-represented in the younger age groups.

Census 2001 & CLSNZ 2001 Mainline Protestant Age Profile

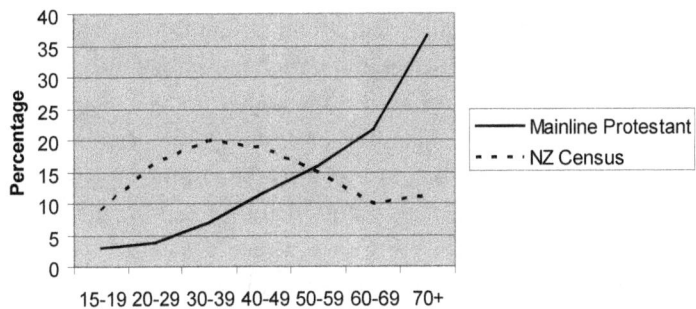

Year
Age Categories for Mainline Protestant Churches
as a Percentage of New Zealand Population
[Statistics from the 2001 NZ Census and 2001 Church Life Survey New Zealand]

Looking at the denominational church groups, we are particularly concerned with the average age of adults over 15 years of age. For Anglicans the average was 58 years, Presbyterians 62 years, Cooperating Parishes 65 years, and Methodists 66 years. This compared with an average age for Catholics of 54 years, for Baptists 43 years, and for the general population 41 years. A further breakdown of the age data indicated the aged and aging profile for these denominations, particularly when comparison is made with the 1997 and 2007 CLSNZ data, as demonstrated in Table 1.

Table 1: Percentage of Attenders by Age Categories across 6 Church Denominations
[Statistics from the 1997, 2001 and 2007 CLSNZ, and the 2006 NZ Census]

Age Categories	15–39			40–59			Over 60		
	1997	2001	2007	1997	2001	2007	1997	2001	2007
Anglican	18	15	11	32	34	24	48	52	65
Presbyterian	20	16	13	28	31	24	49	56	63
Methodist	18	12	11	29	25	22	53	63	67
Cooperating Parishes	18	11	11	29	28	21	57	61	68
Catholic	32	25	23	36	36	25	32	40	42
Baptist	43	41	30	38	37	40	19	22	30
NZ Census 2006			44			34			22

The results of the research indicate that the mainline Protestant churches have in all cases more than double the percentage of attenders over 60 years of age (pre-boomers) than does the general population. The Catholic figure is slightly under double and the Baptist figure about 30 per cent, slightly higher than the general population. It is noticeable that in every case the percentage is significantly higher in the 2007 survey than it was in the 1997 survey. Mainline Protestant churches and Catholics have a somewhat lower percentage of attenders in the 40–59 age group (baby boomers) than the Census profile, while for Baptists the percentage is slightly higher. In all of the groups the percentage in this age group has declined slightly. When we come to the 15–39 age group (post-boomers), they are down to 25 percent of that in the general population for all of the mainline groups, apart from the Presbyterians who are only slightly higher. Catholics are about half and Baptists about 70 percent of the general population profile. In all cases the percentage in this age group has fallen significantly over the decade from 1997 to 2007. The percentages in each category in the general population has changed by only one or two percentage points over this same period of time.

This data reveals that the age profile for all the churches identified is older than that for the general population, and is becoming more aged. While New Zealand's population is aging slowly, the rate of aging for the church has dramatically accelerated. The figures are particularly concerning for mainline Protestant churches. Those for Catholics and Baptists point clearly in the same direction, if with some time lag and a somewhat slower rate. But for mainline Protestant churches the question must be asked as to how tenable even a short term future may be for many local congregations, when over 60 percent of attenders were already over 60 years of age by 2007. It is not that unusual for me to speak on a Sunday in a Presbyterian or Anglican church where there is no one under 50 attending, and only the odd individual under 60.

When I began doing this research in 1999, I identified 2015 as a significant marker because even at that stage 50 percent or more of attenders in those churches were over 60. The trends suggested that, without dramatic change, by 2015 over 50 percent of the attenders would either be over 75, or else have died. The age profile also suggests that, while the rates of decline may have been significant over the past few decades, the rates over the coming years will in all likelihood increase, with so many nearing the end of their lives. The trends indicated by the 2001 and 2007 data demonstrate that to be true. One often hears comments from ministers in these denominations about the numbers of funerals they are now being asked to perform.

The very low percentage in the post-boomer age groups indicates that the number of children born into those churches is relatively small, and also that they are not very successful in recruiting new and younger people. Given these facts, we can only expect this increasingly aging profile to continue. Numbers will continue to decline as older members die and are not replaced by equal numbers of younger age groups. This raises serious questions about the future viability of many of the congregations, and suggests that by 2015 the crisis point will have been reached. My employment is with the Presbyterian Church in New Zealand and I also do a reasonable amount of consultancy work with the Anglican Church. The situations I am involved with in these churches, and the material I receive from the denominational sources of both denominations, corroborate these findings. Indeed, by 2012, not 2015, this crisis point had been reached by many congregations, and discussions of church closures or mergers, with all the pain these entail, are major preoccupations for both denominations.

Many of these congregations, while not viable as churches with full-time or even, in many cases, part-time ministers, have kept going faithfully and often against considerable odds through new and creative ways of providing ministry within their respective polities. This is being done by a small group of aged members for whom loyalty to the church they have known for most of their lives is a key factor in their personal identity. Partially this is a consequence of these people having lived a significant part of their lives within the same local community of which their church is a key element. This has meant that there is both a strong sense of attachment to a particular place, their local church with all its significant memories of important occasions in a person's life, and also very strong social bonds with a group of people with whom they have journeyed for many years, who are also connected with this place.

This is not a significant characteristic for the much more mobile generations that have followed. It also has implications for the future national church of those denominations, given that their relatively centralized and bureaucratic structures depend on the finances flowing upward from local congregations. The CLSNZ 2007 data indicated that 54 percent of Methodist and Cooperating Parishes and 42 percent of Presbyterian and Anglican attenders were retirees. Again, these compare unfavorably with the Catholic and Baptist rates of 28 percent and 20 percent respectively. Given the demographic trends, these percentages will have already increased, and have negatively impacted on levels of financial giving from church attenders. The effect of these trends has begun to bite deeply into the finances of most of these churches. The Presbyterian and Methodist Churches have had to work through significant financial crises which have led to drastic restructuring of their national work. The Anglican Church has been cushioned from this to some extent by large reserves in property and trusts, but is wrestling with significant issues in terms of its cash flow.

The age profile also indicates that the decline in attendance for these churches can be explained to a significant degree by looking at the patterns of the middle of these three age groups, the baby boomers. It is this generation, and their children, the post-boomers, who are largely missing from the ranks of church attenders. In addition, when the historic patterns of attendance are examined the figures begin to show serious decline from the middle of the 1960s, the years that the first of the baby boomers hit young adulthood. The decline can first be seen in youth group and bible class numbers. Then, because baby boomers were significantly absent from church in their child rearing years, Sunday School numbers began to decline in the early 1970s.

This had a particularly strong impact on mainline Protestant churches. For their ongoing vitality they have relied on the repetitive cycle of reproduction in families who belong to the parish. Children are baptized, proceed through Sunday School and youth group, are confirmed, and eventually become adult members who, when married, have their own children—and so the cycle continues. This was the pattern of parish life developed in the settled conditions of Northern European Christendom during the Reformation and centuries immediately following, especially in Great Britain. This pattern of church life was then exported to British colonial settlements like New Zealand.

This cycle, which had been perpetuated for centuries, was broken when baby boomers, as late teenagers and young adults, exited these established churches in large numbers. There was hope that marriage and the arrival of their own families would lead to their returning, as a considerable body of literature indicates that adults are much more likely to attend church when there are children involved. A substantial volume of material was devoted in the late 1980s to helping churches "welcome back the boomers" as adults with their families. However, this never happened, at least not in significant numbers, suggesting that this has been a cohort effect, not an age effect.

Hans Mol found that the majority of church attenders in Christchurch in 1962 were youth.[8] This being the case, it stands to reason that the loss of this age group from church would have a great effect. Indeed, this turned out to be the case, and by 1989 Webster and Perry found that 30–44 year olds (i.e., "boomers") were less linked to church than any other population group. They saw this as being due to the "historical effect" of "the anti-traditional era they grew up in."[9] The data, then, bolsters the conclusion that, with baby boomers in the 1960s, "the socialization process by which religious affiliation is transmitted from parents to the next generation broke down"[10] as they dropped out of church. As a consequence, the significant absence of young adults in their child-rearing years has had a major effect on church participation figures ever since.

One of the reasons for the continuing impact of this effect on mainline Protestant churches is that they have a less "conversionist" understanding of their faith, and less concern with mission and evangelism than have other groups such as the Baptists. In Christendom, mission and conversion were concerns and activities that took place only in places outside of the Christian society. Loren Mead argues that, in applying the name Christendom to the paradigm within which the church operated from the fourth century through to the late twentieth century, this was the critical issue. Beginning with the conversion of the emperor Constantine in 313 A.D., "The world . . . was legally identified with the church. There was no separation between world and church within the Empire. The law removed the hostility from the environment but also made the environment and the church identical."[11]

This paradigm saw church and society as one; mission as an enterprise in far-off places done by professionals rather than the ordinary person; congregations as geographical parishes rather than committed communities;[12] and membership as the result of birth rather than choice.

---

8. Mol, "Church Attendance Survey." He found that 63 percent of Presbyterian and 76 percent of Anglican attenders were under 20. Note that these percentages are of total attenders on a Sunday and so include children in Sunday School and young people in Bible Class.

9. Perry and Webster, *What Difference Does it Make*, 6.

10. Hillard, "Religious Crisis of the 1960s," 223.

11. Mead, *Once and Future Church*, 14.

12. Ibid., 16. "The local incarnation of church stopped being a tight community

A significant consequence of this was that mission was removed from the ordinary life of the church, and the role of the minister or cleric became that of a "chaplain" to care for those in the parish.

While groups such as the Baptists have also been affected by the disengagement of baby boomers in their youth, they have had from their earliest history a more missional understanding of their relationship with their immediate environment, and they have always sought to attract newcomers, especially young people and children, through special programmes specifically developed for this purpose. Classical sociological theory would see this emphasis as a consequence of their sectarian form (membership by choice), rather than the church form of the mainline denominations (membership through birth). Thus they have tended to have a stronger inflow of new, younger people to their ranks. The majority of mainline churches have not developed this kind of approach to their local congregational life, having historically had a sufficient inflow from children born into the parish and socialized in the faith to sustain their continuing life.

The difficulty now is that many of these congregations are beyond the reproductive cycle. There are insufficient people of child-rearing age for replenishment to happen this way, even if they did develop forms which kept the children and young people they already have. Data collected from other questions in the CLSNZ 2001[13] and presented in Tables 2 and 3 indicate that these mainline churches are less successful at doing this than are some other churches, such as the Baptists.

Table 2: Percentage of Attenders' Children (still living at home) Who are also Attending Church [Statistics from CLSNZ 2001]

Denomination	Children (10–14)	Youth (15–25)
Anglican	75	53
Presbyterian	79	59
Methodist	79	55
Cooperating Parishes	71	47
Baptists	87	68
Brethren	92	75

of convinced, committed, embattled believers supporting each other within a hostile environment. Instead it became a parish, comprising a geographic region and all the people in it."

13. 2001 data is used here as the same questions were not asked in 2007. Some of the responses to different questions, however, indicate that the same differences still exist.

Table 3: Percentage of Young Adults (18–25) who are Satisfied or Very Satisfied with what Church Offers for Young People [Statistics from CLSNZ 2001]

Anglican	36
Presbyterian	42
Methodist	36
Cooperating Parishes	30
Baptists	54
Brethren	63

Looking at the percentage of children aged 10 to 14 who are attending church, and whose parents are themselves attending church, the figures for mainline Protestant churches range from 71 percent to 79 per cent. For Baptists it is somewhat higher at 87 per cent, and for Brethren higher still at 92 per cent. When we move to the young people (age 15 to 25) living at home, the figures for mainline Protestants are between 47 percent and 59 per cent, compared with a significantly higher figure of 68 percent of Baptists and 75 percent of Brethren.

In examining how young people feel about what their church offers for them, the results again reveal greater problems for the mainline Protestant denominations in holding on to the youth they have, let alone attracting others. The percentage of those either satisfied or very satisfied with what their church offers for young people ranges between 30 percent and 42 percent for mainline Protestant churches. For Baptists the figure was significantly higher at 54 per cent, and for Brethren 63 per cent. While these figures indicate that retention of young people is a difficult challenge for all churches, they also suggest that the mainline Protestant churches are significantly less effective in this than other more sectarian denominations.

Data from the Youth Ministry department of one of the churches, the Presbyterian Church, illustrates the extent of this challenge. A survey of churches[14] found that there were 5,016 young people aged 11–14 under the pastoral care of churches. This had fallen to 3,327 for those 15–17, and to 1,723 by the 18–25 age group. When we realize that the last age band is more than twice the length of the first, this demonstrates even more the significant challenge these churches face in turning around their aged and aging profile.

As a consequence, congregations in these churches simply do not have the people within their community who are of an age which is going

---

14. Mansill, "PYM Snapshot Data 2005."

to attract younger persons. The generations are so unlike each other that very few under the age of 40 find any appeal or attraction to their style of worship or life together as a community. Research consistently indicates that most new people are attracted into congregations by social connections, and these congregations simply lack the people connections and social networks with younger age groups for this to occur. In addition to the age of congregations, the age of ministers is also an issue. The average age of ministers in these denominations is now well into the fifties, and it becomes difficult for ministers to attract those who are more than two decades younger than themselves.

Believing without Belonging

In researching this question of age effect, the census figures for religious adherence were also broken down into similar age groups to see if this would generate any new information. The results are displayed in Table 4.

Table 4: Percentage of Religious Affiliation for 5 Denominations in Census 1996, 2001, and 2006 by Age Categories (compared with CLSNZ 1997, 2001, and 2007 figures)

Age	15–39			40–59			over 60		
	1997	2001	2007	1997	2001	2007	1997	2001	2007
Anglican									
Census	35	29	24	34	37	37	31	34	39
CLSNZ	18	15	11	32	32	24	48	52	65
Presbyterian									
Census	36	30	24	34	37	39	30	33	36
CLSNZ	20	16	13	28	28	24	49	56	63
Methodist									
Census	39	32	27	33	37	37	29	32	35
CLSNZ	18	12	11	29	23	20	53	66	69
Catholic									
Census	41	45	41	36	34	36	24	22	23
CLSNZ	32	25	23	36	36	25	32	40	42
Baptist									
Census	44	42	38	34	36	37	22	23	25
CLSNZ	43	40	30	38	38	40	19	22	30

In comparing the figures for the percentages for the different age categories from the CLSNZ data (indicating attendance) with Census data (recording affiliation), the same pattern was anticipated. It would be expected that as fewer and fewer young people were raised and socialized in these churches, as they have been from the 1960s on, fewer and fewer would identify with them. However, the results did not bear this out. Age representation was much more evenly spread in the Census figures for affiliation, although these did provide evidence of churches becoming more aged.

Much recent sociology of religion scholarship uses the framework of *believing without belonging*, arguing that to a significant degree religious believing has been detached from religious belonging.[15] This is suggested to be so particularly among younger generations. If census affiliation is primarily an indication of religious belief, and the CLSNZ attendance figures of religious belonging, then this data supports the finding that this pattern of believing without belonging is particularly strong in mainline Protestant denominations (as well as Catholics), but less so amongst Baptists, where the age profiles for each set of data are very similar. Younger people still identify themselves in significant numbers as Anglicans, Presbyterians, or Methodists, even if they do not choose to belong to these churches.

The significance of this is seen even more markedly when the actual numbers are scrutinized. In Census 2006, 116,109 people aged 15–39 identified as Anglicans, 86,430 as Presbyterians, and 29,776 as Methodists, compared with only 17,487 as Baptists. Attendance at Baptist churches in New Zealand on an average Sunday is now roughly equal that of Anglicans or Presbyterians. Given this, the much younger age profile for Baptists suggests that they will have significantly higher actual numbers of young attenders in their churches.

Consequently, the relatively small number identifying as Baptists, compared with the high numbers of Presbyterians or Anglicans, is somewhat surprising. In New Zealand, Baptist churches (along with Pentecostal churches) are seen as the churches which are more attractive to younger people than the mainline churches, and in terms of participation this is clearly true. However, these Census figures indicate that there is still at least some attraction for younger people in what these mainline denominations have to offer. They still identify with them in considerable

---

15. Grace Davie has been influential in developing this perspective. See Davie, *Religion in Britain since 1945*.

numbers. The problem for mainline Protestants is not that younger generations seem no longer to want to identify with them, or even to believe in what their denomination stands for. The problem is that they do not want to belong to them in any significant way. If the somewhat crude analogy of fishing (which is sometimes used for evangelism) is applied, they have a much larger pool of fish to fish for than do, for example, Baptists, but their fish seem much, much harder to catch.

This research provides evidence that the challenge for churches is not so much how they get people to believe, but how they connect with those who have continued to believe in such ways that they might want to belong, a theme I will explore more in the second half of this work. When I first developed this thought, I had in mind primarily baby boomers who had ceased belonging but continued to believe. This data provides evidence to support this, but further indicates that this is also true for post-boomer generations as well.

This has been a surprising finding, as I had presumed that baby boomers continued to hold a religious, and primarily Christian, set of basic beliefs, as a consequence of being socialized in Sunday Schools and youth groups. In 1950, 50 percent of New Zealand's primary school children were enrolled in Sunday Schools in Protestant churches. In 1960, this was still as much as 40 percent (if one adds in Roman Catholics, probably still over 50 per cent), but by 1975 this had fallen to 15 per cent, and by 1985 to 11 per cent.[16]

In fact, it appears that more than the 50 percent of baby boomers had some regular church involvement at some point in their growing up. When asked, a significant majority of my peers (boomers) report that they attended not only Sunday School but also youth group, but left in their teenage years. Australian research found that 67 percent of religious non-attenders could remember attending Sunday School or church weekly or more at some point when growing up, and only 17 percent said they attended less than monthly when growing up.[17] Given the similarities between New Zealand and Australia on most measures of church attendance, it would be surprising if research here did not reveal similar figures.

Not only were people shaped by Christian beliefs in church, but even throughout the 1960s there was a culture of Bible in schools as well

---

16. Dickey, *What's Happening to the Children?*
17. Hughes, Thompson, Prior and Bouma, *Believe it or Not*, 31–32.

as prayers, hymns and bible readings in assemblies in the majority of state schools in New Zealand. It is not surprising, then, that those who participated in these activities retained a significant Christian identity. That culture had by and large disappeared by the end of the 1970s, however, and the figures for attendance indicate that very few of the generation that followed, the under-forties, were brought up in Sunday School. It is then surprising that such a high percentage still identify with the Christian tradition, and in particular with mainline Protestant churches.

This picture is confirmed by a survey carried out with university students in Dunedin in 2006. In this survey of 1,000 students, 59 percent indicated a Christian affiliation, compared with 56 percent of the total population and 47 percent of the 15 to 29 age group in the 2006 Census. The percentage of respondents attending church was also higher than the national averages, with 18 percent indicating weekly attendance and 31 percent at least monthly attendance. These higher figures are not completely surprising, as there is now considerable evidence that levels of religious involvement may well be higher among young people in student populations than among young people in general. Over 50 percent indicated a belief in God, with another 20 percent being uncertain, figures not dissimilar from that for the New Zealand population as a whole.

When it came to what denomination the students identified with, the highest percentages were Anglicans, followed by Presbyterians, and then Catholics. Anglican and Presbyterian numbers were more than double those for Baptists and Pentecostals. What is interesting, however is that when it comes to where these students attend church, very few do so at Anglican or Presbyterian churches. The biggest student churches in Dunedin are mainly Pentecostal, with one significant Catholic church and a reasonably large Baptist church. In other words, the findings reveal that a significant number of students still identify as mainline Protestant, but when they do worship they choose to go elsewhere.

A sign of hope, then, for these churches is that quite significant numbers of younger generations still retain a sense of identity with them and a semblance of Christian belief, and therefore may be seen as favourably disposed toward them. The point of great challenge is that they show increasingly less desire to become involved in the life of these churches.

Conclusion

When analyzing data such as this, which shows declining figures of attendance and an aged and aging profile, it would be easy to paint a picture of complete despair for churches such as the mainline Protestants in New Zealand. Many have done this recently, almost suggesting that they are doomed to disappear and that it is pointless to try to stem the outgoing tide. However, a closer examination of the data does provide a measure of hope, although with their smaller numbers and the more aged profile the Methodists and Cooperating Parishes particularly do appear to be at considerable risk. For the Anglicans and Presbyterians, at least, there are a good number of congregations with healthy age profiles and these are likely to continue to provide places of life and vitality as well as signs of hope.

Numbers overall are likely to continue to decline, perhaps at an even faster rate than the previous two decades, as the remaining generation raised and socialized into the church by baptism as infants, confirmation as teenagers, and membership as adults dies out. This will mean that by 2015 a considerable number of existing parishes will not have sufficient numbers to continue to maintain any form of meaningful life as faith communities. Indeed, this crisis has already hit. The 2010 General Assembly of the Presbyterian Church in New Zealand passed a hotly debated remit requiring parishes with less than 40 regular attenders to be subject to a review by their Presbytery to assess their ongoing viability. This crisis of declining numbers and aging members is also necessitating considerable change in Presbyterian regional and national organizations. Presbytery reform has been underway for about 6 years, with a move to reduce the number of these from 23 to 5, and the national structure has been streamlined and reduced to be almost unrecognizable from what it was 10 years ago.

The Anglican Church has not changed its structures significantly as yet, partly because its reserves have enabled it to continue in much the same ways as before. However, the inevitable pressure of this erosion is now becoming apparent. In Dunedin in June, 2012 the front page of local newspaper in one edition ran the stark headline in large print, "Diocese Near Collapse." It quoted from a letter recently posted to clergy by the Bishop stating, "It is my sad duty to appraise our council . . . that the Diocese of Dunedin in its present form is unsustainable. For many years the diocese has been in decline on any parameter that could be named . . . dropping to the point where several of our parishes are on the very edge of ceasing to exist altogether."[18]

Will these kinds of headlines become increasingly commonplace? Is this outcome inevitable? There are, I believe, two points of hope. One is those numerous parishes, particularly in the Anglican and Presbyterian churches, and increasingly in one newly configured evangelical stream of the Methodist Church,[19] where there is life, energy, and a younger age profile. The second sign of hope is the considerable number of younger New Zealanders who still identify in some way with these churches. Many existing congregations are too aged for these people to ever make a connection with, and rather than pouring most of its time, energy and resources into continuing to keep these unviable congregations going, denominational energy and resources need to be focused on helping those congregations which exhibit life and health to become more effective in this task.

Further to this, new faith communities need to be developed which have forms of belonging that can connect in meaningful ways with the lives of the still considerable number of young New Zealanders who have at least the vestiges of Christian faith, but who have been raised without any connection to the church. This implies a shift in the fundamental understanding of church from that of maintenance—keeping in the faith those born into it and perpetuating forms that relate to their needs—to a more missional understanding that seeks to bring into committed belief and belonging those born outside of the Christian community, by developing forms that are meaningful to their needs and the challenges they present. For some, particularly those committed to an older form of "liberal ecumenical" Christianity, this is a theological as well as a structural issue. Of the mainline Protestant denominations in New Zealand, the Presbyterian Church has most been able to embrace this theological shift. There are signs that the Anglican Church, at least in some significant sectors, is doing likewise, and a stream of the Methodist Church has set up some of its own structures and resources while staying within the denomination. Some of the possible forms these new kind of communities might take will be explored later.

---

18. *Otago Daily Times,* June 12, 2012, 1.
19. The Wesleyan Methodist Church.

5

The Charismatic Movement and the Churches

Modest Beginnings

MODERN PENTECOSTALISM IS GENERALLY regarded as having begun in Azusa Street, Los Angeles in 1906, from whence it spread globally like wildfire, becoming an organized body in New Zealand with the visit of Smith Wigglesworth in 1922. As in most Western countries, Pentecostalism was on the periphery of church life in New Zealand until the 1960s. Pentecostal churches such as the Assemblies of God and Apostolic Church were small, and in 1961claimed only 3,000 on census returns, a mere 0.1 percent of the population. By 1966 this had doubled, and by 1991 stood at 52,000, representing 1.6 per cent. This was not a uniquely New Zealand phenomenon. Ian Breward notes that their growth since the 1960s has been part of a worldwide expansion which "can only be described as extraordinary," and that this has been "obvious in both Australia and New Zealand."[1]

About five decades after its birth, Pentecostal-style religion "spilled over" into the historic churches, its formal beginnings again being traced to California, under the leadership of an Episcopal priest, Dennis Bennett, although this was beginning to happen prior to this time, even in New Zealand. This spill-over into other denominations signified a degree of demarcation between Pentecostalism and the charismatic movement,

---

1. Breward, *History of the Churches in Australasia*, 328.

the latter being among people who generally stayed within their existing churches and assumed a softer form of expression. The charismatic movement was also not necessarily tied to a pre-millennial fundamentalist theology as Pentecostalism was.

Allan Davidson and Peter Lineham suggest that in New Zealand the charismatic movement "began to affect the mainstream churches to a degree paralleled in few other Western countries."[2] Initially it was greeted with suspicion and often hostility, and during the early years many of those who embraced the movement were forced to leave their churches and join Pentecostal churches. This was particularly so amongst the Brethren, who specifically rejected it in 1964, and in Baptist churches, where those who had embraced Pentecostalism were encouraged to leave. The editor of the *New Zealand Baptist* wrote, under the heading "Members We can Do Without": "Baptists who accept Pentecostalist views should . . . sever their connections with their church, and link up with like-minded people in one of the several Pentecostal bodies in this country . . . love and honesty demand that they resign their membership, rather than remain as agents, no matter how unwilling, of Satan himself."[3]

Many people from these churches became leaders of independent Pentecostal and charismatic churches. A Baptist report in 1969, while noting some beneficial effects of Neo-Pentecostalism, emphasized its harmful influences.[4] In 1967 a Presbyterian report warned of the dangers of divisiveness and an unbalanced Christian life and doctrine. The Anglican churches seemed to be more open from the beginning, perhaps reflective of the diversity that has long been embraced by that church, although there were tensions within some dioceses and, in one case, terms such as "evil," "extreme fundamentalists," and "arrogant and proud" were used to describe charismatics. From the 1970s onward the other denominations became more tolerant, and increasingly people found they could embrace a charismatic or Pentecostal dimension without having to leave their churches.

---

2. Davidson and Lineham, *Transplanted Christianity*, 324.

3. "Members We Can Do Without," 2.

4. Many of these reports referred to here can be found in Worsfold, *History of the Charismatic Movements in New Zealand*.

A Growing Influence

By the end of the 1970s, the charismatic influence was widespread in most Protestant churches. "Life in the Spirit" seminars had a considerable impact on Anglican parishes. A report to the Anglican General Synod in 1976 reported that, by the end of 1974, it was estimated that in the Auckland Diocesan Synod between 40 percent and 50 percent of clergy were either participants in renewal or were open to the possibility of a charismatic experience. In Christchurch it was reported that, by the same year, 30 percent of Anglican clergy in the diocese were either participants in renewal or had shown considerable interest by regularly attending charismatic prayer meetings. "It would be true to say that in most (if not all) Anglican churches in Christchurch there are charismatic Christians."[5] Significant in the growth of charismatic renewal amongst mainline churches were the Summer Schools organized by Christian Advance Ministries[6] during the 1970s. Participation grew rapidly, and by 1975 half of those attending were Anglicans.

The Anglican report also looked more briefly at the influence of the movement in other churches. "The extent of the charismatic renewal in the Presbyterian Church is widespread . . . nearly 20 percent of Presbyterian parishes in the country are affected to some degree."[7] In 1973 the Presbyterians received a report which made a much more positive response to the movement than it had in 1967. This "agreed that those of our Church who have had some form of pentecostal experience need to be recognised as contributing members of the body."[8] A report the following year encouraged the church to go beyond "passive acceptance" and "create a climate of sharing."[9]

Jim Veitch notes that, by the end of the 1980s, "the charismatic influence was strongly represented in many parishes throughout the country."[10] In his view this development brought a new enthusiasm to the life and worship of parishes, "strengthening the conservative strand"

---

5. *Provincial Commission on the Charismatic Renewal*, 67.

6. Formed to further renewal amongst Anglicans, Catholics, Presbyterians, and Methodists.

7. *Provincial Commission on the Charismatic Renewal*, 75.

8. *Presbyterian Church of New Zealand*, 1973, 91.

9. *Presbyterian Church of New Zealand*, 1974, 143.

10. Veitch, "1961–1990: Toward the Church for a New Era," 172.

in the church."[11] There were also centers of charismatic renewal in the Methodist Church, but it had "minimal impact" on the church as a whole.[12] Commenting on Protestants in general, Veitch notes that by 1990 "Charismatic Christianity . . . has a strong hold and influence on mainline churches, and exerts tremendous influence on the leadership and on policy development."[13]

Despite the initial misgivings and often strong opposition, there is no doubt that the church influenced the most by the charismatic movement was the Baptist church. Indeed, by the end of the 1980s those opposed to it were a clear minority in the church. Significant in furthering the movement and gaining acceptance of it was Spreydon Baptist Church and its minister, Murray Robertson, who emerged as a key leader for charismatic renewal nationally. By the mid-1970s it was estimated that 25 percent of Baptist ministers were baptized in the Spirit and the majority of students at the theological college were charismatic. In 1981 there was a strong move to accept diversity and move toward cooperation, and by 1989 69 percent of Baptist churches identified with the charismatic movement.[14]

What was the impact of this strong influence of the charismatic movement on churches such as the Baptists, Presbyterians, and Anglicans? Certainly the impression was often voiced that it is those churches which embraced the charismatic dimension that have grown. In the Baptist scene there does seem to be significant truth in this. A 1984 study of the twenty fastest growing Baptist churches in New Zealand in the period 1973 to 1983 found that "the best combination for growth seemed to be . . . conservative, evangelical and charismatic."[15]

These findings are confirmed by Elaine Bolitho's research, which found that between 1968 and 1988 54 percent of charismatic Baptist churches grew at a rate faster than the rate of growth for all churches. This was almost double that of non-charismatic churches. In that period of time, charismatic churches added around 6,700 new members while others added about 700, and planted 32 new churches out of a total of 36. Looking at other indicators of effectiveness, they had more children and youth and attracted more people under 40 than did non-charismatic churches.

11. Ibid.
12. Bolitho, *In This World*, 70.
13. Veitch, "Protestants Since the 1960s," 96. Veitch is to some degree reflecting his experience in the Presbyterian Church.
14. Bolitho, *Meet the Baptists*, 37.
15. Ng, *Focus on the Fastest Growing Baptist Churches*.

Regarding the Presbyterian Church, Veitch noted in 1990 that, over the previous two decades, "Charismatic and evangelical orientation seemed to be the stimulant in the majority of growing churches."[16] Two different research projects carried out by the Presbyterian Church, in 1985 and 1991, both found that the churches which were growing "classified themselves as charismatic, conservative and evangelical."[17] There does not appear to be any research done in the Anglican Church to confirm these patterns, but impressions gained through observation certainly seem to confirm that those churches which had embraced charismatic renewal were also more likely to have grown over the period.

Explaining Charismatic Vitality

One reason for the apparent influence of the charismatic movement on church vitality is likely to be its reinforcement of strong orthodox or conservative beliefs. As we have already identified, the experience of the church in New Zealand confirms international findings that this is a significant factor in the likelihood of growth. A number of the studies cited argue that a combination of evangelical beliefs with the charismatic dimension was most likely to lead to growth.

Support for this contention may be seen in the experience of the Methodist Church. As noted above, it was the mainline church least influenced by charismatic renewal. Bolitho found that only 20 percent of Methodist congregations held a charismatic orientation, compared with 69 percent of Baptist congregations. It is also seen as the church most influenced by liberal theology and a strong commitment to a "social agenda."[18] The Methodist Church, then, may have missed the strengthening influence of the charismatic movement on the beliefs of its members, and consequently suffered the greatest decline of the mainline Protestant churches. Liberal is not a word that could really be applied to any Bap-

---

16. Veitch, "1961–1990: Toward the Church for a New Era," 151, 153. He also notes that "not all charismatic parishes were growing."

17. Bradley, *Who's in the Pews*, 257.

18. Perry and Webster's research indicates, for example, that Methodists showed the lowest percentages of any church for people believing personally in God, life after death, a soul and heaven, but the highest percentage believing in reincarnation. Perry and Webster, *The Religious Factor in New Zealand Society*, 134. Bolitho sees a move "from evangelical to liberal theology" and the "collapse of neo-orthodoxy" and "decline in evangelical theology" as being factors leading to decline.

tist churches in New Zealand. It is evident, however, that those churches which had a tradition of being more tolerant and open, with a more intellectual and questioning approach to the faith, tended to be those least influenced by the charismatic movement.

While this is important, an even more significant impact of the charismatic movement and Pentecostalism is that it helped to make Christianity and church life more relevant to the changed social and cultural context of New Zealand life that emerged from the mid-1960s—the other dimension identified as being more likely to foster a growing church. It is often suggested that the charismatic movement had more impact on mainline church life in New Zealand than in any other Western country. The *Operation World* Handbook, for example, in its entry on New Zealand for 1978, states: "Charismatic renewal has brought about widespread changes. Nearly every denomination has been affected. The impact has been greater than any other English speaking nation."[19]

Murray Robertson likewise has claimed that "What has happened in the Charismatic movement in New Zealand probably hasn't got many parallels elsewhere in the world."[20] Here he is referring to the widespread impact of the movement across so many different churches. Certainly this is so compared with the country most similar to New Zealand—Australia. While there is clearly a strong Pentecostal stream of church life in Australia, there is nothing like the dominant influence of charismatics amongst Baptists, nor is there a very strong stream in the Anglican, Uniting, or Presbyterian Churches. The evangelical sector of the church in Australia is much more heavily influenced by a strong Reformed tradition, which is often quite anti-charismatic and anti-Pentecostal in tone.

Part of the reason for this strength of influence in New Zealand may be the extent to which its church life is readily influenced by trends from overseas. There was certainly a steady stream of both Pentecostal and charismatic leaders visiting New Zealand in the 1960s and 1970s. The relatively small geographical area of New Zealand as a country also aids in the rapid spread of ideas. At the same time, the extent of the movement's reach in New Zealand may also be partially due to particular changes in New Zealand society over this period. In 1974 Colin Brown observed that the rapid growth of Pentecostalism in New Zealand coincided with the rise of charismatic renewal, and postulated that "this

---

19. Johnstone, *Operation World*, 318.
20. Cited in Bolitho, *Meet the Baptists*, 31.

suggests that both were a response to changes in society in general at that time."²¹ Some twenty years later Elaine Bolitho, noting that the rapid changes of the 1960s and 1970s "caused a sense of discontinuity," argues that in this context the charismatic movement can be seen as "providing continuity of God experience."²²

It is clear from looking at the age make-up of Pentecostal and charismatic churches, compared with mainstream non-charismatic churches, that the appeal of this form of Christianity over this period was largely to baby boomers. Bolitho claims that the "keys to interpreting the complementary differences between the charismatic and non-charismatic Baptist groups appear in the different values held by pre-war and baby boom New Zealanders."²³ In other words, it appears that the Pentecostal and charismatic movements from the mid-1960s to the 1980s helped to adapt Christianity to forms and styles that were particularly relevant to the post-war generation, as they emerged into young adulthood over that period. It appeared to do this in New Zealand to an even greater degree than most other Western countries. Why was this?

Examining Pentecostalism in Australia, Alan Black writes:

> Insofar as it opposes moral permissiveness and upholds patriarchy, Pentecostalism is at odds with the expressive revolution. But in many other respects it is in harmony with that revolution. Indicative of this are its stress on self-validating experience; informality in dress, forms of worship and interpersonal relationships; spontaneity, immediacy and instant (religious gratification); anti-intellectualism, some degree of expressive disorder; involvement of the body; excitement and novelty; the use of popular rather than classical music forms; and in characteristics such as these, a deliberate contrast with more conventional religious institutions.²⁴

In researching Spreydon Baptist Church, it became obvious how much the forms and styles which the church developed, especially in the 1970s and 1980s, were congenial to the baby boomers who moved into the church in significant numbers. The experiences of many other churches were similar, albeit often to a lesser degree. The more relaxed and experiential style of worship, use of more contemporary music, with

21. Brown, "The Charismatic Contribution," 102.
22. Bolitho, *Meet the Baptists*, 36.
23. Ibid., 38.
24. Black, "Australian Pentecostalism in Comparative Perspective," 117.

keyboards, guitars and drums replacing the organ, rapid development of small groups, valuing of individual gifts, and widespread participatory roles all affirmed the more informal and expressive culture which developed. There was considerable emphasis on the need to develop closer and more intimate personal relationships. Especially in the charismatic movement, less hierarchical and more informal forms of leadership evolved, compared with the traditional models. Particularly in New Zealand, this emphasis on greater informality and more egalitarian relationships[25] was well in touch with larger social trends.

Other commentators on the phenomenon highlight a number of distinctive and important dimensions of this movement. Perhaps most significant is the more expressive and experiential elements. Steve Bruce, in his study of the charismatic movement in Britain, highlights the much greater prominence given to these elements as the key difference between it and traditional Protestantism.[26] Brown sees this as being "especially important" in the New Zealand setting: "There is a general tendency, especially among younger age groups, toward a much freer expression of emotions in all sorts of situations, not merely in words but in gestures also. This is closely related to the tendency to prefer immediate experience to rational reflection . . . greater frankness, fewer inhibitions and increased demonstrativeness are more common than in the immediate past at least."[27]

Referring back to our studies of congregations in Christchurch, I found in researching the two more traditional and non-charismatic congregations, when interviewing people even 25 years later, a great deal of reserve, inhibition, and formality, which is likely to have mitigated against creating the relaxed, informal, expressive culture attractive to youth in the 1960s and 1970s. One member of these churches, speaking of this, expressed it in these terms: "My generation wouldn't just drop in on someone. You almost had to make an appointment to have a cup of tea with someone. There was a very reserved and formal culture that was just increasingly out of touch with the uninhibited and informal style for example of my children and their friends. They don't go to church. They haven't for years." It appears, then, that while the more relaxed, informal, expressive culture that developed in charismatic churches fit well with the

---

25. Egalitarianism is seen an important culture trait in New Zealand.
26. Bruce, *God is Dead*, 179–80
27. Brown, "The Charismatic Contribution," 108–9.

cultural and social changes happening among young people, the more controlled and formal culture of many mainline Protestant churches created a barrier for them.

Brown also identifies the desire for more intimate forms of community life as being significant at the time when the movement took off. He suggests that the "level of pastoral care and mutual support in Pentecostalist [and charismatic] circles is quite high," and that this probably adds significant appeal.[28] By and large, charismatic and Pentecostal churches embraced the small group movement more readily than other churches, and the sense of community and mutual caring in these was a significant factor.

Bruce identifies another "major theme of the charismatic movement that chimes well with the secular climate" as "its attitude towards the individual self."[29] Andrew Walker, a leader in the movement in Britain, and more recently a researcher on it, writes: "People in the renewal were in touch with themselves as well as God. As the Hobbesian and hedonistic individual replaced ascetic individualism in the larger culture so the Renewal reflected these changes."[30] In New Zealand, Bolitho suggests that for young New Zealanders the kind of life and forms that developed in charismatic churches "affirmed the individualistic cultural milieu to which they belonged."[31]

It can be seen how much these characteristics are in touch with the kind of social and cultural values that emerged in Western countries like New Zealand—individualism, privatism, pluralism, relativism, and anti-institutionalism—as part of the counter-cultural movements of the 1960s and 1970s. "The charismatic movement in the churches reflected the idealism, the heightened experience, and the hedonism of this counter-culture."[32]

Perhaps this dimension in itself also explains some of the appeal of the charismatic and Pentecostal movements. They were outside of and therefore counter to the established church culture. Pentecostalism was outside of, and often in opposition to, the mainline churches. The charismatic movement in some ways set itself up as a protest movement,

---

28. Ibid., 109.
29. Bruce, *God is Dead*, 180.
30. Walker, "Thoroughly Modern," 30.
31. Bolitho, *Meet the Baptists*, 39.
32. Walker, "Thoroughly Modern," 30.

seeking to usher in a new vision of Christian community in place of the established forms of institutional religion. This in itself was appealing to young baby boomers in New Zealand in the 1960s and 1970s. A number of writers point to the significance of the Jesus Marches of 1972 in the main cities of New Zealand in terms of popularizing charismatic and Pentecostal Christianity. Support largely came from Pentecostal and charismatic-evangelical churches, and those joining the marches who were not involved with churches largely found their way back into those kind of churches.[33]

Two groups of churches which rejected the charismatic movement and suffered significant decline over this period were the Brethren and the Churches of Christ. Commenting on this, Breward notes that "Churches of Christ and Brethren, who were inclined to believe that they were the most authentic form of Christianity, also found that a number of their most ardent members left."[34] The Brethren fought bitterly over this issue during the 1960s. Peter Lineham writes, "It is difficult to estimate the extent of Brethren losses through the dispute. They were certainly extensive. Beside the people who departed from the assemblies in the period from 1963–65, many more have drifted out, then or later, through Brethren intransigence."[35]

In the early 1960s attendance at Brethren churches may have been similar to that of the 14,000 who attended Baptist churches. But by 1986 Baptist attendance of over 26,000 was considerably higher than the Brethren figure of about 11,000. One cannot explain the growth of one and decline of the other entirely in terms of their response to the charismatic movement, but as it appears this movement helped the growth of Baptist churches, so it is logical to infer that the Brethren rejection of it was a factor in their decline. It made it difficult for them to change in ways relevant to the new cultural values and social attitudes of young post-war New Zealanders. In a similar vein, the Churches of Christ, who before 1960 were not dissimilar to Baptist churches in form, declined both in census figures and in membership from about 4,300 in 1961 to approximately 2,250 in 1986. Rejection of the charismatic movement again appears to be one explanatory factor.

---

33. Davidson and Lineham, *Transplanted Christianity*, 325.
34. Breward, *History of the Churches in Australasia*, 330.
35. Lineham, "Tongues Must Cease," 206.

Evaluating the Movement

In identifying charismatic churches as more likely to have grown over this period of overall church decline, it is important to ask where the people coming into these churches came from. In my research on Spreydon Baptist Church, I found a repeated concern expressed by Murray Robertson, during its time of most rapid growth, that so many new people were coming from other churches, and a desire to see more "unsaved people" coming to faith. When descriptions were given of the kind of people being baptized, it was obvious that the majority of these people came from churched backgrounds.

Reflection on my own experience as a pastor of a charismatic Baptist church, which also grew rapidly in the late 1970s and into the 1980s, reveals a similar pattern. The vast majority of new congregants either came from other churches, or were young adults who had been brought up in church and were now returning after a time away. As indicated in the congregational studies, research on Spreydon as well as other charismatic and Pentecostal churches confirmed this, with the largest proportion of newcomers being from mainline Protestant churches and another significant group from older conservative churches.

It is thus clear that the growth of charismatic and Pentecostal churches has largely occurred through people moving to them from mainline or conservative churches, both of which have experienced significant losses. The decline of one group has fostered the growth of the other. In 1982 a report in the New Zealand evangelical newspaper, *Challenge Weekly*, suggested that the rapid growth of Pentecostal church raised a question regarding ". . . how much of the Pentecostal success has been at the expense of other churches, by drawing off not only members, but many of the keenest members, in fact weakening the other churches. How much of this increase in numbers has been made by inroads into the godless community?"[36]

The answer from this research is clearly "not much." It appears that little of the growth has in fact been through previously un-churched New Zealanders embracing the Christian faith for the first time,[37] an issue

---

36. Thompson, "Just how Alive are our Churches," 15.

37. A paper published by Signposts Communications in the 1990s asked the question, "Has the New Zealand Church grown in the past 20 years?" They bemoaned the fact that "good consistent data on church attendances in New Zealand is minimal," such that they had to rely on "observed trends." They suggested these indicated four

which will be explored further in the next chapter. In a similar vein, Steve Bruce, commenting specifically on the charismatic movement in Britain, states that while there is no survey data to point to, "a very large number of institutional histories and personal biographies show most of the growth . . . was a result of Christians moving spiritual home."[38]

If this were the pattern, we would expect to see a slowing down of the growth of these churches as the pool of New Zealanders raised in mainline Protestant churches, and to a lesser degree older conservative evangelical churches, began to age and diminish. Trends in the 1990s seem to bear this out. Many leaders of these churches talk about the heyday of the 1970s and 1980s, the years of easy growth. Whereas, from the mid-1960s through the 1980s, Baptist churches had shown overall steady growth, in the 1990s this tended to plateau. A census return of about 70,000 in 1991 had fallen to about 56,500 in 2006. An attendance average of round 31,500 in 1991 had risen only slightly to around 34,000 in 2006, not even keeping pace with population growth.

For Pentecostals, census affiliation continued the pattern of increase they had shown since 1961, although at a slower rate, with an increase from about 52,000 in 1991 to approximately 76,000 in 2006. Gordon Miller, who has kept track of attendance trends, writes that the "explosive growth slowed in the late 80s, declined further in the early and mid-90s, and has now almost disappeared."[39] He notes that the Pentecostal peak of the 1970s and 1980s was "during the sharpest decline of the mainline churches." It is no coincidence, then, that as the Pentecostal and Baptist growth has slowed in the 1990s and 2000s, the decline in the mainline Protestant churches has similarly slowed.

These findings show that the significant growth of Pentecostal and charismatic churches from the mid-1960s to the mid-1980s, which was largely as a result of people transferring from mainline Protestant

---

insights: (1) Some of the decline in mainline churches since the 1976 has resulted from people transferring to Evangelical or Pentecostal churches. (2) Much of the drop in Brethren churches has resulted from the transfer of large numbers to independent Christian fellowships, Baptist churches, and other Pentecostal/charismatic churches, especially in the 1960s and early 1970s. (3) Much growth in the Baptist church between 1978 and 1986 was transfer growth from mainline churches and other Evangelical churches. (4) A significant amount of growth in Pentecostal churches has resulted from transfers from mainline and Evangelical churches. The research reported here indicates their observations were very accurate.

38. Bruce, *God is Dead*, 175.

39. Miller, "Leadership Letter," 1–6.

churches, has slowed significantly since, as the tide of people leaving mainline churches has slowed. Partly this has been because many of their congregations have developed similar characteristics to Pentecostal and charismatic churches, in the two crucial dimensions of a stronger adherence to orthodox beliefs and a willingness to adapt to make themselves more relevant to the changing culture and social patterns. Veitch sees this as being partly due to the widespread impact of the charismatic movement. "By . . . 1990 Charismatic Christianity had continued to grow in strength throughout all the churches, and became a major factor in maintaining the life and vitality of individual congregations."[40] People of those denominations who wished to embrace this kind of "orthodox and relevant" Christianity no longer needed to leave their denomination to do so.

In addition to this factor in explaining the declining trajectory of the charismatic movement, we need also to evaluate how it related to its social and cultural context and how that changed over the period. I have argued that, to a significant degree, its rapid growth can be explained by the way it helped churches adapt to the cultural changes that emerged in the 1960s and 1970s. While I would not want to discount the activity of God in this vitality and growth, examining it through the lens of sociology and cultural studies, as well as historical analysis, can explain much of what happened in human terms.

If one has a strong incarnational perspective this does not create a theological problem, as it leads to a belief that God has chosen primarily to work within the world He has created, rather than as an external force acting upon it. As Paul Fiddes puts it, "God never acts wholly immediately and directly on us and through us, because natural life is never dissolved by grace."[41] Divine and human agency are often hard to distinguish, either in such micro matters as the exercise of spiritual gifts or at a more macro level of explaining historical movements. Having worked significantly in the area of social sciences, I believe we should seek to explain phenomena as much as possible using these approaches, while acknowledging that when we have done that we have not explained everything about those phenomena.

This principle of the incarnation is of course most fully expressed in Jesus Christ, who provides the model for all we do. In Jesus God took

---

40. Veitch, "Protestants since the 1960s," 99.
41. Fiddes, "The Theology of the Charismatic Movement," 37.

the human social, cultural, and historical context seriously, in all its particularity. Jesus was chronologically, geographically, religiously, and culturally a first-century Jew. He neither repudiated his humanity nor his Jewishness. The early church continued this principle as the gospel moved out of the language and culture of Jesus and his disciples into that of Graeco-Roman culture. Ever since, those most effective in mission have "assumed that any culture can be host to Jesus Christ."[42]

The charismatic movement can thus be understood as an incarnation or contextualization of the gospel and church within the emerging baby boomer culture of the 1960s and 1970s. It was therefore effective in enabling many of those who felt alienated by the culture and expressions of a previous age, which were still maintained in many churches, to sustain their faith and feel at home in church in this very different world.

At the same time, the critical point to note in an authentic contextual or incarnational approach is that there are limits to how far culture can set the agenda or determine the shape of the church. Andrew Walls reminds us there are two important principles. On the one hand, there is the "indigenizing" principle, which affirms that the gospel is at home in every culture and every culture is at home with the gospel. But there is also the "pilgrim" principle, which warns us that the gospel is never fully at home in any culture and will put us out of step with every society.[43] So while there is much in every culture from which the church can take its forms and practices, there are elements of culture which it must critique and resist. The danger of becoming deeply embedded in any particular culture is that, like the frog in the kettle, we become unaware of changes that may be taking place.

One of the characteristics of the emerging new culture of the 1960s and 1970s was its growing individualism, which put more focus on the self and the fulfilment of one's own individuality—what Walker described as the "hedonistic individual." This shift was to some extent ameliorated by the idealism and desire to create a better community and world that went with many of those socialized in the 1960s and early 1970s, both in the wider culture and the charismatic movement. These characteristics helped to turn people outward rather than inward as the narcissistic tendencies of the culture encouraged, and many of those who had discovered a new sense of freedom and empowerment were motivated to become engaged in significant missional and community activism for the sake of others.

42. Jacobs, "Contextualization in Mission," 236.
43. Walls, *The Missionary Movement*, 7–9.

However, as the 1970s turned into the 1980s, a stronger form of self-centered individualism emerged, and the rampant materialism of what novelist Tom Wolfe called the "decade of money fever" took grip. According to Walker, "The charismatic movement has followed the same contours of secular modernity from its early to its late phase; it has in fact been for the spirit of the age rather than against it. It has perhaps, in David Harvey's understanding of late capitalism, capitulated to the consumer and experiential hedonism of late modernity and become commodified and corrupted."[44]

He notes that a narcissistic streak of American hedonism emerging as Christianity was repackaged so that increasingly there was little emphasis on asceticism—what I can do for God—but, rather, an orientation toward self-gratification—what God can do for me. He also notes Jamison Davison Hunter's demonstration in the 1980s that American evangelicals in general, and charismatics in particular, were borrowing heavily from secular therapeutic models and looking for life-enhancing satisfaction. It is interesting that at this time there is growing evidence of American influence in the charismatic movement in New Zealand, which up to this stage had largely drawn on sources from the U.K.[45]

This was soon to become a major factor with the arrival of John Wimber. Following the first of several visits in 1986, Wimber and what some termed "Wimberization" became the dominant force in the charismatic movement in New Zealand and this, combined with the increasing influence of American Pentecostalism, led to an unhelpful captivity of this sector of the church by certain cultural trends which should have been more strongly resisted, or at least engaged with more selectively and critically.

In researching the charismatic movement in the U.K, I found significant similarities. Douglas McBain, who was the leader of Baptist charismatic renewal there, discusses the phenomena popularized by Wimber's ministry, which were identified as "responses to the action of the Holy Spirit . . . including shaking, trembling, falling over, apparent drunkenness, bodily writhing, laughter, sobbing and prolonged praise."[46] McBain suggests these manifestations may be nothing more than the conditioned

---

44. Walker, "Thoroughly Modern," 34.

45. This shift is also identified in New Zealand society as a whole in the most recent major history of the country." Belich, *Paradise Reforged*, 392. He sees the colonial relationship with Britain as being "weakened substantially" from the 1960s and had "virtually disappeared in the late 1980s." The danger he saw was of re-colonization by the U.S.

46. McBain, *Fire over the Waters*, 104–5.

results of the heightened excitement in which Wimber's ministry is usually conducted. He refers to the view of Martin Percy that "in exciting religious meetings, the body releases endorphins, which produce the religious feel-good factor, and so we feel changed."[47]

A significant cultural and social trend over this period was growing consumerism and the development of what has come to be called a consumer culture. One manifestation of this was the growing materialism of the 1980s. But in a culture that increasingly valued feelings and experiences, as the 1980s moved into the 1990s there was a shift from consuming goods to consuming experiences. In some ways material goods and money came to be valued not so much as an end in themselves as for the experiences and feelings they could provide. Stephen Hunt, Malcom Hamilton, and Tony Walker write:

> Post-modern society produces a culture of the consumer, a culture in which what matters is not what is true or what is meaningful, but *pzazz*, what catches the eye, for only that which catches the eye will sell. If religion is to compete in a post-modern world it too must offer eye-catching wares, which is precisely what neo-Pentecostalism does. God has to top last year's eye-catching interventions in this world with something even more eye catching this year.
>
> The movement has increasingly appealed to members of a society who have grown up with the three minute culture of the television and have come to expect instant satisfaction. It offers spiritual excitement through what Wilson calls 'proximate salvation.' It satisfies an impatient demand to consume experience 'now,' tending towards what might be termed an over-realized eschatology . . . But the 'now' and the 'new' have no sense of continuity nor church history, no patience with dogma nor ecclesial authority.[48]

Tom Smail, who was a key leader of the charismatic movement in the UK and very influential in New Zealand, which he visited several times, wrote an article in 1996, reflecting on his own experience with the movement. Unfortunately, he wrote, "the subjectivist and inward looking tendency has made the beneficiaries of the renewal: more interested in personal healing then in mission; their own spiritual development than in the establishment of God's rule in society; exercising gifts rather

---

47. Ibid.
48. Hunt, Hamilton and Walter, "Tongues, Toronto and the Millennium," 16.

than carrying crosses; exuberant praise than committed intercession; triumphing in the Spirit rather than repenting at the cross."[49]

This increasing captivity to the wider culture gradually shifted the focus and culture of the movement itself so that, instead of being a movement seeking to renew the church for the sake of its mission in the world, it gradually became more and more focused on the health, well-being and experiences of the individual. Certainly in some of the best examples of the renewal in New Zealand in the 1970s and 1980s, a focus on the church's mission was still central in what developed. The emergence of a very significant community ministries focus with Murray Robertson at Spreydon Baptist Church, and the Kingdom focus of another key leader, Brian Hathaway of Te Atatu Bible Chapel in Auckland, were highly publicized examples of this.

As the later 1980s led into the 1990s, however, this focus in most places seemed to disappear, although at Spreydon it was continued. In noting this, it is not insignificant that Robertson slowly moved away from an emphasis on the charismatic movement. In a recent interview with him about this movement he said, "It was very significant in the '70s and into the '80s, but as it moved on to the '90s it became problematic, losing its way, particularly around the loss of a mission focus."

At the end of the 1990s, Martin Percy argued that the "charismatic renewal finds itself reacting to an increasingly postmodern society. Naturally following Niebuhr, its self-perception is that it leads the way in asserting 'Christ above culture' but the movement would be more adequately expressed as representing the 'Christ of culture.' . . . The movement taps into contemporary preoccupations with empowerment, fulfilment, healing and meeting individual needs."[50] This shift led to a loss of the energy, idealism, and dynamism which characterized the movement in its first two decades, significantly lessening its impact.

In addition, there was another cultural shift that impacted on this movement. We have seen how the movement in New Zealand fit particularly well with some of the values of the baby boom culture. But what would happen as young people emerged who were no longer of that generation but of a generation with somewhat different values? It was noted earlier how Donald Miller's research in *Reinventing American Protestantism* identified how American churches which could be described as

---

49. Smail, "Renewal of the Anglican Church," 6.
50. Percy, *Power and the Church*, 195.

"charismatic" to some degree were dominated by the baby boom generation, as they "adapted to the needs of that generational segment, as opposed to either their parents' or their children's generation."[51] Miller later did further research with Richard Flory on churches that were made up of the generation which followed, GenXers. They found that while there are similarities between boomers and GenXers' approach to religion, especially in their suspicion of institutions and authority, there are also several significant differences.[52]

This means that the new forms of church which developed from the mid-1960s to the 1990s, which were effective in meeting the needs of baby boomers, have not been as effective in the 1990s in meeting the needs of GenXers. This was a perspective I found in the research on Spreydon Baptist, with its increasingly aging leadership and membership. While there was a significantly sized youth group, they were loosely attached to the church and large numbers drifted out in their mid and late twenties.

My own observations, anecdotal evidence, and research done by both Baptist and Presbyterian Youth Ministries indicates that this is a common pattern in Protestant charismatic churches. The now aging leaders and membership of these churches have remained trapped in forms of church life, worship, and music that were relevant to the culture of the 1970s and 1980s but are disconnected from the culture of those who have grown up since. This also helps to explain the slowing and eventually plateauing growth rates overall for Baptist and Pentecostal churches in this latter period. Many of the churches which were large and significant charismatic churches in that period are now considerably smaller, and often going through the same routines with little of the dynamism apparent 20 or so years ago.

Thus while the charismatic movement had a significant impact in fostering vitality in Protestant churches from the mid-1960s to the mid-1990s, indications are that its immediate influence has steadily declined since that period. Those who saw in "the renewal" the hope for the future of a new church in Western societies have now had to begin looking elsewhere.

---

51. Flory and Miller, *GenX Religion*, 232.
52. Ibid., 242–44.

6

Emerging from the Shadow of Christendom

DESPITE THE CONSIDERABLE DROP in participation in organized religion over the past half century, data such as the New Zealand census figures mentioned earlier continue to indicate that in New Zealand the majority of people persist in maintaining a religious identity and orientation. Even the secular media in New Zealand seem to have finally accepted the fact that, despite an ongoing decline in church-going, New Zealanders are not becoming secular atheists, as the older strong secularization thesis postulated. This view had informed almost all media comment in New Zealand for at least the past 25 years.

Not only has the frequency of stories about religion increased since the beginning of the twenty-first century, the content and tone of those stories has begun to shift. The most influential and highest circulating newspaper in the country, the *New Zealand Herald*, began and ended 2006 with articles on religion. The first, in early January, ran with the heading "Most Avoid Church but Still Believe"[1] and reported, with comment by various religious leaders, on a poll which indicated that 70 percent of New Zealanders believed in God, 30 percent prayed often, another 30 percent did so at least occasionally, but only 20 percent attended church often. Then, in late December, the newspaper ran an article entitled, "Free-range Soul Searching Replacing Organised Religion in NZ."[2] As well as reporting many anecdotal stories reflecting the importance of spirituality or religious beliefs to people, it also reported on a national

---

1. Boyes, "Most Avoid Church but still Believe."
2. Harvey, "Free-range Soul Searching."

poll which found that over 60 percent indicated spirituality was important to them.

As with most Western societies, then, New Zealand reflects the paradox of a highly spiritual culture in the midst of the apparent decay of organized religion. In other words, it appears that people who are seeking spiritual or religious experience and meaning in their lives are not finding it presented in a form that meets their aspirations regarding what the church has continued to offer. The research I have carried out over a number of years indicates that this has occurred because while the values, attitudes, and styles of the surrounding culture underwent a profound change beginning with the counter-culture of the 1960s, and came home to roost with a vengeance in the 1990s—in what is now known as postmodernity—the church has continued to be shaped by a set of values, attitudes, and styles that belonged to a previous era. As a consequence, whenever it has knocked on the door of the vast majority of the under-50s they have responded, "no thanks, I'm shopping elsewhere."

All of this means that an increasing gap has grown between religious believing and belonging. While people are apparently increasingly concerned to nurture the spiritual dimension, find answers to questions of meaning in life, and prepare for whatever happens at the end of physical life, they see organized religion in the form of the institutional church as being largely irrelevant to those issues. Increasing numbers are "believing without belonging." Wade Clark Roof writes that "A decade ago these questions were raised by Boomers who felt at odds with the religious culture of the churches; today these same concerns are most likely raised by those younger, the Generation Xers. In either instance, it is less a protest of religion in the deepest sense than a response to institutional styles that are unfamiliar or seemingly at odds with life experiences as these people know them."[3]

Conservative Growth and Mission

It is not hard to find theologians and sociologists who warn that the crisis confronting institutional religion in Western countries like New Zealand is massive, if not terminal. However, many Christians within the evangelical tradition argue that their experience does not match these gloomy predictions and immediately point to all kinds of evidence to contradict

3. Roof, *Spiritual Marketplace*, 56.

them. It may be the case that the mainline church is facing crisis, but an evangelicalism enlivened by the fires of charismatic and Pentecostal renewal can point to ample evidence that contradicts this generally negative assessment. The success of the Alpha courses, the surge of new ethnic churches, the growth of some large Pentecostal and charismatic churches, the rise in "born again" religion, and the growth of mega-churches in the U.S. are all cited as signs that a robust evangelicalism seems immune from the trend toward decline and secularization afflicting more traditional forms of institutional Christianity.

An example of this can be found in a letter to a Christchurch newspaper as part of a debate in the national media following the awarding of New Zealand's highest honor to controversial theologian Lloyd Geering for his contribution to religion in New Zealand. The correspondent claimed that "As fast as people are leaving traditional churches they are flocking to Christchurch's largest congregations, where a variety of contemporary styles of worship can be found."[4] This is a claim I come across frequently from my evangelical, charismatic and Pentecostal friends; however, my own research makes me rather sceptical.

Klaas Blockmuehl, an evangelical himself, has argued that Christians in general have given very little thought to the challenges posed by secularization, and that evangelicals have been "often content if they add to their numbers even when the overall state of Christianity deteriorates."[5] Diana Butler Bass, who for many years had focused her work optimistically on helping churches in the U.S. to become successful and vital, has come to the conclusion, after analyzing wider trends since 2000, that "vital churches might well be only islands of success in the rising seas of Western unbelief, and the high tides of cultural change are leaving traditional religion adrift."[6] To put it bluntly, having a larger share of a shrinking pie may be of some comfort to those in that sector, but it neglects the larger issues upon which those of us concerned about the future of the Christian faith should be focused.

A significant factor in the rather unrealistic perspective of many evangelical leaders has been the focus on church growth. This movement operates by basically looking at churches that are growing, trying to draw out reasons for the growth of those particular churches, and then claim

---

4. *Christchurch Press*, January 15, 2000.
5. Blockmuehl, "Secularization and Secularism," 50.
6. Bass, *Christianity after Religion*, 15.

that if all churches would only apply these principles they could all grow. The problem is that they have never really looked hard enough at either how the growth of those particular institutions fits into the broader patterns of religious and cultural change in society, or at where the people entering into these churches have come from.

When we speak of the decline of the church, then, it is somewhat problematical. The rates of decline have been somewhat uneven, and in general the patterns indicate it is more accurate to speak of the decline of liberal and mainstream Christianity. As Steve Bruce puts it with regard to the U.K., we find a general pattern of resilience as we move from "left" to "right" across the Protestant spectrum. This has been highlighted in his recent work on the church there, *Church Growth in Britain*. While acknowledging overall decline in church involvement, the book highlights the fact that this does not tell the full picture, as "substantial and sustained church growth has also taken place across Britain over last 30 years."[7] The cases examined confirm this picture. We have highlighted this in New Zealand with data indicating the very rapid growth of Pentecostal churches since the 1960s, and the overall vitality and growth in some sectors of the Protestant churches which have retained an evangelical orientation and been influenced by the charismatic movement.

When I began researching churches in New Zealand in the late 1990s, my major motivation was my hope that by studying these kinds of churches, and finding what it was that made them effective, it would provide material that could be helpful for the church in New Zealand in understanding how to go about its mission and lead people to faith and a sense of belonging in the church. However, as I gathered data, interviewed people, and observed how the patterns in these particular churches fit into the wider patterns of religious and cultural change, I became less confident that the research findings would actually serve this purpose. What I found was not quite what I had thought I would find. There was quite a gap between what they perceived themselves to be achieving and their long-term efficacy (a perception, I should add, that I also held to at least some degree then). While these churches have played a very important role in helping to maintain and conserve a vital and living Christian faith within an increasingly post-Christian New Zealand, I became increasingly less certain that they would provide the models for effective mission to the growing percentage of New Zealanders who are genuinely non-churched.

---

7. Goodhew, ed., *Church Growth in Britain*, 3.

My first thoughts in this direction came out of reflection on my own experience as minister of a charismatic Baptist church which grew rapidly in the late 1970s and 1980s and saw a significant number of baptisms. As I moved into theological education and training leaders for ministry, and in the light of that work reflected back on my own experience of ministry, I realized that the majority of those who came to us either came from other churches, or were young adults who had been brought up in church and were now returning after "sowing their wild oats." While the former group came probably equally from mainline and conservative churches, the latter were primarily from mainline Protestant churches.

This dynamic began to emerge as a serious issue to consider when I came across Canadian research which indicated that the vast majority of those who were in growing evangelical, charismatic, or Pentecostal churches actually came from other conservative churches or were the children of church members. These made up around 90 percent of the total, 70 percent and 20 percent respectively. Only 10 percent came from outside of this churched community. The reason for the growth of conservative churches, the researchers claimed, was because conservative churches had higher than average birth rates, did a better job of retaining children, and attracted more people ready to switch churches. It was not because they were more effective in mission, as many conservative church leaders believed.[8] As mentioned earlier, my research on Spreydon Baptist Church furthered this impression, firstly by finding in the written material a repeated concern that so many new people were coming from other churches, and a desire to attract more "unsaved people."

This led me to research the backgrounds of those now attending the church. The results were even more marked than I had imagined. What it showed was that 87 percent of those attending the church had been attending another church as adults before they came to this church. Of the remainder, about 9 percent had attended either Sunday School or youth group at this church or elsewhere, and only 3.9 percent came from a genuinely non-churched background. Interestingly, the largest group of attendees at this Baptist church, 33 per cent, came to it from mainline Protestant churches. I then looked at three other churches which had grown, where similar results were found. In all cases, at least 75 percent

---

8. Bibby and Brinkerhoff, "The Circulation of the Saints," 273–82. This study was followed up by further studies which confirmed the same patterns. See *Journal for the Scientific Study of Religion* Vol. 17, No. 2 (1978) 129–37; Vol. 22, No. 3 (1983):253–62; and Vol. 33, No. 3 (2007) 273–80.

of new members came from other churches, and only between 2.7 percent and 4.0 percent came from a non-churched background. Again, the largest numbers were from mainline Protestant churches.

The next question was whether this phenomenon was also typical of other Western countries. Research in the U.S. on the sources of growth in conservative churches concludes that "the majority of the recruits to our [new evangelical movements] have come from other churches," and that the majority "come from liberal Protestant or Catholic churches."[9] William Chadwick, in a research project for the School of Church Growth at Fuller Seminary, demonstrates that up to 90 percent of the growth in model "church growth" churches is by transfer from other churches.[10]

Sally Morgenthaler has explored the question, "How do we explain the growth of the mega-church? Simple: musical chairs—church-hopping growth. And it represents more than 80 percent of the people who have come in our doors in the past decade . . . The mega-church's feeder system is the smaller church, and disgruntled believers who have quit their churches."[11] In Canada, additional research by Don Posterski and Irwin Baker has found that 5.5 percent of church attendees come from an unchurched background, and that there is no difference between mainline and conservative churches.[12] Finally, in Australia the NCLS research has found that 7 percent of church attendees are newcomers, of which 4 percent are returnees to church life after a period of time away, and only 3 percent are actually involved in attending church for the first time. Again, no significant differences were found between Pentecostal and Anglican churches.[13]

These rather disturbing figures indicate a basic flaw in the logic of church growth thinking. This claims that the way to have effective churches is to look at those churches that are being successful (in terms of numerical growth) and then seek to copy what they do. It stands to reason, however, that if most of the growth in growing churches comes from other churches it is impossible to conclude that if all churches applied the same principles, all churches would grow. The problem is that we have confused the growth of some churches with growth of *"the"* church.

9. Perrin, Kennedy and Miller, "Examining the Sources of Conservative Church Growth," 73, 75.
10. Chadwick, *Stealing Sheep*.
11. Morgenthaler, *Worship Evangelism*, 26.
12. Posterski and Baker, *Where's a Good Church*, 53–54.
13. Kaldor, *Build My Church*.

We have confused growing churches with being effective in mission. What has happened is merely a reconfiguration of existing church-goers. Where people go to church has changed, and some churches have grown at the expense of others.

In New Zealand in the 1950s, the vast majority of the 20 percent or so who regularly attended on Sunday went to either mainline Protestant or Roman Catholic churches. By 2006 the percentage in church had halved to about 10 per cent, and over half of these had moved to evangelical, charismatic or Pentecostal churches. While it is true that some of these people had stopped going to church for a time, it is a mistake to confuse the awakening of their faith for the first time as an adult, or the renewal of a lapsed faith (though both of these are to be celebrated), as effective mission to the large and ever growing percentage of New Zealanders who have never had Christian faith as part of their story and are therefore the genuinely non-churched.

If most of the growth of evangelical, charismatic and Pentecostal churches in New Zealand over the past three decades has been from people leaving mainline Protestant churches (as the research clearly indicates), what will happen when that pool runs dry? The indications are that in New Zealand, as well as in Australia, the rapid growth of Pentecostal churches came to an end in the late 1990s. Peter Brierley's research indicates that in fact this has happened in Britain as well, and indeed worldwide.[14] In the U.S. George Barna's research also confirms that numbers of the boomers who moved into the mega-churches in the 1980s and early 1990s are now drifting away, disillusioned.[15]

It appears, then, that how we do church, and consequently how we communicate the gospel, only makes sense to those who have "church" somewhere in their history. The problem is that this is a diminishing percentage of the population, so in the retail terms increasingly applied to the church in a culture where everything is commodified, the market for church is shrinking rather than increasing. Michael Moynagh, after noting that thriving churches in Britain flourish mainly because they attract individuals with some church experience, states that "few churches are making headway amongst those with no church background. Yet this will soon be—if it is not now—the new mission field."[16]

14. See Brierley, *The Tide is Running Out*; also, *Global Analysis of the Christian Community*.
15. Gibbs and Coffey, *Church Next*, 150, 173.
16. Moynagh, *Emergingchurch.intro*, 208.

In Britain research has shown that by 1990 only 14 percent of children had contact with a church during their childhood,[17] and that by 2004 only 4 percent were attending church.[18] In 1960, as we have seen, 40 percent of New Zealand children were enrolled in Protestant Sunday Schools, but by 1985 this was down to 11 per cent, and is in all probability somewhat similar to the British figure now. The consequence of these changing patterns is that, as one moves through the generations, there is an increasingly diminishing percentage of each succeeding cohort attending.

In the U.S., the generation known as "builders" make up 10 percent of the population, and 60 percent are affiliated with church. Boomers are 29 percent of the population and around 40 percent are affiliated with church. GenXers make up 28 percent but only 18 percent are affiliated with church. The generation behind them, sometimes known as "millennials," make up 21 percent of the population, but only 12 percent are affiliated with church,[19] a figure tracking down to somewhere near the levels for children in Britain and New Zealand. In an earlier chapter we demonstrated this same pattern in the church in New Zealand—that while there is a decline in the percentage identifying with Christianity as one goes down the generations in the census data, when it comes to church involvement the CLSNZ data highlights the low representation of the younger generation, especially in mainline Protestant churches. The trends over time also confirm that this decline is becoming more marked.

Robin Gill, in *Church Going and Christian Ethics*, presents research demonstrating quite clearly that in Britain those who went regularly to church as children or young people, but did not now attend as adults, held to higher levels of traditional Christian belief than those who never went to church. He writes, "It really does seem that people who never go to church now, but yet who were brought up doing so, have residual beliefs and affections for Christian belief and practice. In contrast the never-nevers [those who have never attended] are distinctly more distant from Christian culture."[20] John Finney's research in Britain, documented in *Finding Faith Today*, also found that over 90 percent of those who came to faith as adults were actually coming back to something they had experienced previously in childhood.[21]

17. Finney, *Finding Faith Today*, 11.
18. Williams, *Mission Shaped Church*, 36–41.
19. "Generational Differences."
20. Gill, *Churchgoing and Christian Ethics*, 129.
21. Finney, *Finding Faith Today*, 13.

In the U.S., George Barna concluded as a result of his research that "if people do not make a commitment to Christ by the age of fourteen the likelihood of ever doing so is slim."[22] With only a very small percentage of New Zealanders being exposed to Christianity in their formative years over the last three decades, this finding has serious implications for the church here. Callum Brown, in *The Death of Christian Britain*, shows that until the 1960s people in Britain still constructed "their identities and their sense of self" from a broader culture that was fundamentally Christian. Since the 1960s this has rapidly broken down, and thus churches find it more and more difficult to connect with people raised in a cultural milieu that is radically different.

Consequently, Brown claims that "missions of the new millennium will fail amongst the young because of their unfamiliarity with discursive Christianity due to its disappearance from the family and youth media, and the young's absence from Sunday Schools."[23] The figures we have looked at for New Zealand indicate that this may have already been true here over the past two decades or more. These rather sobering facts present many significant challenges for the church and I want to focus on two of these for the remainder of this chapter: our understanding of conversion, and our understanding of the forms which church life takes.

Conversion

A significant area of research in sociology of religion since the 1960s has focused on the attempt to understand conversion. Johann Lofland and Rodney Stark[24] were the first to actually observe people in the process of converting to a new religious movement. Up until that point, most scientific explanations saw conversions as an attempt by individuals to address the deprivations they felt. What Lofland and Stark found was that attachments lie at the heart of conversions, and that conversion therefore tends to proceed along social networks formed by interpersonal attachments, and is a process rather than a sudden event.

Since then many studies have found the same to be true in an immense variety of religious groups around the world. In their analysis of how people make religious choices, Stark and Finke propose that in

---

22. "Evangelism."
23. Brown, *The Death of Christian Britain*, 229.
24. Lofland and Stark, "Becoming a World Saver," 862–75.

making those choices "people will attempt to conserve their social capital [interpersonal attachments], and so under normal circumstances most people will neither convert nor reaffiliate."[25] This explains why children usually adhere to the faith in which they were raised. By doing so they protect their relational and kinship ties.

Similar research shows that most people who are in religious organizations have stayed within those in which they were raised. Darren Sherkat has studied religious orientation and participation among baby boomers and finds that "traditional socialization factors have a dominant influence on future religious beliefs and participation . . . that radical changes in religious orientations or behaviors will be uncommon, and that individuals will follow the beliefs and patterns of participation established by their parents and religious groups . . . Stated in terms of theories of religious commitment, religious desires and understandings are learned through social ties."[26]

On the basis of these patterns some have applied social learning theory, widely used in psychology, as an explanation of how religious commitments are made. This emphasizes the role of observational learning and the modeling of behavior, suggesting that socialization occurs when important cultural agents model and reinforce certain attitudes and behaviours.[27] It seems clear, then, that people in Western countries are essentially socialized into the faith, and that very few are to be found in churches who have not received a basic understanding of Christian beliefs and behavior during their upbringing as children or adolescents, or both.

How then are we to understand the process of conversion, something that has traditionally been so central to conservative, evangelical, and Pentecostal Christianity? Again, sociology provides some helpful insights. A number of researchers on conversion prefer to use the term "alternation" rather than "conversion" when discussing some kinds of religious transformations.[28] In most cases the use of the term "alternation" recognizes that some religious changes in people's lives are significant

25. Stark and Finke, *Acts of Faith*, 119.

26. Sherkat, "Counterculture or Continuity," 1087–1115.

27. See Bandura, *Social Learning Theory*. This is examined in the context of religion by Hungsberger, "Apostasy: A Social Learning Perspective," 21–38. Also Roof and Hoge, "Church Involvement in America," 405–26.

28. See, for example, Pilarzyk, "Conversion and Alternation Processes," 379–405; and Richardson, "Conversion to New Religions," 104–23.

but are not full-blown conversions. Rather, they involve the integration of a series of elements that result in less disruptive life changes than traditionally defined by conversion. In fact, a general conclusion from the social-psychological literature is that the nature of personal transformation is rarely radical enough to qualify as a conversion.

The term "alternation" was originally suggested by Peter Berger to refer to the possibility that "an individual may alternate back and forth between logically contradictory meaning systems."[29] Berger preferred the term "alternation" to the more religiously charged term "conversion." Richard Traviasano, however, has suggested that conversion and alternation be used to refer to two quite different types of transformation.[30] He defines conversion as the negation of a former identity. Conversion is a radical and fundamental shift in identity that results in clear changes in values, ethics, morals, and lifestyle behaviors. Alternation, on the other hand, implies some linkage and continuity between the past and the present. The ensuing identity and lifestyle grows naturally out of its predecessor.

This distinction is helpful in understanding the kinds of transformations or changes that people undergo. In alternation a supportive network and an ideological framework is already present. In conversion a whole new world is entered into; the past no longer has a direct bearing on the present. Conversion is non-cumulative. Alternation is cumulative. Our analysis suggests clearly that most of what is reported in church growth stories and counted in "conversion" statistics are actually alternations rather than conversions.

An additional difficulty is that, in much church growth literature, conversion and recruitment are confused in the focus on gaining new members. Since most come from within "the tradition," rather than outside the church, very few have actually been converted. As a consequence, particularly within the evangelical tradition, we need to rethink the metaphors and symbols we use to describe the kinds of changes to which we are calling people and the kinds of commitments we are asking them to make. We have used the language of dramatic conversion to describe what is in reality either a consolidation of some existing identity, or a reaffirmation of a previous identity, perhaps after a period of experimentation with alternative identities.

---

29. Berger, *Invitation to Sociology*, 65.
30. Traviasano "Alternation and Conversion," 237–48.

This has deluded many church leaders into believing they have been seeing a constant stream of "new converts to Christianity" coming into their churches, when in reality they have been witnessing some significant milestones in the ongoing journey of those who were already in the fold of faith. It has made us feel comfortably successful and has hidden from us just how difficult are the real challenge of seeking to convert people to the faith who have never been a part of it.

As previously argued, a key theme of recent research on religion in Western culture is that religious believing had increasingly become separated from religious belonging. Historically orthodox Christian faith has encompassed both dimensions. Faith needs to be communally expressed; it has both social and cognitive dimensions. In our examination of religious commitment and conversion, we have suggested that faith can be explained largely in terms of socialization. Sociologists claim that faith is both socially transmitted and socially maintained. If this is so, then it is clear that the critical challenge we face today is not how to find better explanations of the faith, a sharper apologetic and more polished presentation, so that people through understanding might come to believe. Nor do we need to radically change the nature of what we believe in order to make it more palatable to people, as liberalism has attempted. The rapid decline of most liberal churches clearly indicates that is not the critical issue.

This focus on belief is part of the legacy of the Enlightenment with which we are still shackled. A number of thinkers have argued that the church in the West, in both its evangelical and liberal forms, tied its coattails to and was basically shaped by the values of the Enlightenment. As the church generally resists change, rather than engaging positively with it, it has continued to hang on to this paradigm much longer than the rest of the society in which it exists. Scottish theologian John Drane suggests that churches are "the last modernist, Victorian bureaucracies that are left."[31]

One of the strongest illustrations is the whole evangelistic crusade movement that reached its peak with Billy Graham. For Graham the gospel was reduced to a matter of individual belief and conversion to a matter of a rational choice. It was buying into the beliefs of Christianity, clearly and logically presented. It thus became "Steps to Peace with God" or "The Four Spiritual Laws." People were asked to "only believe." In a culture

---

31. Drane, *The McDonaldization of the Church*, 54.

where people still belonged within a basically Christian community, and had social networks that reinforced those beliefs, making a commitment to affirm or consolidate those beliefs which were already a part of their "ideological framework" was relatively easy. Many responded, as was demonstrated in the large crowds and high number of responses during Graham's 1959 Crusade in New Zealand. During the twelve days of the crusade, combined attendances exceeded 25 percent of the population, and more than 17,000 made public Christian commitments.[32]

However, as the culture changed from the beginning of the 1960s, and baby boomers moved out of church in increasing numbers, the social networks that maintained a sense of belonging were fractured. When Graham returned to New Zealand in 1969, the social connection to church—the sense of belonging—was much weaker, and consequently crowds were considerably smaller and responses dramatically reduced. This situation became even worse, as research on the evangelistic campaigns of Graham's successors Leighton Ford and Luis Palau, in 1978 and 1987 respectively, has shown. These were essentially "in house" affairs, with convinced Christians speaking to convinced Christians, rather than attracting and converting those from outside the church scene.[33]

As I was working on a first draft of this chapter I was reminded of the failure of church leaders to grasp our very changed reality when a church newsletter arrived by e-mail, advertising the latest crusade by an overseas evangelist in New Zealand as possibly "the greatest event in New Zealand since Billy Graham's visit in 1959." The culture in which that kind of approach to mission had any significant impact has long since passed, and only when church leaders come to a sober acceptance of this reality will energy be put into developing forms that are relevant to our social and cultural context, rather than longing nostalgically for a repeat of the past.

Research by sociologists on baby boomers and their religious journeys[34] indicates quite clearly that the reason the majority left church was not to do with disagreement over belief, but rather because of a disengagement from the way they were being asked to belong. In other words, the forms in which belonging was expressed, and the behaviors in which

---

32. 574,300 attended, 23,257 sought counseling, and 17,493 recorded decisions. Hutchinson and Wilson, *Let the People Rejoice*, 142.

33. Gilling, "Convinced Christians," 77–96.

34. See especially Roof, *Spiritual Marketplace*, and *A Generation of Seekers*. Also, Wuthnow, *Christianity in the 21st Century*, and *After Heaven*.

they were asked to engage, became increasingly disconnected from the style and forms in which they expressed their belonging and behavior in other areas of their life. It became irrelevant. For all the talk about church change and renewal, for all the energy expended, the ways in which we belong have remained fundamentally unchanged over 50 years of the most rapid change in human history.

Eddie Gibbs suggests that the "popular models of church today, such as the 'mega-church' concept, the 'seeker church' and the new 'cell' church model are only tactical attempts to breathe new life into old structures."[35] They may make church more appealing and attractive to those who already belong or have recently departed. They still, nonetheless, have a form of life that is increasingly distant from and irrelevant to those who are one, two, three, or even more generations removed from the church, as the majority of those in countries like New Zealand, Australia, and Britain now are.

This is a significant point of difference between these countries and the USA, from which much of the material for new forms of church to "reach the unchurched" emanates. In the U.S., where about 50 percent of the population claimed to attend church weekly in 1960, and where occasional attendance may have been around 80 per cent, a very significant proportion of the population still has close "belonging" links to the church, although this is rapidly changing. In New Zealand, Australia, and Britain the weekly attendance figure was about 20 percent in 1960, and it seems that occasional attendance, for all of the twentieth century at least, could never be claimed for much more than 40 percent of the population. This means that a much higher proportion of the population is much more distant from any belonging links to the church.

If conversion comes about primarily through socialization, as we have suggested, then belonging needs to happen before believing can occur. Without a social connection, it is unlikely to happen. Hence the critical challenge we face. How do our churches become the kinds of communities to which those outside may make some kind of connection, and therefore might possibly someday end up belonging, and so eventually come to believe? I think there are three key areas of challenge with which the church in countries like New Zealand, Australia, Canada, Britain and, I would suggest increasingly, the U.S., need to grapple: the shadow of Christendom; the stranglehold of clericalism; and the idolatry of church. Let us examine each of these in turn.

35. Gibbs and Coffey, *Church Next*, 168–69.

The Shadow of Christendom

The forms of church life that exist today have been shaped for eighteen hundred years in what has been known as Christendom, a period in which Western culture and society was fashioned by a Christian understanding, with the church a significant player in determining the values and mores of that society. While that state began to break down in the nineteenth century, it still continued to be given lip service, at least, until the latter decades of the twentieth century. What has emerged in the West since the end of World War II, and particularly since the "cultural revolution" of the 1960s, is a society whose values and culture are no longer shaped by a Christian understanding.

The church meanwhile has continued to maintain forms, values, language, and rituals that were shaped by that framework. These are intensely meaningful and helpful to those brought up within that churched (or Christendom) culture, and it is their concerns that largely shape what churches do. However, they are meaningless (when they can actually be understood) and irrelevant to the vast majority of those brought up in post-sixties Western culture. Hence the diminishing involvement in churches, as we have seen, amongst baby boomers and, even more so, amongst the generations that have followed them.

Most of the attempts to renew or build new kinds of churches are still largely determined by the inherited forms and patterns of the past. A case in point that illustrates this is the strong emphasis still placed on coming to worship on Sunday morning as the primary point of commitment for Christians. Sunday as the one designated day for worship was a product of Christendom. In the post-Christendom culture in which we live, it is just another day of the week for increasing numbers of New Zealanders, particularly the young, and for many attending a church service is not possible given work, family, or sporting commitments.

I became fully aware of this one Sunday morning in 2000, when my three young adult children were still living at home. I was getting ready to go to church and was aware that, of the five people living together, I was the only one who could go to church that morning, as the other four were all working. Yet for so many churches Sunday is still the only real worship option offered. We must also consider what happens in these Sunday services. Shaped by our Christendom heritage, the main fare is worship in the form of corporate singing and listening to a 20 or 30 minute monologue, with no opportunity to interact. Where else in our society do we attempt to create a sense of belonging and community in this way?

We need to create new forms of church that are not shaped by the values and forms of Christendom but by a genuine mission encounter between the gospel and culture of twenty-first century New Zealand (or any other culture). My belief is that these cannot be developed by those of us who have lived in the church for thirty or twenty or maybe even ten years, and so are already shaped by the inherited culture. One of the things that is most discouraging is the degree to which, when young people who have been raised in the church come into leadership positions, generally end up simply modifying the model into which have been socialized, with a bit more current cultural expression.

Rather, our models of church must be developed by those who have been brought up in the context of that culture and who have come to faith out of it. In other words, we need to change from a patronizing "come" mentality—this is what we have developed to meet your needs—to a "go" mentality, where by incarnationally dwelling with people living in communities outside of established churches we allow the seed of the gospel to be sown and take root. Only then can authentically new forms and shapes create new life.

Graham Cray, now the Director of Fresh Expressions, speaking about the challenge that youth culture provides for the gospel, argues that ministry to young people involves entering their worlds in order to plant the gospel and church there. "It does not necessarily intend to draw young people back into a church culture which is alien to them . . . it is not a 'bridge' strategy but a genuine commitment to new forms of church for a new cultural era."[36] This of course raises all kinds of issues of authority and control and so brings us to the second point.

The Stranglehold of Clericalism

Fundamental to Christendom is the distinction between clergy and the laity, wherein "A professionalized cast of Christians, with its own hierarchical gradations, is separated from other Christians by various forms

---

36. Cray, *Youth Congregations and the Emerging Church*, 7. Fresh Expressions in an organization which largely arose out of the Church of England, to facilitate the development of new and different expressions of church life. See www.freshexpressions.org.uk.

of ordination and induction."[37] Some would suggest that the Reformation changed this, but in effect, as one critic expressed it, it took off the "sacerdotal gown" and put on the "professorial gown," with nothing fundamentally changing. While the markers of this separation may have changed—from "priest" to "preacher" to "senior pastor," from "Roman tunic" to "Geneva gown" to "blue suit and white shoes," and from "confessional" to "study" to "corner office"—it is still kept firmly in place. Everyone knows who calls the shots and who gets the money.

Richard Thomas claims that "much of today's formal expression of Christianity . . . continues to express a form of Christian imperialism that has come down to us directly from the days of Christendom."[38] As we have seen, one of the core value changes of the 1960s was a deep seated anti-institutionalism. Roof, writing about this in a religious context, concluded on the basis of his long-term research that "Boomers in great numbers questioned religious authority when they were growing up and have remained somewhat distrustful of institutions, even as they had aged."[39]

All of the indicators are that this attitude is even stronger among GenerationXers, who see boomers as having created their own, albeit quite different, institutions. While many contemporary churches endeavour to disguise any signs of hierarchy and speak a language of tolerance and "permission giving," to outsiders they appear dominated by hierarchies and deeply concerned over issues of control. In most churches, whether something is allowed to happen or not, whether it is some new venture by young people or a new ministry that someone wants to begin, permission has to be sought from the appropriate authority before it can begin—usually, in the end, the "man" at the top.

In a culture which encourages you to "do your own thing" and "follow your own dream," people bristle at this kind of control over what often seem to be fairly minor things. Often people suspect the real issue is that the leaders are afraid of losing control of what people think or do. One of the values that has become central in our culture is that people resent being told what to do by others, and want to have a say in decision-making. Most innovative and growing companies achieve this by devolving much decision-making down to small groups and teams.

---

37. Kreider, *Change of Conversion*, 95.
38. Thomas, *Counting People In*, 133.
39. Roof, *Spiritual Marketplace*, 127.

In most churches, however, there is still a small and central decision-making body dominated by the minister, staff, vestry, or elders. Feeling they have no say in what is happening, increasing numbers of thinking church-goers are drifting off. Given the postmodern suspicion of control, few are attracted into an organization that smacks of this kind of culture of control. As we look for new forms of church life, we need to look for new forms of ministry that are non-hierarchical, inclusive, and open, forms which will loosen controls in church life and free up resources to be used in helping people, rather than supporting and meeting the needs of the institution.

The Idolatry of Church

I recently talked with someone who had just begun as the pastor of a church. He had spent his first period of time meeting with people in the church and asking them how they viewed the church at the moment. What he heard repeatedly went something like this: "I am just absolutely flat out and stressed out at the moment. My job is taking about 50 hours a week, my wife is working a fairly pressured job, and the demands of the children both in their education and leisure activities just seem to increase all the time. And all I ever hear from the church is they want more. We should be supporting their programmes more. We need to be giving more."

That perspective is not unique to that church. It is a refrain I hear repeatedly from people who are married with significant work and family commitments. I believe that one of the problems we face today is that the local church has become an idol. This is a consequence of the church growth and church management approaches, which have interpreted the gospel in terms of what happens to the church. It becomes the focus and center of attention. A church leader in Canada[40] told me, "We keep asking the wrong question. We keep asking 'what is the right form for the church?' We should be asking, 'what does it mean to be an authentic follower of Jesus today?'— and the church should take its form out of that."

It seems that so often today our preoccupation is with the church as an institution instead of living out the gospel. We become focused on keeping the institution going, on making it bigger and better, on what is

---

40. His church, largely made up of GenXers, had grown from 120 to 2,000 in the past 6 years.

happening at church, inside the institution. It becomes idolatrous, and in the end any idol takes from life rather than gives life. Research on church leavers indicates that this has been the experience of many,[41] and those looking in from the outside say "I don't want to have any part of that."

The gospel is not primarily about building churches; it is about living in the world with a spirituality shaped by gospel values. The local church exists in two modes: gathered and scattered. It is gathered when we meet together to worship corporately, to encourage and disciple each other so that when we are scattered in the world we can authentically live as Christians and so bear witness to the gospel. Jesus is primary, the church is secondary. The problem is that we have made the church in its gathered form all-pervasive and have forgotten that it loses its rationale if it is not primarily resourcing its members for their life when it is scattered. When this happens people conclude, as they are in increasing numbers, that it is simply irrelevant to their lives.

What is desperately needed is a whole change of perspective about "church" as an institution (in other words, when it is gathered) that actually puts it in its right perspective. Rather than the church demanding that people serve it, it should be seeking to serve people by resourcing them so that they can live as authentic followers of Jesus in the world, at work, at home, in education, or in leisure, and so point others to him. Martin Robinson puts it this way: "The challenge for the church now is to stop thinking merely about methods to reverse the decline but to reconsider the basic purpose and call of the church. To return to mission as the *raison d'etre* of the church will inevitably mean that the shape of the church will change . . . What flows from mission will be the church but it will be a very different kind of church."[42] Dietrich Bonhoeffer described Jesus as "the man for others," the one who was willing to give away his own life that others may live. The church that goes by his name is called to follow his pattern and give away its own life that others may live.

Churches that Connect

For the church to be the church in New Zealand and other Western societies in the twenty-first century, I believe these are three of the major issues with which we need to wrestle. What will the church be

---

41. See Jamieson, *Churchless Faith*.
42. Robinson and Smith, *Invading Secular Space*, 56.

like when it manages to break free of the shadow it has inherited from its form in Christendom, when it is no longer dominated by the control of its leadership, and when, rather than demanding that its members serve it, in fact seeks to serve them so they can live their lives in the world as Christ intended?

Peter Brierley, perhaps the leading researcher on the church in Britain and a deeply committed church person, said to me in an interview, "I believe we are entering a time of churchless Christianity." What he meant was not that Christianity will no longer exist in communal forms—it inevitably must if it is to survive let alone thrive—but that the forms of Christian community it will take, and the way belonging is expressed, will bear little resemblance to "church" as we have known it. I do not know exactly what it will look like, but I do believe it will be vastly different from the form of even the most innovative of those churches regarded as contemporary.

Roof, who as we saw earlier claims that the absence of baby boomers and GenXers from churches is less a protest of religion in the deepest sense than a response to institutional styles that are unfamiliar or at odds with their life experience, suggests that three key parameters will be that such a church "privileges open discussion, shared experiences and attention to spiritual development."[43] Alan Jamieson, in his research on the faith journeys of those who have left churches, sees the trend as part of "the postmodern desire to escape organized structure," but above all that "People are saying 'I want to set my own path.'"[44] The qualities suggested by Roof seem a good place to begin.

One final helpful sociological insight comes from looking at the nature of "sets." Sets refer to the way in which we group categories of people or things together. Mathematicians speak about a variety of different types of sets, and one helpful distinction is that between "bounded" or "closed" sets, on the one hand, and "fuzzy" or "open" sets on the other.[45] A closed set has a clear boundary, and things either belong inside the set or are outside it. Open sets, on the other hand, have no sharp boundary and categories flow into one another. In Western society after the Reformation, the church has often functioned as a closed set. It was clear who was in and who was out, there were a variety

43. Roof, *Spiritual Marketplace*, 189.
44. Jamieson, "Free-range Soul Searching."
45. See Hiebert, *Anthropological Reflections on Missiological Issues*, 107–36.

of boundary markers, and for someone to come into the set they had to come through these markers, often defined in terms of belief and the various rites associated with it. The usual institutional factors of hierarchy, control, and sanction come into play and only people who subscribe to the particular beliefs, values, and behaviours are part of it. This model is most marked in the conservative evangelical and Pentecostal stream, although a leading Anglican churchman told me that, whereas the Anglican Church had historically been an open set communion, in order to compete with the seemingly thriving conservative churches it had moved to a more closed set mentality.

In an open set, in contrast, the focus is not on the boundary—on who is inside and who is outside. Rather, the nature of the set is determined by a focus on the center, which holds the set together. In the case of the church this is obviously Jesus Christ. Thus the concern is not on who is in and who is out (institutional concerns), but rather on whether or not people are moving toward the centre, toward Christ (gospel concerns).

The church here is an inclusive community rather than an exclusive community. Anyone who wants to identify with the church, because they want to identify with Christ, is in some way included. People are not excluded because they do not hold to a particular doctrinal belief, or have not been through a particular rite, or behave in a certain way. If conversion is regarded as a process, and belonging needs to be experienced before believing happens (and hopefully behaving eventually results), then it is obvious that this model of church needs to be that which is embraced. The church is then an open community of people who are seeking to help each other along their life journeys.

7

Is the Future Churchless?

THIS BOOK BEGAN WITH John Lennon imagining in the early 1970s a world in which there was "no religion," and theologian Lloyd Geering suggesting as the twentieth century ended that we were seeing "the death of religious institutions, the death of organized religion." Four years later, post-9/11 and all the religious hype that has followed, he again asserted that that "conventional religion is coming to an end."[1] Geering, along with many others in New Zealand, has consistently made this claim since the erosion in church statistics first became evident in the late 1960s. In one sense it is interesting that he still continues to make the claim, rather than looking back posthumously on its funeral, as he had earlier predicted its demise would come before we entered the twenty-first century. While Lennon's imagination of a world without religion is clearly not going to be reality in any imminent future, are the prophets of doom right about organized religion, even if its death is being rather prolonged?

That church-going has been in decline in all Western countries, particularly since the 1960s, is beyond dispute, as the data we have examined so far clearly demonstrates. Whatever statistics one uses, and however one looks at them, they all point in one direction—down. In New Zealand church attendance as a percentage of the population has been approximately halved since 1960, and continues to decline even if the rate has slowed a little. But the figures certainly raise the question as to whether, at some point in New Zealand's future, the church will sink from view and we will, for all intents and purposes, be a churchless society.

---

1. "Beyond Belief."

However, if the data are beyond dispute, the interpretation of and explanation for them are subjects of significant divergence and contestation. In brief, the dispute can be summarized as between those who argue that with the onslaught of modernization religious belief has become implausible for increasing numbers—and hence they have ceased belonging to religious organizations (classical secularization theory)—and those who claim that, while people have stopped belonging, they have still continued to believe.

Theoretical Perspectives

A review of the literature of the past fifty or so years suggests there are basically three different theories of church-going:

1. *Secularization:* Under the acids of modernity, religious believing withers and, as a result, religious practices decline, especially church-going. An activity that was once sustained by deeply-held religious beliefs becomes largely pointless. This view is represented by Bryan Wilson and the early Peter Berger, and was the dominant view until the 1990s.

2. *Persistence* theories hold that, even in the modern world, religious beliefs and practices remain abiding features. There may well be relative shifts from one form of religious belief or practice to another, yet viewed as a whole, religious belief persists today as it always has in every society. They are part and parcel of the human condition. This opinion is represented by David Martin and Andrew Greeley. The distinction between these two positions has become more blurred since the 1990s. The work of Jose Casanova[2] is especially important. He accepts that church-going is declining in most parts of Europe, and that a process of separation, or differentiation, of church and state has happened or is likely to happen everywhere. Nevertheless, there is evidence, even within Europe, and certainly elsewhere in the world, of a de-privatization of religion, of its taking on a significant public role. "Religious resurgence . . . is as much a feature of modern societies as is religious decline."[3] Even though secularization theorists are usu-

---

2. Casanova, *Public Religions in the Modern World.*
3. Gill, *Churchgoing and Christian Ethics*, 61.

ally less dogmatic today than in the past, they do still tend to see church-going as the dependent variable and religious belief as the independent and declining variable. As modern people become less religious in belief, so church-going will continue to decline. Many who argue for persistence also hold that religious belief is the independent variable, but argue that while this may change it will not disappear and is likely to find expression in ritual form.

3. More recently a third theory, *separation*, has developed. This is based on the conviction that late modernity, or postmodernity, is characterized by growing fragmentation and religious pluralism. Reginald Bibby, Peter Berger, and Anthony Giddens[4] have all been important in expressing this. The work of Grace Davie[5] has also been very significant in shaping this view. She argues that in Britain the data indicate that believing and belonging have become increasingly separated. While Christian "belonging" has clearly declined, Christian beliefs nonetheless persist. Charles Taylor, in his large and influential work, *A Secular Age*, sits somewhere in this group, rejecting orthodox secularization theory and arguing that the "story is not simply one of decline but also of new placement of the sacred or spiritual in relation to individual and social life."[6]

Secularization theory has had a rather difficult time lately, despite a rigorous defence by Steve Bruce. It is now difficult to find sociologists prepared to defend it. Indeed, many are now writing about post-secular societies. We have mentioned Peter Berger's significant change of position, and a later work is titled *The Desecularization of the World*.[7] Rodney Stark and Roger Finke title their chapter on the topic "Secularization: RIP."[8] And the person most influential in the theological popularization of the secularization theory, Harvey Cox, now calls it "the myth of the twentieth century."[9]

Certainly in its classic form, as the death of religious believing, such statements contain substantial truth. However, to dismiss the whole theory is unjustified. "Secularization" is one of those evasive words which

4. Bibby, *Fragmented Gods*; Giddens, *Modernity and Self Identity*; Berger, *A Far Glory*.
5. Davie, *Religion in Britain since 1945*.
6. Taylor, *A Secular Age*, 437.
7. Berger, ed., *The Desecularization of the World*.
8. Stark and Finke, *Acts of Faith*.
9. Cox, "The Myth of the Twentieth Century, 135–43.

almost means different things to every person who uses it, and at some levels of meaning it is unquestionably true. Casanova puts it well: "The core of the theory of secularization, the thesis of the differentiation and emancipation of the secular spheres from religious institutions and norms, remains valid. These function 'as if' God would not exist. This forms the unassailable core of secularization."[10]

However, as Danièle Hervieu-Léger has observed, this process of "exiting from religion" is not to be equated with the renunciation of belief. "Secularization of belief is not the end of belief but the movement by which the elements of belief break free of the structures prescribed by religious institutions."[11] In this sense, belonging and believing need to be seen as separate variables. Religious belonging has indeed declined significantly in Western countries, but religious believing has not suffered to anywhere near the same extent. This view is also articulated by Taylor, who in line with the perspective developed in this book, argues that "the cultural revolution of the 1960s destabilized earlier forms of religion, followed by the development of new forms."[12] In the age of "expressive individualism," religious belief and practice is a personal choice and "finding a place in the broader church is no longer relevant."[13]

This decline in belonging should be understood in relation to the parallel observation that virtually all voluntary associations have been finding it difficult in the last few decades to attract and retain members. An article in a widely read New Zealand magazine, *Metro*, outlined the decline in all kinds of voluntary organizations.[14] My own research has shown the decline in involvement in New Zealand's national sport of rugby, from 400,000 in the 1970s to 120,000 by the early 2000s, despite belief in rugby remaining incredibly strong in our culture, even during a long period of repeated failures of the national team.[15]

Perhaps the most significant research of this trend is that carried out in the United States by Robert Putnam and published in *Bowling Alone*.[16]

10. Casanova, *Public Religions in the Modern World*, 6, 40.
11. Hervieu-Léger, "The Twofold Limit of the Notion of Secularization," 119.
12. Taylor, *A Secular Age*, 526.
13. Ibid., 486.
14. "Death of the Samaritans," 24–28.
15. Ward, "Rugby and Church," 26–30. The period finally ended when the All Blacks won the coveted Rugby World Cup in 2011, 24 years after their only other success.
16. Putnam, *Bowling Alone*.

He surveyed a wide variety of organizations in all kinds of fields, and found a decline in virtually all voluntary and membership organizations. These included attending political meetings, attending public meetings, serving as an officer or committee member in any local clubs or organizations, participating in local meetings of national organizations, attending club meetings, joining unions, playing organized sport, and attending religious services. In other words, belonging has been simultaneously losing its popularity in other fields as well as in religion. Loss of belonging is part of a broader pattern of change which happens to affect religious organizations amongst others. It is therefore not a uniquely religious problem, and does not in itself indicate that religion is necessarily dying out. "Trends in religious life reinforce rather than counterbalance the ominous plunge in social connectedness in the secular community."[17]

My own doctoral research on churches in New Zealand[18] indicated that their loss of young people in the 1960s and 1970s, the root cause of the malaise which the churches face, was because they no longer wanted to belong in the ways that churches of that time demanded, rather than because they no longer believed. Wade Clark Roof's research among baby boomers in the United States has indicated a similar pattern,[19] as has Alan Jamieson's more recent research among church-leavers in New Zealand. Those who leave do not do so because they no longer believe, but for other reasons. They continue to have faith outside of the church, a "churchless faith."[20] Their believing has become separated from belonging, or, in the distinction increasingly used, they are spiritual but not religious. A 2006 survey by the Barna organization found that while 76 million Americans never attended church, 77 percent considered themselves to be Christian and 62 percent prayed.[21]

Numerous surveys indicate the resilience of religious belief in secularized Western societies. Some of the more interesting research was that carried out in Britain by David Hay and Kaye Hunt on the spirituality

---

17. Ibid., 79. Putnam in fact suggests that decline in religious community may be somewhat slower than that of other kinds of community. A British observer in fact argues that, "If we take into account the widespread flight from any kind of community, especially small-scale local voluntary community in our society, congregations may be judged to be doing quite well." Willmer, "The Collapse of Congregations," 249.

18. Ward, "Losing My Religion."

19. See Roof, *A Generation of Seekers*; also, *Spiritual Marketplace*.

20. Jamieson, *A Churchless Faith*. This is based on his Ph.D. thesis of the same title at the University of Canterbury.

21. www.Barna.org., March 20, 2006.

of non-church-goers. Previous research showed that in 1987 48 percent admitted to a form of religious spiritual experience. In 2000 this had increased to 76 per cent.[22] In the U.S. a 2008 Pew study found that about 90 percent believed in God, and a General Social Science Survey found that 75 percent said they pray at least once a week.[23]

Both of these figures are similar to those found consistently over recent decades. Reg Bibby finds that research unfailingly shows that "Canadians, in large numbers, are expressing spiritual needs and interests" and "see themselves as spiritual."[24] A group of Australian researchers, after analyzing a raft of data, write: "What this research makes clear is that many of those who are not attending are nonetheless religious, oriented to God, open to those aspects of life which are beyond the material."[25]

In New Zealand, the International Social Science Surveys[26] carried out in 1991, 1998, and 2009 confirm that overall religious believing has persisted. There have been both rises and falls in the percentage believing in God, in life after death and praying. In 2006 close to 60 percent of the New Zealand population still identified as Christian in some form or other. This is scarcely a culture of unbelief, the truly secular condition that many predicted would be here already, and the findings indicate, as Taylor expresses it, that "our age is very far from settling into a comfortable unbelief."[27]

However, it is important not to assume that because people are continuing to believe, their beliefs have remained the same. "Religion has refused to die as so many had predicted . . . but it certainly is not like it used to be," as it has "escaped the confines of formal organizations."[28] As people have left organized religion in increasing numbers, they may not have renounced belief, but they have certainly changed it. Davie observes that "belief begins to drift further and further away from Christian orthodoxies as regular practice diminishes."[29] Research by Gill, Hadaway and Marler demonstrates that in Britain support for distinctively Chris-

---

22. Hay and Hunt, *Understanding the Spirituality of People who Don't Go to Church*.

23. Bass, *Christianity after Religion*, 49, 55.

24. Bibby, *Restless Gods*, 190. Later research by Bibby finds that "spiritual needs and fragmented beliefs and practices persist." "Restless Gods and Restless Youth."

25. Hughes, et al., *Believe it or Not*, 1.

26. *International Social Science Survey Programme*.

27. Taylor, *A Secular Age*, 727.

28. Bouma, "Mapping Religious Contours," 5.

29. Davie, *Religion in Britain since 1945*, 76.

tian beliefs appears to be declining.[30] They summarize their findings as demonstrating a decline in several traditional Christian beliefs, a confusing pattern of persistence and some slight increase in New Age beliefs.

One indicator of this is belief about God. Whereas in 1947 more believed in a personal God than an impersonal God (as Spirit or Life Force), by 1993 the balance had shifted so that belief in a personal God was the minority understanding. The New Zealand ISSSP survey indicates the same preference. Alan Webster, the director of the study, writes that "belief seems to be evolving rather than fading away."[31] Reginald Bibby, while emphasizing the continued religious orientation of Canadians, points out that "many Canadians have conceptions of spirituality that are fairly foreign to religious bodies and especially to Conservative Protestants. The two sides may have little more than a word in common."[32]

While the U.S. shows stronger attachment to traditional Christianity, the 2008 Pew survey found that only a bit over half now think of God as a person with whom one could have a personal relationship; this trend is consistent with other Western societies. Robin Gill, in postulating a "cultural" theory of church-going, as an alternative to the three presented earlier in this chapter, argues that regular church-going reinforces distinctive beliefs and values, which in turn sustains individual identities. His theory predicts that a "decline in Christian beliefs will follow rather than precede a decline in church-going and Sunday School attendance."[33] The research presented throughout this work would certainly give credence to this argument.

There are two critical issues which emerge out of this brief overview of data and interpretive theories. The first is that secularization was a modern meta-narrative, which, as we know, are being widely abandoned. It is also a narrative of decline, and sociology is increasingly abandoning this perspective, instead describing what has been happening as simply change, which is often multidimensional and at times apparently contradictory.

The second issue is the question of how one quantifies religion or the religious. Narratives of religious decline did two things. They counted church attendance or membership, and these clearly have been in decline. They also pointed to census returns, which showed an increasingly

---

30. Gill, Hadaway and Marler, "Is Religious Belief Declining in Britain?"
31. Webster, *Spiral of Values*, 168.
32. Bibby, *Restless Gods*, 199.
33. Gill, *Churchgoing and Christian Ethics*, 66.

higher percentage ticking "no religion." These two sets of figures were then interpreted to mean that people were "losing their religion." This is the line consistently taken by Lloyd Geering and James Veitch, to whom the New Zealand media have returned again and again, until the last few years, for comment on religious trends.[34]

Both of these conclusions are being challenged. The first equates religion with belonging to an institutional church and attending regularly. We have seen that this is going out of fashion in all kinds of spheres, but this does not mean that the activity itself is going out of fashion. I offer another sporting analogy: I spent many years, when I got too old and fragile for rugby, running competitively, particularly in marathons. In the mid-1990s I retired from that, but after an absence of six years returned. What I noticed was a great difference. Numbers in events for registered runners were much smaller, veterans sections were by far the largest, clubs were much smaller, many had merged in order to survive, and others were seeking to amalgamate. The club I joined had one senior man (under forty) and one woman. All the rest were veterans. There were no youth.

This sounds very much like many churches. However, come the City of Christchurch Marathon and Half Marathon, there are record entries, and considerable numbers of young people. The same is true for the Dunedin Harbour Half Marathon, and the Round the Bays Run in Auckland continues to attract upwards of 80,000 participants. If one goes running around the popular running places in New Zealand, like Ross Creek in Dunedin, Hagley Park in Christchurch, or One Tree Hill in Auckland, there are more people running than ever.

While writing a first draft of this book I was running in Hartford, Connecticut, preparing for the Boston marathon. The parks were full of runners, and of course the great marathons like Boston continue to attract far more entries then organizers can accommodate. In other words, running is thriving, more people than ever are doing it, but few want to join organized institutions to do it. It would be a huge mistake to equate the state of running in New Zealand solely with clubs and events organized under Athletics New Zealand, and my impression is that the same is true elsewhere.

---

34. I should make the point at this stage that, in a number of personal conversations with Jim Veitch over recent years, he has clearly modified his position and has engaged energetically with the life of the church.

is the future churchless?

Preoccupation with institutional expressions of religion can be seen as part of the modern focus on institutions and specialization. Only what is in that sphere equates to religion. But "the religious" is much broader than that. Martin Percy notes that "religion as a differentiated category only emerged within Europe in the seventeenth century. Culturally what many describe as postmodernity may be nothing more than religion's return to non-differentiation."[35]

This line of argument has long been sustained by Greeley and Martin in challenging the standard secularization thesis. Greeley argues that, in the late medieval period, regular church-going was not particularly high, and that religion operated in very diffuse cultural forms.[36] Martin shows that the popular image of a sacred medieval society is the product of history written from the perspective of medieval élite society, controlled by the church. There is no reliable evidence that religious life in Europe has declined since the Middle Ages.[37]

High church attendance itself was a result of the institutionalization and compartmentalization of life in modernity and, as Percy shows, reached its peak in England in the Victorian era. So there was no long period of high church involvement which has steadily declined since the onset of modernity. Rather, this was an unusual period, part of the institutionalization of all of life, and the changes that have occurred in the second half of the twentieth century may in fact be a return to a more "normal" and less institutionally-located religiosity. David Lyon makes the important observation that "Secularization may be used to refer to the declining strength of some traditional religious group in a specific cultural milieu, but at the same time say nothing of the spiritualities or faiths that may be growing in popularity and influence. If we view religion in typically modern, institutional fashion, other religious realities may be missed."[38]

The second critical issue, census returns, is also very interesting as it raises the question of what people mean when they tick "no religion." The assumption has been that they mean they are not religious—that they are "secular atheists." In New Zealand the number indicating this, or "object to state," has increased from 9 percent in 1961 to 32 percent

---

35. Percy, *The Salt of the* Earth, 24.
36. Greeley, "The Persistence of Religion," 24–41.
37. Martin, *The Religious and the Secular.*
38. Lyon, *Jesus in Disneyland*, 21.

in 2006. A similar trend can be found in Australia, where this group increased from 11 percent in 1966 to 29 percent in 2011. In the United States, although relatively small, those in this category doubled in the 1990s from 7 percent to 14 per cent. These increases are frequently cited in support of the secularization thesis. However, more detailed research done on the beliefs of those who now define themselves as having "no religion" throws this assumption into question. Hout and Fischer note, again, that the most significant factor in the increase in this category was the "cultural experience of coming of age in the 1960s,"[39] and find that "religious scepticism proved to be an unlikely explanation."[40] Most people with no religion "hold conventional religious beliefs, despite their alienation from organized religion."[41] They argue that

> In a country with as much emphasis on religion as we see in the United States, . . . the growing detachment of a significant proportion of the adult population from organised religion is important. Equally important is the evidence that indicates how the new religious dissenters have distanced themselves from the churches, not from God . . . The majority of adults who prefer no religion continue to believe in God and an afterlife. Few are atheists or agnostics. Most pray. Many reject the 'religious' label, but they think of themselves as 'spiritual' . . . In short, the critical feature of most such people is not their beliefs, or personal piety, but their estrangement from organised religion.[42]

These findings are supported by the American Religious Identity Survey 2001, which found that 19 percent of Americans did not identify with

---

39. "The cohorts born prior to 1935 are more religious than those that came after, each cohort from 1935 to 1950 is increasingly less religious than the one right before it, and those born after 1950 are at the same (low) level of religious attachment as the 1950 cohort. We think that this pattern of cohort difference reflects a 'sixties effect' . . . that people who were old enough in the 1960s to have well-established religious identities were less affected by the changes of those times than were cohorts just coming of age then. Thus the cohorts that were over 30 years old in the 1960s less often expressed preferences for no religion in the 1990s than did cohorts that were in their teens and twenties then." Hout and Fischer, "Why More Americans Have No Religious Preference," 183.

40. Using an analysis that includes a "six statement belief-in-God item" they find that the "increase in no religious preference is concentrated among those with the firmest beliefs, not among sceptics." Ibid., 187–88.

41. Ibid., 188.

42. Ibid.

a religious group. Interestingly, however, of these 35 percent described themselves as religious and 45 percent believed in God.[43]

Similarly, in Australia the National Social Science Survey data shows that "most people who have dropped out of church life or who were nominal in their involvement had not rejected belief in God."[44] In New Zealand, research by A.C. Neilsen among people who did not attend church, but had some previous experience of church, found that "despite not currently attending a church or other formal religious institution, spiritual belief is still strong."[45]

All of this research indicates that the decline in church belonging cannot primarily be explained by people losing their religious belief. They have not embraced a fundamentally non-religious stance, or lost their religion in the deepest and most fundamental sense. Claiming that the principal characteristic of the religious landscape of today is that faith or religion has diversified rather than declined, Charles Taylor argues that "The modern cosmic imaginary is uncapturable by any one range of views. It has moved people in a whole range of directions from the hardest materialism through to Christian orthodoxy . . . The salient feature of the modern cosmic imaginary . . . is that it has opened a space in which people can wander between and around all these options without having to land clearly and definitively in any one."[46] Half a century earlier, with prophetic insight, Richard Wright wrote in *The Outsider*, "Since religion is dead, religion is everywhere . . . Religion was once an affair of the church, it is now in the streets in each man's heart. Once there were priests; now every man's a priest."[47]

From 'Religion' to 'Spirituality'

The gradual awareness of the media that there is another story about religion than that of decline in New Zealand was illustrated in an article in *The Press*, documenting the increasing popularity of home altars, a

43. Keysar, Mayer and Kosmin, "No Religion: Profile of America's Unchurched," 40–44.

44. Bentley, Blombery and Hughes, *Faith without the Church*, 70.

45. *Attracting New Zealanders to Spiritual Life*, 5. The open-ended qualitative research was carried out among forty people who indicated in preliminary research that they considered themselves either religious or spiritual but did not attend church.

46. Taylor, *Secular Age*, 351.

47. Wright, *The Outsider*, 359, cited in Ostwalt, *Secular Steeples*, 189.

tradition of ancient cultures. John McGuckin, Professor of Early Church History at Union Theological Seminary in New York, noted that "In rural parts of medieval Europe, home altars were kept by Christians who could not easily travel to church," but that now "the altar's popularity has less to do with physical distance than with the spiritual gulf that separates many people from organized religion."[48]

There is, then, some support for each of the three theories outlined: there are some signs of decline, several signs of persistence, and clearly belief has become increasingly separated from belonging. The situation is increasingly described as a change from "religion" to "spirituality."[49] The 2000 survey, carried out for the BBC's "Soul of Britain" series,[50] found that whereas in 1990 54 percent called themselves "religious," by 2000 that figure had fallen to 27 per cent, while 31 percent preferred to call themselves "spiritual." Roof's research among baby boomers found that 73 percent preferred to use the language of "spirituality" rather than "religion."[51]

The words in this shift signify different realities. "Religion," according to these findings, connotes rigid, authoritarian, oppressive institutions; dogmatism and lack of openness to alternative perspectives; and cold formalism or ritualism. "Spirituality," by contrast, suggests flexibility and creativity; tolerance and respect for alternative insights from others; room for doubt and searching; and an emphasis on personal experience.

Robert Wuthnow also tracks this change in American spirituality since the 1950s.[52] He suggests that a spirituality of "dwelling" or "place" has given way to a spirituality of "seeking" or "journey." He defines the former as an orientation that links spirituality to participation in institutional religion and is marked by sharply drawn symbolic boundaries. Spirituality is indicated by membership in the organization and "being there"—by belonging. This kind of spirituality, he suggests, flourishes in times of social and cultural stability.

With the social and cultural upheavals of the 1960s, however, people began to shift to a spirituality of seeking or journey. "The 1960s began with theologians declaring God was dead; it ended with millions of Americans finding that God could be approached and made relevant to their lives in

---

48. "Altars of Intimacy," B-5.
49. See, for example, Heelas, "The Spiritual Revolution," 357–77.
50. "Soul of Britain."
51. Roof, *Spiritual Marketplace*.
52. Wuthnow, *After Heaven*.

more ways than they had ever imagined."[53] A spirituality of seeking views the spiritual life as an ongoing journey or quest, with the process as important as the destination. It is more ambiguous, with vague and open boundaries and loose connections, if any, to religious institutions. Roof describes it as a "quest culture,"[54] and Taylor argues that in our "pluralist world, in which many forms of belief and unbelief jostle, and hence fragilize each other," we have a "spirituality of search" or "quest."[55]

Two other terms are helpful in understanding the nature of this change. The first is what has been called "detraditionalization." Paul Heelas defines this as a "shift of authority from 'without' to 'within.'"[56] In religion, "The shift in authority [is] from faith in, or reliance/dependency on, that which lies beyond the person to that which lies within. "Voice" is thus displaced from the establishment of traditions to the creativities of the spiritually/religiously inspired self."[57]

In tracing this "flight from deference," Heelas sees it as part of the shift from religion to spirituality which is having a widespread effect on all kinds of religious traditions. It means that, even in traditional religious institutions, the authority of the institution has less hold on the individuals who belong to that institution as they take more account of their own personal convictions and beliefs. It can be found, for example, in the work of Donald Miller on "new paradigm churches" in the United States, such as Vineyard and Calvary Chapel, where it is repeatedly emphasized that personal conviction counts more than doctrine, the Holy Spirit more than external tradition. Heelas holds that

> Crudely, detraditionalized people want detraditionalized religion: a 'religion' which is (apparently) more constructed than given; with practices which emphasize the authority of participants; which enables participants to be personally responsible for their salvation; which says that 'sacred texts should confirm what is in you' . . . ; which provides guidance and personal

---

53. Ibid., 53.

54. Roof, *Spiritual Marketplace*.

55. Taylor, *A Secular Age*, 531–32.

56. Heelas, "Detraditionalization and its Rivals," 2. This fits with Anthony Giddens' notion of change from "traditional" to "post-traditional" society in many parts of the Western world, with the centre of authority being moved from socially accepted traditions to the self. Giddens, "Living in a Post-Traditional Society," 56–109. He describes the "emergence of an internal referential system of knowledge and power."

57. Heelas, "The Spiritual Revolution," 375.

experience rather than beliefs; which does not demand that one should belong to a particular organization.[58]

Taylor develops a similar theme, arguing that in the age of authenticity the "spiritual as such is no longer intrinsically related to society," and that individuals "only accept what rings true to [their] own inner self."[59]

What we are seeing, then, is not so much a decline in religion as an evolution of religion as its cultural context changes. This means that it is now much less located in institutions, which consequently carry considerably less authority in determining how people express it or the resources they draw on to shape it. This is the basic theme of Dianna Butler Bass's *Christianity after Religion,* to which we have referred several times, and which carries the subtitle "The end of the church and the birth of a new spiritual awakening."

The second helpful framework for understanding the changes over this period is provided by the writings of Ernst Troeltsch on mysticism. Troeltsch built on Max Weber's well known distinction between church and sect as the two basic social forms of Christianity, by adding a third, mysticism. He argued that Christianity can assume any of these three basic social forms and that all have existed throughout Christian history.[60] What is most significant for us is that he held that mysticism was the most rapidly growing type and was likely to come to predominate in the modern world.[61]

Unfortunately, mysticism was omitted from most subsequent analyses of religion, as it is only rarely found in institutional form. In particular, H. Richard Niebuhr, in his highly influential *The Social Sources of Denominationalism,* eliminated it from the church-sect discussion.[62] This is regrettable, as the church-sect distinction has become increasingly difficult to maintain, with newer forms blurring the differences, and discussion centered on it has often been unhelpful in seeking to understand religious change. Much of what has been described in the research

---

58. Heelas, *The New Age Movement,* 172.
59. Taylor, *A Secular Age,* 489–90.
60. Troeltsch, *The Social Teachings of the Churches.*
61. Ibid., 381.
62. Garrett, in noting this, also suggests a further factor may have been the hostility of some Protestant theologians, and in particular the hugely influential Karl Barth, to mysticism. Garrett, "Maligned Mysticism," 211.

analyzed throughout this work, however, clearly fits within Troeltsch's understanding of mysticism.

These two frameworks of detraditionalization and mysticism place the changing nature of religion within the increasingly individualistic character of Western societies, especially since the 1960s. A significant number of social commentators see this process as continuing, with devastating consequences. Many church leaders, faced with a seemingly more and more difficult task as they lose church members, also subscribe to the analysis. Modern and postmodern culture, especially its individualism, is the enemy to be resisted at all costs before it swallows us all down the sink hole.

More recently this worst-case scenario is being challenged. In the 1970s Berger and colleagues wrote *The Homeless Mind*.[63] What happened in the counterculture was that people lost faith in the primary institutions of society—government, education, business, religion, family—where people had previously found belonging—"homes"—and ended up with minds with nowhere to park—"homeless"—except for the self. This contributed to the dubbing of the 1980s as the "me decade." However, many are now suggesting that since the mid-1980s there has been a reconnecting with belonging, a quest for new forms of community.

Some sociologists speak of a new communitarian age. But this is not occurring by people going back to those primary institutions through which older generations belonged, but in what Berger termed "secondary" institutions. These are face to face, open, tolerant, inclusive, non-judgmental and democratic,[64] and much looser. Wuthnow, in researching the now incredibly widespread small group phenomenon—which fits this category—suggests that this is bringing together two important contemporary searches: the quest for the sacred, and the quest for community,[65] believing, and belonging.

This is the essence of the challenge faced by the church in societies like New Zealand. Sociology holds that faith is both socially transmitted and socially maintained, a perspective I would maintain is also consistent with Scripture. The relationship between Christian belonging or community and personal faith or spirituality has become increasingly disconnected, and as it has done so the latter has become less Christian, at least in

---

63. Berger, et al., *The Homeless Mind*.
64. See also Heelas, "The Spiritual Revolution."
65. Wuthnow, *Sharing the Journey*.

an orthodox sense. Is a reconnection possible, or do we face a future which, while it may be religious in the broader sense, is churchless and therefore ultimately may be without Christianity in any traditional sense?

The Church and the Future

If we ignore the perspectives from either end of the spectrum (that the death of Christianity is inevitable because of secularization, or that the churches need to return to more traditional beliefs and practices and people will flock back[66]), there are two main schools of thought. First, there are those who argue for the reformation of existing forms. There is still a growth dynamic in the semi-traditional congregation, so long as it is done well. On the other hand, there are those who are increasingly suggesting that the inherited mode of being church has had its day, and that tinkering around with it cannot reverse the decline. Something more drastic is required; a new beginning with completely new forms not weighed down by the baggage of outmoded forms and traditions. My contention is that we need to do both, but there is also a third and even more important challenge.

Reformation: Making Existing Forms of Church more Effective

In analyzing international studies which attempt to characterize effective churches, and comparing these with the congregational studies summarized earlier, we have been able to identify some common characteristics of "effective churches." However, in further researching these growing churches, we also found that most of the people in them came from the

---

66. This latter response has been labeled fundamentalism, and a move in this direction is popular in some of the more conservative sectors of the church. It is a response to the fragmentation of life and values in an increasingly pluralistic society. Baumann argues that fundamentalism will thrive under the conditions of postmodernity: "The allure of fundamentalism stems from its promise to emancipate the converted from the agonies of choice; here one finds, finally, the indubitably supreme authority to end all other authorities. One knows where to look when life-decisions are to be made, in matters big and small, and one knows that looking there one does the right thing and so is spared the dread of risk taking. Fundamentalism is a radical remedy against that bane of postmodern/market-led/consumer society—risk-contaminated freedom." Baumann, *Postmodernity and its Discontents*, 184. While it will be attractive to some, it is unlikely that it will ever attract a majority in modern liberal democratic societies such as New Zealand, and is therefore an ultimately unhelpful response.

already churched sector of New Zealand society. This group, who have belonged to the Christian church in some way during their life, is still a significant sector of society, as the number still identifying as Christian on census returns indicates.[67]

The church has often been compared to a boat or ship afloat on the sea. Using this analogy, if the ship is leaking on the ocean of contemporary culture, then the most sensible initial task is to endeavor to stop, or at least slow down, the leaks. Those churches that have reformed along the lines of this research have, to some degree, been clearly successful in this, and have therefore played an important role in conserving Christianity, in the best sense of that word. It is important that they continue to do so.

Two factors, however, put a limit on how effective mere reformation will be. First, those socialized within the church, and therefore still identifying with its specific beliefs and forms, are an increasingly aging sector, most of them over fifty. Second, research indicates that most of those who are going to return have done so by the age of forty.[68] Thus, if the churches are going to rely on reform alone, they will be appealing to an increasingly limited market. Australian researchers, after noting that many of those who do not attend are nonetheless religious, go on to state that "it is [however] unlikely that they will be brought into the ranks of church attenders in large numbers."[69] I believe this is the reality which the church in New Zealand and elsewhere faces. The majority of the under-fifties, while they may be interested in spirituality and religion, are not going to be attracted into the kind of social institutions which existing forms of church represent, however contemporary the packaging may be made. It is just not their social world.

Revolution: Creating New Forms of Church

We have highlighted throughout these reflections the paradox of a strongly and perhaps increasingly spiritual culture and the continued decline in church belonging in countries like New Zealand. Michael

67. Hadaway and Marler contend that data from a number of studies indicate that "people with heavy levels of childhood religious involvement usually retain the denominational identity they held in childhood—in spite of religious inactivity as adults . . . In a sense they were 'imprinted' as children through religious involvement." Hadaway and Marler, "All in the Family," 104–5.

68. Bibby, *There's Got to be More*, 75.

69. Hughes, et al., *Believe it or Not*, 1.

Moynagh asks the critical question of whether this interest in spirituality will "remain, as now, largely private, individualized and unfocused, or will it once more be channelled into church;" he goes on to suggest that the "church may connect with our more spiritual age if it offers not only a spiritual map, but the freedom for people to select the route most helpful to them."[70]

There seem to be two key parameters for new forms of Christian community. First, in line with the pluralism and fragmentation of the culture, there will be a great variety of congregational forms that need to emerge, either within the structures of existing churches or as new churches. Second, in line with the increasing individualism and freedom, these new forms will need to give space to individuals to make their own choices from a selection provided, rather than prescribe what is expected in a standardised way. Along this line, Roof argues that

> High levels of religious individualism do not necessarily undermine spiritual vitality. Individualism often does erode certain forms of institutionalized religious participation—usually the older more acculturated styles that have lost touch with everyday life—but it also opens up 'free space' for forming new activities and solidarities as individual proclivities evolve in a seemingly endless kaleidoscopic fashion . . . That people today are bonding more around their emotions, experiences, and yearning need not spell the demise of traditional structures, but it does mean that such structures, as well as any new type of spiritual movements now taking form, must accommodate, indeed, actively embrace, personal concerns in its formation of community.[71]

Many have identified the cultural and social change over the second half of the twentieth century as being from a modern to a postmodern society, characterized by looser, less structured, less hierarchical, and more fragmented forms of society. Zygmunt Bauman uses the suggestive analogy of the "solid" structures of modernism becoming liquefied—hence he describes the emerging culture as "Liquid Modernity."[72] In this liquid world, he argues, the old certainties, stable institutions, and predictable linear ways of thinking no longer make sense, and in so many spheres what was once stable and predictable is increasingly fragile, friable, and liquefied.

70. Moynagh, *Changing World, Changing Church*, 87, 89.
71. Roof, *Spiritual Marketplace*, 163.
72. Bauman, *Liquid Modernity*.

is the future churchless? 127

Along similar lines, Manuel Castells uses the term "network society" to describe the new type of social structure that has emerged in the last two decades of the twentieth century. He defines a network as a "set of interconnected nodes" and points out that "networks decentre performance and share decision making. By definition a network has no centre."[73] Tracing these trends, Wuthnow finds a shift to "porous social institutions" with permeable structures and a society marked by "loose connections," where people have much greater flexibility and limited commitments in a wider variety of networks. He quotes from a follow-up study of the "organization men" of the 1950s, which found that their "children utterly lack their fathers' loyalty to a specific organization, [and] are more inclined to join many ever-shifting networks than to seek a niche in one immortal hierarchy."[74] It is obvious that forms of church which effectively contextualize the Christian faith within this fluid and shifting culture will be markedly different from those that did so for a previous solid and stable culture. They will be marked by fluidity rather than solidity.[75]

If the church is to resemble more this kind of social and cultural context, to be fluid rather than solid, what will these forms look like? Harvey Cox suggests that, "So far, only faint harbingers of the new era are discernable. If the qualities of most of the new religious movements presage anything, we may expect a world that prefers equality to hierarchy, participation to submission, experience over abstraction, multiple rather than single meanings, and plasticity rather than fixedness."[76]

If churches do embody these principles, then the forms they take will undergo a process of significant further change. Church leaders could do worse than to reconfigure the catchphrase from Mao Tse-Tung's Chinese revolution and seek to "let a thousand flowers bloom." Some will wither and die very quickly, some will doubtless become non-orthodox or heretical, but among those that thrive are likely to be found the new social groupings needed to contextualize our faith into the new world of

---

73. Castells, "Materials for an Exploration of the Network Society," 5–24. His work is detailed in *The Rise of the Network Society*.

74. Wuthnow, *Loose Connections*, 49.

75. Roof also picks up on this concept of liquidity or fluidity in his chapter, "On Being Fluid and Grounded," in Roof, *Spiritual Marketplace*, 111–44. He refers to a style of religion "privileging themes of individuality, adaptability and fluidity." 112.

76. Cox, "Myth of the Twentieth Century," 143.

post-Christian, postmodern and post-secular New Zealand. This is the approach of the "missional church movement."

In our current context, where many of our old frameworks have been undermined and so no longer work, the way ahead is uncertain and uncharted. Hence a significant part of what this movement encourages churches to do, once they have understood the challenge their new context provides, is to begin experiments that may make connections with what the Spirit is doing in the lives of those living in their local communities.[77]

Resourcing: The Social and Cultural Role of the Church

With the drift of values and beliefs in our culture away from those that have been shaped by centuries of Christian orthodoxy, it is also obvious that connecting believing with belonging will be increasingly challenging. This is the main argument of Callum Brown in *The Death of Christian Britain*, which sees the critical issue as the loss of "discursive Christianity," and the death of the "Christian-centered culture" from which people found guidance as to how they "should behave and how they should think about their lives."[78]

It is also obvious that if "belonging" is in itself less of a cultural value, a focus by the church which is primarily directed at those concerns will mean that its role will be both increasingly diminished and less and less effective. If, however, the church sees as part of its role the shaping of the values and beliefs of the wider culture and society in which it exists, then it needs to put energy and resources not only into connecting with people's beliefs in order to move them toward belonging, but also with connecting in order to help shape those beliefs and values. Unfortunately, the focus of church leadership has seen a preoccupation with institutional concerns and a neglect of the wider kingdom role of the church as salt, light, and leaven in society.

In doing this the church faces a complex and challenging task. Not only must it be shaped by the culture as it seeks to incarnate the Christian message into forms that are indigenous to it, but it must also seek

---

77. Roxburgh and Boren, *Introducing the Missional Church*, provides a good introduction to this. In the U.K., Fresh Expressions also encourages a similar approach. See www.freshexpressions.org.uk.

78. Brown, *The Death of Christian Britain*, 193.

to shape the culture by those gospel values that transcend it. It must be faithful to both its "context" and to its "text." Cox writes that

> In many places in Europe today one gets the distinct impression that although the institutional forms of religions may be weaker than they once were, religion still plays a strong role in public culture. References and allusions appear in such widely disparate places as poetry and drama, film, political debates, and even popular music . . . Could Christianity in Europe be moving away from an institutionally positioned model and toward a culturally diffuse pattern, more like the religions of many Asian countries . . . ?[79]

In a similar vein, Martin sees the religious, the spiritual, and the sacred "leaking" into ordinary life at every level,[80] and Berger finds the world "dripping with reactionary supernaturalism."[81] As a consequence, in this changing location of religion we are finding that new vehicles for religious expression are coming from outside of religious institutions, drawing upon other cultural forms that are not formally related to religious institutions (in other words, secular); and so we find popular cultural forms taking on some of the tasks of traditional religions.

Some have described what we are seeing as the sacralization of the secular. Conrad Ostwalt writes: "If the modern era of secularization promised the disappearance of religion, the new era, the postmodern era of secularization, promises the increasing relevance of religion expressed through popular cultural forms."[82] Consequently, many are now claiming that secularization, rather than leading to the disappearance of religion, actually encourages a return of religion to ordinary life, leaving it more powerful, diffuse, and omnipresent, and so "we might even view the age of secularization as the age of religious saturation."[83]

Given these changes, it is "nowadays better to conceptualize religion as a cultural resource or form than as a social institution."[84] Even in its institutional form, it needs to operate to resource the culture rather than to preserve an institution. All revolutions go through first a destructive and

---

79. Cox, "The Myth of the Twentieth Century," 138–39.
80. Martin, *The Breaking of the Image*.
81. Berger, "The Desecularization of the World," 4.
82. Ostwalt, *Secular Steeples*, 25.
83. Martin and Ostwalt, *Screening the Sacred*, 158. In addition to these authors, Harvey Cox, David Martin, and Martin Percy share this view.
84. Beckford, *Religion in Advanced Industrial Societies*, 171.

then a constructive phase. There is increasing recognition that, especially since the 1960s, we have seen the collapse of modern society, aided by the postmodern deconstructive critique of modernity. Many[85] are suggesting that we are now entering a phase where the emphasis is increasingly on reconstructing new forms of society. This lies behind the new quest for community we have identified and also, I suggest, behind the renewed interest in spirituality.

Walter Brueggemann suggests that in this process the task of the church is "to *fund*—to provide the pieces, materials, and resources out of which a new world can be imagined."[86] It is important to recognize, however, that in this changed world the role of the church in this regard is not the same as the role it held in Christendom. That world has gone forever, despite the longing for its return by some. And so Brueggemann argues that "The work of funding consists not in the offer of a large ordered coherence, but in making lots of pieces that admit of more than one large ordering."[87] There are many areas that could be explored in this regard. I want to note three here.

1. Resourcing the personal spiritualities and faiths of people: An increasing theme in religious research in Western societies, as we have seen, is that many of those who do not attend churches regularly still have religious beliefs. In addition, these are significantly shaped by the Christian tradition. As we have noted, in New Zealand almost 60 percent still identify with the Christian faith. In England, where church attendance is even lower than New Zealand, 73 percent indicated in a recent poll that they regarded themselves as a Christian.[88] These figures suggest a level of openness and some allegiance to the churches and their beliefs and values. While they may not be regular worshippers or "belongers," there are still times when they wish to express that identity through liturgy or worship, or a chance to reflect on life or events helped by religious symbols, stories, or sacred spaces.

   A poll at Easter 2005 found that 46 percent of New Zealanders indicated they attended church at least once a year, apart from weddings and funerals.[89] Death and marriage themselves are perhaps

---

85. Such as David Tracey, Alister McGrath, Keith Ward, and John Drane.
86. Brueggemann, *Texts under Negotiation*, 20.
87. Ibid.
88. Thomas, *Counting People In*, 19. The survey was carried out in 2001 by Opinion Research Business.
89. TV3/Colmar Brunton Poll, March 24, 2005.

the most obvious particular rituals for these people, with a significant proportion of funerals and marriages still taking place in religious settings, whether inside or outside churches.[90] Also important for some are births. The church needs to consider ways in which it can offer religious resources in more accessible and relevant ways to those who may be interested in religious expressions at such events.

In the more public sphere, the interest in Christmas, Easter, and Anzac Day as public religious rituals offer opportunities for the church to seek to connect with the spiritual dimension of our culture in ways that can help to fund and shape it. All of these events are attracting increasing numbers of participants. Another indication of this desire of many for religion to play at least some role in their lives is the way in which church schools[91] always have far more students applying for entrance than they are able to take. The vast majority of these come from families who are not regular attenders at church.

Then there is the increasing demand for the church to play a role in significant public tragedies and deaths. This has been well documented in Britain,[92] but there are also ample examples in New Zealand, when "the church takes center stage in a civic religious role as chaplain to the nation."[93] The response to the death of Princess Diana and "9/11" are international events in which significant numbers of New Zealanders turned to the church. In New Zealand, the death of Charles Upham,[94] the murder of Police Constable Duncan Taylor,[95] the killing of Mark Parker in the Bali bombing,[96] the multiple deaths in a Christchurch plane crash, services held in churches

90. Exact figures are difficult to find, but indications are that it is still about 50 per cent.

91. In New Zealand, as well as the state school system, there are many private or integrated schools, most of which are part of the Anglican, Catholic, Presbyterian, or Methodist churches.

92. See, for example, Davie, "From Obligation to Consumption," 5–6.

93. Davidson, "Christianity and National Identity," 16–35.

94. Charles Upham was New Zealand's great military hero. His funeral in November 1994 in Christchurch Cathedral saw over 5,000 people cramming the cathedral and the streets outside.

95. Taylor was murdered in Palmerston North on 5 July, 2002. The Roman Catholic Cathedral in Palmerston North was used for people to pay tributes and for a large public funeral. In Timaru, his hometown, the Roman Catholic Church was used for the public to pay tributes.

96. His funeral in his hometown of Timaru was performed by an Anglican priest, Mike Hawke, with over 1,000 people attending.

to commemorate New Zealand's worst peace-time tragedy, the 1979 air crash on Mount Erebus,[97] and the call by the Prime Minister after the Asian *tsunami* to recognize Sunday, January 17, 2005 as an official memorial day[98]—all of these are examples of the church engaging positively in a public religious role. This trend reached new levels with the Pike River mining disaster in 2010 and the Christchurch earthquake in 2011, where the church had a very public role in the period following and large nationally televised memorial services were held, with the Prime Minister taking an active role and other leading political figures also attending

Clearly, religion is still in demand in New Zealand society, and the church needs to respond to this with a confidence born of an awareness that our society refuses to leave religion alone and so "continue[s] to offer a ministry and a faith to a public that wishes to relate to religion without necessarily belonging;" to do this, it needs more approaches that "engage with contemporary culture in interrogative, empathetic and critical-friendly ways."[99] We have seen that most now see spirituality as a journey or quest, hence the tremendous popularity of films such as *Lord of the Rings*, *Star Wars*, *Harry Potter*, and *The Chronicles of Narnia*. This understanding also resonates with the ancient and once again contemporary notion of pilgrimage, a concept which will be explored further in a later chapter. It may then be better to conceptualize the local church as a way station for pilgrims rather than as an institution to which they "belong."

2. Connecting with the spiritual and religious questing that is taking place in our culture in all kinds of ways, especially in popular culture—film, literature, art, music, tourism, and even sport. Film provides a powerful illustration of this.[100] Stories are one of the main ways in which we make sense of the often chaotic and haphazard world in which we live. There is no doubt that film is now the principal storyteller in our culture. George Miller, producer of *Babe*, *Mad*

---

97. These services in November 2004 were headed by the Governor General of New Zealand.

98. The Prime Minister herself spoke at a service in Auckland's Anglican cathedral, attended by the Governor General, the leader of the opposition, and several cabinet ministers.

99. Percy, "Things Are Not as Bad as You Think," 9–10.

100. In 2006 I began teaching a new course at the University of Otago, "Spirituality in Film."

Max, and *The Witches of Eastwick*, has suggested that cinemas have become our covert new cathedrals.

> I believe cinema is now the most powerful secular religion, and that people gather in cinemas to experience things collectively the way they once did in church. The cinema storytellers have become the new priests. They are doing a lot of the work of our religious institutions, which have taken so much of the poetry, mystery, and mysticism out of religious belief that people look for other places to stimulate their spirituality.[101]

Films do entertain, but they also do so much more, and the millions who go to watch them are going for more than just a bit of light relief. As Catherine Albanese has stated, films express or reinforce "the powerful beliefs about life and provide a web of fundamental beliefs." They act like sacred stories because they establish a "world that makes sense and give people a feeling for their place in the scheme of things" and introduce "what the world means and how it means."[102] One only needs to examine the nature of so many of the most popular films. I have already referred to *Lord of the Rings*, *Harry Potter*, *Star Wars*, and *The Chronicles of Narnia*. But one could mention many others: *Forest Gump*, *Sixth Sense*, *Matrix*, *The Lion King*, *Dogma*, *Keeping the Faith*, *Bruce Almighty*, *As It Is in Heaven*, *Gran Torino*, and, from a New Zealand context, *Whalerider*. Their mythic and religious qualities are self-evident, their spiritual questing clear.

Robert Wuthnow, in a recent book on music, art, and religion,[103] finds that part of the reason for the vitality of religion in the face of secularizing forces is the increasing role of the arts in our culture. His studies show that, rather than being incompatible with active church involvement and the Christian faith, as they are often portrayed, "those with greater exposure to artistic activities are more likely than those with less exposure to be seriously committed to spiritual growth."[104]

If in our world spirituality is increasingly disconnected from institutions, and people are exploring it and fostering it through the arts, then it is critical that the church and our theological institutions

101. Miller, quoted in Frost, *Eyes Wide Open*, 100.
102. Albanese, quoted in Martin and Ostwalt, *Screening the Sacred*, 156.
103. Wuthnow, *All in Sync*.
104. Ibid., 19.

enter into and engage with that world. They must do so, firstly, in ways which create opportunities for people to engage with Christian perspectives and voices in their "reflection" on it. *The Da Vinci Code* phenomenon illustrated profoundly the level of interest in religion, something demonstrated even further when it made the silver screen.

It was interesting to watch how different sectors of the church engaged with this, but it certainly created a tremendous point of connection with the culture. Unfortunately, the defensive and antagonistic way many responded simply confirmed for significant numbers the suspicions they already had about organized religion.[105] For some, however, engaging in an empathetic way, acknowledging the truth of some of the issues the book and film raised about the "dark side" of religion, while pointing out in an informed way the difference between what history actually records and what fiction tells, led to helpful conversations with those outside of the church.

Secondly, the church needs to engage with society, in ways that allow the Christian tradition to enter into that world and inject Christian narratives into broader conversations. Excellent recent examples of this are the Christian film producers Tom Shadyac, in *Bruce Almighty*, and Andrew Adamson, in *The Chronicles of Narnia*. Of course a more direct illustration of this is Mel Gibson's *The Passion of the Christ*. Whatever one may think of the portrayal of religion it conveyed, the huge audiences again illustrated the interest in religion that still exists within our cultures, and this film certainly put the central narrative of Christianity into the culture in a highly accessible way.

If Callum Brown is right, and there is a loss of discursive Christianity in the culture—and while he overstates the case, there has clearly been a significant loss—this is in some ways an even more urgent challenge than that of getting bodies into churches. Weber talked about people becoming musically tone-deaf so far as religion is concerned. Clearly he was wrong and people can still hear religious and spiritual tones in the culture. But perhaps many of the under-forties *are* tone-deaf as far as the Christian religion is concerned. We need to connect with the broader culture not only to help them interpret these tones in light of the Christian gospel, but also to ensure that some of those spiritual tones in the culture are Christian.

---

105. Unfortunately, this mirrored the similar response some decades earlier to *Jesus Christ Superstar*.

3. A reawakening of the voice of the church in the public arena: The response of the newly installed Dean of the Christchurch Cathedral, Peter Beck, to derogatory remarks made about immigrants by the leader of the New Zealand First Party, Winston Peters, and the subsequent criticism of the Dean—that the church should stick to religion and stay out of politics—led to a striking editorial under the title "Turbulent Priests" in the *Christchurch Press*, one of New Zealand's most respected newspapers:

> The notion that the church should limit its activities exclusively to the ecclesiastical realm contradicts the teaching and life of the Jesus of the Gospels and the spirit of a faith that demands of its adherents an engagement with the world. A Christianity that did not speak about the moral dilemmas society faces would be a vacuous creed . . .
>
> For decades the pulpit of all denominations was a force in public life, and the nation was the better for it . . . [our] regret should be universal that they are so timid in engaging in the life of the nation.
>
> They alone can fill the spiritual and moral gap that exists in a society, not just secular but also lacking articulated common beliefs. No other force than religion exists which is capable of proclaiming a comprehensive ethical doctrine . . . No other force is so deeply entrenched in the history and culture of the world, so enmeshed in the great journey of the human race. Religion . . . has a store of wisdom that needs to be drawn on if we are to avoid the catastrophes that tempt individuals and communities on all sides.[106]

As our fragmented society seeks to redefine its common values and beliefs, without which it cannot function, the church can play a significant public role. A positive example of this was the "*Hikoi of Hope*," a protest march beginning simultaneously at both ends of the country and ending in the capital city, Wellington, in September 1998, organized by representatives of the churches of New Zealand to raise awareness of the impact of government policy on the poorer sectors of society and the growing gap between rich and poor.[107] One consequence of this march, besides raising public awareness for the

---

106. "Turbulent Priests," A–8.

107. The Hikoi involved over 40,000 people during its duration, and between 15,000 and 20,000 people were present on October 1st when leaders of various political parties were presented with a compilation of poverty stories.

issues raised, and respect for the church, has been the establishment of regular meetings between the heads of the churches and representatives of the government.

Other examples have been the positive role of the churches in the Royal Commission on Genetic Modification, and their significant contribution to the government's "Statement on Religious Diversity" issued in 2007, which encourages education about New Zealand's diverse religious and spiritual traditions, respectful dialogue, and positive relationships between government and faith communities.

This re-emergence of the church and religion to a more significant public role in other Western countries has been described by Casanova: "Religious traditions throughout the world are refusing to accept the marginal and privatized role which theories of modernity as well as theories of secularization had reserved for them. They 'went public.'"[108] He is clear, however, that this is not a return to the dominance of the church of Christendom. Even where the Catholic Church has played a significant role, such as in Spain and Poland, it has accepted the fact of the secular society, the separation of church and state, and the removal of religion from the control of public life. This means, for countries like New Zealand, that the church has to accept that it is no longer at the center of society, and must learn to function and speak from the margins, as one voice among many.

Conclusion

Several writers have used the model of liminality developed by anthropologist Victor Turner to understand the process of cultural and social marginalization which has been one of the processes of change affecting the church in many Western societies since the 1960s. The word "liminal" comes from the Latin *limen*, meaning to be on the margin or threshold. Alan Roxburgh in particular has used this concept and applied it to the church: "Liminality is a term that describes the transition process accompanying a change of state or social position . . . It is the conscious awareness that as a group (or individual) one's status-, role-, sequence-sets in society have been radically changed to the point where the group

---

108. Casanova, *Public Religions in the Modern World*, 2, 5.

has now become largely invisible to the larger society in terms of those previously held sets."[109]

This is a helpful concept for understanding what has happened to the church in New Zealand. Given the fragmented nature of postmodern New Zealand society, the church cannot hope to regain its former position. Instead, it must learn to work as just one piece in the cultural mosaic, but a piece that is called "to act as salt, leaven and light, bridging and permeating other pieces of the Mosaic."[110]

To return to our original question—"will we find a church in a future New Zealand?"—I hope I have clearly articulated that we will do so, that our future is not in fact "churchless," as some have argued. There will still be churches, but there will also be a wider and more diverse religiosity and spirituality outside of the church, a "churchless faith" beyond its control. Many of the increasing numbers who hold this perspective will still be open to connect with church at a range of levels and in a variety of ways, so the church can continue to have an important role in resourcing and seeking to give some Christian shape to their faith. This will not be a churchless society, but it will be one with "less-church," to reverse the order of the words. The church will be less—in its form less institutional, in its role less central, and in its authority less powerful—but it will still be present. Learning how to function positively in this new social and cultural reality is, I believe, the central challenge that we who still identify as "belonging" face—belonging not only to the Christian faith but also to the Christian church.

---

109. Roxburgh, "Pastoral Role in the Missionary Congregation," 23–24. This is developed in more detail in Roxburgh, *The Missionary Congregation*.

110. Gibbs and Coffey, *Church Next*, 220.

8

Being the Church in a Fragmented World

IN HIS ANALYSIS OF changes in the global church over recent decades, Peter Brierley makes the point that if churches are divided into two groups, institutional and non-institutional, very different patterns are found. Institutional churches, those which are the state church in at least one country, made up 87 percent of Christians in 1960, but had declined to 77 percent in 1995. Non-institutional churches, on the other hand, had increased from 13 percent to 23 percent over the same period.[1]

Included in this understanding of institutional churches are the two major mainline Protestant churches in New Zealand, Anglican and Presbyterian. In these institutional churches the locus of authority has tended to be tilted toward the national church rather than the local congregation. In the non-institutional churches, the balance of authority tends to be tilted, often very strongly, toward the local. One exception to this framework among non-institutional churches is the Methodist church which, while not qualifying under Brierley's definition as an institutional church, shares many of their characteristics. It is the third of the mainline Protestant churches in New Zealand.

While most churches in recent history have been denominational, the form and structure of denominations has been quite varied, with those in the first group having the centralized church leadership playing a much stronger role and many aspects of their life tending to flow from the center down to the local congregation. In the second group, the local congregation plays a much stronger role, and belonging to the

---

1. Brierley, *Future Church*, 30–34.

denomination tends to be much more voluntary, with power being more likely to flow from the local up. Given this framework, a strong case can be made to argue that the more strongly denominational churches have been considerably more likely to decline, whereas those which are denominationally much looser have shown greater vitality and often considerable growth. Perhaps the idea of denominations, at least as it has been practiced in these churches, has been part of the problem.

Certainly in his analysis of why churches like Calvary Chapel and Vineyard experienced such growth in the U.S., while those such as the Episcopalian and Presbyterian Churches declined, Donald Miller sees this as a partial explanation. Defining the historic denominations as "highly routinized, bureaucratic institutions that were stylized in another era,"[2] he argues that baby boomers have left these in large numbers and are unlikely to return for the following reasons: (1) "brand" loyalty has little meaning; (2) tradition is generally a negative; (3) they want to be involved in running their own organizations; (4) they tend to be local in their interest and fail to see the value of remote denominational organizations.

A Post-denominational Era?

Given these trends, which can be amply illustrated in almost all Western countries, many people, especially leaders of conservative churches, have argued for some time that the denominational era is over and we are entering a new "post-denominational era." Of course this is not a new argument, at least in New Zealand, following on from the more liberal ecumenical stream who argued similarly from the mid-1960s, as church union plans unfolded. The projected end was of course very different. For the latter the vision was, if you like, one super denomination,[3] whereas for conservatives today it is the supremacy of the local congregation.

Despite all this discussion for the past four decades, denominations are still here, and it is interesting to note that in Canada, Bibby, having for long predicted the ongoing decline of mainline Protestantism, which seemed in "numerical free fall," now asserts that "rumors of the death of mainline Protestantism in Canada appear to have been greatly exaggerated," with signs of "a measure of denominational resurgence."[4]

2. Miller, *Reinventing American Protestantism*, 12.

3. These plans collapsed in the late 1970s, with the result that there is no United or Uniting Church in New Zealand as there is in Australia and Canada.

4. Bibby, *Restless Gods*, see especially 74–78. Similarly, in the USA a recent book by

Many, however, continue to talk about a post-denominational era. Does this have any meaning, or should the term be dropped? In an overview of the history of denominations in America, Russell Richey writes that

> ... like democracy or capitalism, denominationalism persists as a complex of theory and practice, of process and form, and has taken very different complexions over its life ... Denominations as we know them may well be breaking up. If so it does not mean the end to religious movements now denominated, many of which had a pre-denominational ecclesial existence and have no reason to confuse their essence with its current denominational expression. Denominationalism is a relatively recent phenomenon and may have outlived its usefulness. It may, on the other hand, be simply going through another of its metamorphoses.[5]

Steve Stookey, a Southern Baptist historian, speaking at a conference on post-denominationalism, claimed that "Post-denominationalism doesn't mean denominations are going to die; they're just changing. We're talking about a transition. The question we should be asking is, 'What are they going to look like in the twenty first century?'" He prefers the phrase "neo-denominationalism."[6]

Richey outlines different stages in the development of denominations, and as with all organizational forms these stages were influenced by patterns in the wider culture. In the late nineteenth and early twentieth centuries, corporate or managerial organization came to typify many denominations as it did government and industry. In this period the personnel who administered denominations changed also, with clergy becoming more professionalized, requiring more elaborate credentialing and accrediting processes, including the requirement of a seminary degree.

As is typical of large modern organizations, local initiative and lay leadership were sometimes considered a threat. Demands for control and approval often outweighed the need for creativity and grassroots involvement. Beginning in the late 1960s, mainline denominations became national religious regulatory bodies, devising complex guidelines and procedures for their respective bodies. Rather than looking like a

---

Bacher and Inskeep, *Chasing Down a Rumor*, suggests that the rumor is premature, with signs of hope and significant activity. While it is true there are signs of vitality and hope and it is not all decline, nevertheless the overall trends have been mainly downward.

5. Richey, "Denominations and Denominationalism," 76.
6. Stookey, "Post-denominationalism."

gathering of like-minded believers, they came to look more like a religious regulatory agency. These trends can also be discerned in the history of denominations. Certainly in my own experience, coming from the free church tradition into the Presbyterian Church in New Zealand, the 256 pages of the *Book of Order* are a daunting reminder of this.

Jim Kitchen, in a helpful book entitled *The Postmodern Parish*,[7] lists as one of the three markers of the new context for church "post-denominationalism" (the others being "postmodernity" and "post-Christendom"). He points to the fading importance of denominations, with power having shifted from formal denominational structures to affinity groups within mainline churches, evangelical, charismatic, liberal, and so on. People often feel a closer connection to those who share the same affinities, but belong to a different denomination, than they do with those of a different affinity group who belong to the same denomination. There is a loss of brand loyalty among younger generations who engage in church shopping, and the critical issue is the character of a local congregation rather than the denomination to which it belongs.

Jackson Carroll, in *Mainline to the Future*, points out that we are witnessing considerable blurring of denominational distinctives as congregations borrow from one another. There is a growth of localism in congregations, so that increasingly local concerns take precedence over those of the denomination, as these lose their "long familiar adhesive and dynamic principles."[8] A number of researchers speak of "de facto" or "creeping" congregationalism: "Regardless of their denomination's polity, whether it is hierarchical or connectional, many congregations are essentially voluntary gathered communities."[9] Congregations borrow from one another across denominational lines and even across faith traditions, which leads to great variety. These differences are less and less dictated by denominational distinctives and are rather influenced by local circumstances, de facto congregationalism, and borrowing models that others have found to be successful.

In *Tattered Trust: Is there Hope for your Denomination?* Schaller argues that the critical issue has been that of trust versus control. He suggests that a crucial question in any society is, "do we trust people or do we trust the institutions people have created?" In an earlier era, people

---

7. Kitchen, *The Postmodern Parish*.
8. Richey, "Denominations and Denominationalism," 55.
9. Carroll, *Mainline to the Future*, 5–6.

answered with the latter and so built denominations, labor unions, political parties, and so on. This assumption began to change from the 1960s, and people began to trust only those whom they had learned to trust or who had earned their trust, but not institutions staffed by strangers. Numerous surveys across a wide range of Western societies have indicated declining levels of trust in the major institutions in recent decades.

Schaller sees the core question for the future direction of denominations as being focused on whether they try to regulate or resource. If the central culture of the denomination is (a) structured around vertical lines of authority, (b) based on the assumption that institutions, not people, should be trusted, (c) designed to perpetuate a European heritage, and (d) organized on the assumption that congregational leaders cannot be trusted, the answer is obvious. The number one responsibility of a denominational system is to regulate the role, behavior, and beliefs of individuals, congregations, and regional judicatories. This normally calls for a legalistic policy designed to facilitate permission withholding. If, however, the core culture of that religious tradition emphasizes (a) horizontal lines, (b) trusting people, and (c) a democratic philosophy, the natural result is to focus on ministry and missional goals for both congregations and regional judicatories. Here the primary role for denominational systems will be to resource congregations and regional judicatories.[10]

A few years after joining the Presbyterian Church, I was invited to be a consultant with a task group working on how the Presbyterian Church in New Zealand needed to change in response to both a significant financial shortfall and pressure from many local congregations for a much looser and smaller denominational organisation. There is no doubt that the Presbyterian Church has belonged to the first of Schaller's groups, and that the Book of Order has been used in a legalistic way to regulate and control congregations. The challenge was how it could move into the second category, while still retaining its essential identity as standing in the Presbyterian tradition, characterized by being both connectional and confessional.

In an increasingly postmodern world, whose values include widespread diversity, the rejection of hierarchy, suspicion of institutions, and a strong emphasis on personal choice, it is clear on which side the balance needs to be weighted for denominations to have a strong, but different, future. For many, including Presbyterians, this will mean considerable changes in the way they are structured, as well as the way they operate. At

---

10. Schaller, *Tattered Trust*, 59–60.

the deepest level it means a significant change in their culture. It is hopeful to note that in New Zealand the Presbyterian Church has managed to move some considerable way in this direction, a reality bemoaned by a number who see it as being no longer truly Presbyterian.

To add to the plethora of "posts" by which to describe our contemporary context, I would suggest that, while all three mentioned by Kitchen are helpful, increasingly I find the most helpful term is yet another—"post-traditional." This helps to explain much about the others. What it means is not that we are beyond tradition, but that we have moved to the place where inherited traditions play less and less decisive roles in the way we understand and order our lives. If traditions remain important to us, they do so because we *choose* to seek their guidance in the changed and changing contexts in which we live. We often reinterpret and change them in the process.

Such responses to tradition are quite different from the inevitable, taken for granted ways in which individuals have previously experienced tradition. This is not to say that traditions are no longer important, but that something significant is happening in how we relate to them. For increasing numbers of people, traditions no longer carry the authoritative weight they once did. This involves a shift of authority from something "out there" and external to us (scripture, appointed leaders, the Book of Order) to authority that resides "in here," in the self. As a result, we live *reflexively*, not abandoning traditions but not following them uncritically. This means testing them by one's own knowledge and experience as well as in dialogue with other traditions.

This has a profound impact on ecclesiology, as all forms of church are discovering, to the considerable consternation of many. Karl Barth said of the church that ". . . in every age and place its constitution and order have been broadly determined and conditioned by political, economic, and cultural models more or less imperatively forced on it by its situation in world history . . . It has had and still has to adapt or approximate itself to these in order to maintain itself . . . in respect of the form of its existence . . . there is no sacred sociology [of the church]."[11]

In other words, there are no sacred forms of church, either at a congregational or denominational level, regardless of how sacrosanct these may appear to some long-serving stakeholders. There are, to be sure, traditions we should honor and value, and we ignore or treat these lightly

---

11. Barth, *Church Dogmatics,* IV/ 3/2: *The Doctrine of Revelation,* 739.

to our own impoverishment. Yet we must recognize them as human constructions. Churches and church leaders need to give full expression to the reformation principle, *ecclesia reformata semper reformanda*—"the church reformed is always being reformed"—as they develop ecclesiastical practices that are both faithful to our tradition and appropriate to the social and cultural realities of our post-traditional, postmodern and post-Christendom society.

This means that we need to recognize the difference between valuing "traditions" and "traditionalism." There is an important place for good traditions. In a rootless, disposable, plastic world many people are looking for good traditions that have stood the test of time as anchors. In religion we see the current vitality of the Catholic and Orthodox traditions, which were the only two Christian groups to show an increase in New Zealand census returns between 2001 and 2006. Recent research by Donald Miller and Richard Flory on post-boomer spirituality speaks about the "return of ritual" among a significant group of young adults who are "reappropriating ancient rituals and symbols."[12]

At the same time, the way they relate to tradition will be different from how previous cultures have done so. Rather than strictly following a single uncontested tradition, they are more likely to choose selectively and to draw on other traditions as well. Those of us who identify with a particular ecclesiastical tradition must therefore ask, "What is the essence which this tradition is trying to live out, and how do we live that out now in our very different context, rather than slavishly adhering to the forms it took in an earlier context?" We must be willing, if forced with a choice between following some well-worn, customary, and cherished path of church practice, or innovating to adapt to a new cultural and social context, to opt for the latter. As with the apostle Paul, in his trans-local leadership of congregations in the New Testament, our choice must be on the side of freedom.[13] This requires that we break with the "but we've always done it this way" mentality that infects so many leaders at both a congregational and denominational level—a mentality which honors the vision of our forebears but does not necessarily embrace a contextually relevant vision for the present.

In other words, this challenge necessitates a process of reflective discernment in which we examine our cherished practices in the light of our

---

12. Flory and Miller, "Expressive Communalism," 31–35.
13. See especially 1 Corinthians 8–10. Was he the first denominational leader?

new realities. This does not mean throwing out our traditions with abandon. Many are important means of grace that we ignore at considerable cost. They embody a collective memory and wisdom without which we would be impoverished. Carroll writes, "What is called for is the selective retrieval of those aspects of our traditions that were forged in previous times and places as Christians attempted to be faithful to the gospel, and that, appropriately adapted, may help us today in our search for fidelity. Such traditions . . . can be reflexively drawn on and re-traditionalized in ways that keep them living rather than dead."[14]

In this regard, Kitchen adds that the awareness that we are entering a post-denominational era can encourage us to "try to understand our own traditions at a deeper level so that we can separate the tradition's wheat from its chaff."[15] Again, this requires a different stance toward tradition. Rather than residing in the tradition itself, authority has now moved more to the individual, or the local community, making it important that we exercise our freedom to choose those traditions that will guide us individually or as communities, and seek to adapt them to the realities of our current context.

Stephen Warner, in arguing for a new paradigm in understanding religion in America, saw as central to this process the fading of denominational structures and the rise of "de facto congregationalism," as local congregations developed a new group vitality.[16] Part of this drive, according to Loren Mead, has been the necessary recognition that, in our post-Christendom context, the frontier for mission is now the community outside the congregation's door rather some distant or foreign context.[17] Given an increasingly diverse and pluralistic society, those in the local situation are obviously better able to understand and respond to the particular needs of their own changing context than are distant denominational staff.

I have argued elsewhere that this may be one of the reasons that congregations in the Free Church tradition were able to respond and adapt more rapidly to the changing context they faced in the period following the 1960s than those that belonged to more "institutional" denominations.[18] They had considerably more freedom than those who required

---

14. Carroll, *Mainline to the Future*, 81.
15. Kitchen, *The Postmodern Parish*, 23.
16. Warner, "Work in Progress toward a New Paradigm."
17. See chapter 4 for an explanation of this.
18. Ward, "Losing My Religion?"

permission from regional, national, or in some cases international bodies. One of the congregations I researched, Spreydon Baptist Church, experienced ongoing growth and vitality over this period, partly facilitated by its ability to continually change to adapt to its changing context. I am currently working on a book which tells the story of this church and its minister for 40 years, Murray Robertson. Robertson trained as a Presbyterian minister in Edinburgh, but went into a Baptist church when he returned to New Zealand. One of the reflections he has made to me several times is that he believes he would not have been able to do what he had done at Spreydon if he had gone into a Presbyterian church, because of its more regulative and controlling polity.

The End of the Local?

Over this period, however, even the nature of the local has changed considerably. As indicated in chapter two, one of the most significant social changes has been the loss of the local community where, prior to the 1960s, a substantial part of life took place. The mainstays of these communities were married women who lived within the confines of the local community with their children during the week. Without a car, they walked to the shops to buy their food which, with smaller refrigerators and the absence of freezers, they needed to do much more frequently than today. They met other women at the shops and the school gates, and socialized primarily in the churches, in the auxiliaries and women's groups. Their friendships were local and they shared the community with their husbands during the weekends.

Married women began entering the workforce in large numbers in the 1960s, and the significance of the local community began to decline. As families bought a second car, shopping, business, entertainment, and leisure activities all began to be done outside of the local community. Television also played a major role, making much entertainment an individual matter in the privacy of one's home, rather than playing cards, listening to music or dancing with neighbors, gathering at the local club or church, or visiting the local movie theatre. As local communities became less significant, so did local community churches, and many left the church altogether. There are still pockets of local community life in suburban and rural churches, remnants from the post-war years, but they are now rapidly disappearing as the people who had made up and maintained them either move into retirement villages or pass away.

With increasing mobility many people find today that they are involved in many diverse groups and activities, all with different geographical locations, and that there is little overlap in terms of the people they meet in our these varied groups and networks, based around work, sport, education, ethnic or cultural identities, religion, or other leisure pursuits. Indeed, there is little which might indicate that we all belong to one community. We experience community in a thousand little fragments. For many people their significant friends and relationships are found outside of the geographical community in which they "sleep"—they scarcely know their neighbors, and certainly do nothing communal with them.

Given this change, there is now a widespread recognition that geographical communities are giving way to networks of interest, although Richard Tiplady may overstate the case when he writes that "geography is history."[19] People do not relate to others so much in the same place but to individuals with similar interests from much further afield. Increasingly the talk is about community "across space" rather than "within place." These changes have also been furthered by the rapid growth of telecommunication, so that even when individuals are located within a particular geographical place, all their significant community relationships and contacts are taking place with people outside of that locality. As one person put it, "you are more likely to know a stranger in California in an internet chat room or on Facebook than you are to meet your neighbor two doors down." In other words, especially in urban areas, we no longer have many "comprehensive communities" where people in same area, across a spectrum of ages, vocations, and leisure pursuits, do a whole variety of things together.

All of these changes have implications for church life in its local form, but also for the ways in which they are structured denominationally. The traditional parish structure was based on a centralized denominational structure, and mainline churches in New Zealand and elsewhere are still fundamentally organized on this basis. In this understanding, the church was made up of those who were born into in the local community—the parish. However, as we have argued, people no longer identify with those communities but, rather, belong to communities of people of their culture, or with similar interests, concerns, and preferences—communities of choice rather than communities of birth.

19. Tiplady, *World of Difference*, 5.

This is the underlying premise of Lyle Schaller's book, *From Geography to Affinity*. He argues that for millions of church shoppers, instead of choosing a new church home "on the basis of the geographical location of the meeting place, they join with others who share a major point of commonality."[20] This is one of the reasons why what have traditionally been identified as "sectarian churches" have done better in contemporary society. They have realized that people join by choice and so have engaged more in marketing approaches, and in doing so have often been more sensitive to what they perceive as being the needs and desires of potential customers. They have not assumed that they can serve the needs of all the people in their district but have rather focused on those who are likely to identify with them.

As a consequence, an approach to church life that is primarily geared around having standardized churches established on a geographical basis, trying to meet the needs of all in the local community with the same menu, determined by some central body—the parish church model—is by and large no longer workable. Nancy Ammermann, writing about the postmodern denomination, notes that modern organizations were premised on mass production, and so the modern denomination assumed that one approach, one set of programs, could serve everyone. Postmodern organizations are premised on finding niches, assume diversity, and make room for pluralism.[21] As Michael Moynagh puts it,

> By and large the church is still stuck in the standardized world. It approaches evangelism with a mass mindset. 'Come and join our church' is the invitation which assumes 'our church' is suitable for the people we invite. 'We like it so other people will.' That is typical one size fits all thinking. The church could get away with this in a mass society, but in an it-must-fit-me world it won't wash any more. A different approach is needed—one that is more sensitive to the differences between people, to their suspicion of organizations, and to their expectations of choice. The reaction of other organizations is to draw closer to people, to listen to them, and to respond to their individual preferences. Can the church afford to stand aloof?[22]

20. Schaller, *From Geography to Affinity*, 15.
21. Ammermann, "SBC Moderates and the Making of a Postmodern Denomination," 896–99.
22. Moynagh, *Changing World, Changing Church*, 33–34.

In our diverse, fragmented, networked society we need a diverse, fragmented, networked church that lives within the networks in which people live. There is still a place for some "traditional local churches," if I can use that phrase, especially for older, less mobile people. Alongside these, however, we need to develop a whole variety of diverse, culturally and socially specific congregations, which people join from a wider geographical area on the basis of personal preference. "Instead of building the public image of a congregation around the real estate," there is a need to build that image "around the congregation's distinctive role in ministry."[23] If society now consists of a mosaic of fragments or niches, then we must do church in fragments or niches. Moynagh, in developing the consequences of our new context for the shape of the church, sees four significant changes in our approach, from standardized to customized, from top-down to bottom up, from come-and-join-us to we'll-come-to-you, and from Sunday to any day.[24]

Congregations in a Networked World

For mainline Protestant denominations, still structured on the parish model, it appears that alongside maintaining a significantly smaller number of traditional local churches, most of the energy needs to be put into two quite different approaches. It is interesting that, of the churches based on the parish model, the one which has maintained the greatest strength and vitality in New Zealand is the Catholic church, and there are considerably fewer parishes in this church than in the Anglican and Presbyterian churches. The consequence is larger attendance and greater vitality for Catholic parishes.

Peter Lineham identifies the kind of typical Protestant parish church as being like the old general store of the Four Square or I.G.A. type; like these, they face considerable difficulties in sustaining viability today.[25] Many researchers have found that, in numerous areas of life today, it is mid-size organizations that are experiencing the most difficulty; the smaller and larger organizations seem to be doing much better. This is

---

23. Schaller, *From Geography to Affinity*, 17.
24. Moynagh, *Changing World, Changing Church*, 137–38.
25. Lineham, "Three Types of Churches," 199–204. Four Square and IGA were the two major franchises of this kind of grocery store in New Zealand.

true of churches also,[26] so the first option is to endeavor to develop larger churches which have several quite different congregations within them.

In my own Presbyterian denomination these are now being called regional churches, following Lyle Schaller's definition, but the more popular terminology is mega-churches. In the U.S. a figure of 2,000 attenders is commonly used to define these churches, although in New Zealand a figure of 800 would be more realistic. These churches are somewhat controversial, and perceptions of how significant a role they will play in the future are vigorously debated. They certainly have been very attractive to baby boomers and this will ensure a significant place for them for some time.

However, anecdotal evidence as well as some research suggests that these churches have less appeal to the post-boomer generations, who are looking more for community and greater participation. It also seems that mega-churches of the Crystal Cathedral and Willow Creek style, with their huge auditoriums, require a large, reasonably homogenous population to draw on, something which is difficult to find in New Zealand, and is perhaps limited to parts of Auckland and Christchurch. Indications are that now most larger churches in the U.S., and often those which are most vital, are multi-congregational rather than multi-service. That is, within the umbrella of a large church they offer a variety of different communities or congregations, each with its own leadership and style.

Rick Warren, pastor of Saddleback Community Church, one of the largest of the mega-churches, sees the future of his church as the "cineplex concept"[27]— multiple venues and worship styles rather than two or three offerings of the same fare in one large auditorium. The analogy of the cinema industry is interesting. In the 1980s a long-term trend of attendance decline was coming to a head and many were predicting the demise of cinemas. The trend was reversed by building cinemas that were smaller, more attractive, and had more screens. Cinema complexes replaced individual theatres. No longer did people simply have to take or leave the one show that was on offer, but could make their own choice from the variety available. Movie theatres as I knew them while growing up have largely disappeared, but new and better forms have arisen.

---

26. "The middle is shrinking. These congregations, whose average worship attendance is from forty to two hundred, appear to be in trouble." Naylor and Willimon, *Downsizing the U.S.A.*, 149.

27. Parks and Stafford, "Shockingly Ordinary Purpose-Driven Life of Rick Warren."

Rather ironically, and perhaps indicating the culture lag of the church, a number of the older large theatres have been converted into churches, which are often becoming inhabited by smaller and smaller audiences. Certainly this trend to a "cineplex church" fits in with the trends of diversity and pluralism we have identified, and many are now developing off-site venues, in effect operating as mini-denominations.

This, then, is one way for churches to diversify in order to fit in with the various niches and fragments of our culture. This has the advantage of being able to run a variety of specialized ministries and services because of the larger critical mass, alongside offering a variety of congregational styles. It is interesting that Spreydon Baptist Church, which was a multi-congregational church from the mid-1980s, pulled these back in to one large central worship service in the mid-1990s, but over recent years has changed to become multi-congregational again, although in significantly different ways.

The second approach is smaller niche churches that have incarnated the gospel for particular socio-cultural groups. In some ways these may be seen to be doing what one particular congregation in a larger church is doing, but providing a number of other functions as well. If we look at the dominant group of New Zealanders, primarily European New Zealanders, these groups with which a particular church may identify include the following:

1. Older adults, probably in their late sixties and beyond, pre-boomers, who were brought up in the Christian tradition and have largely remained within it, for whom the traditional style is helpful. For many of these people, the local church is a significant place of life and family memories, and the rituals and liturgy of the church tradition have been a significant part of their life journey, identity, and security as they move on in the last phase of life. Some who have drifted out of the church want to identify more closely again in their later years.

2. Baby boomers, now in their late forties to mid-sixties, who are churched and have remained in the church for most of their life, although they may have had some brief period(s) away from it. Earlier we looked at how the charismatic movement helped to adapt church life to the needs of this generation in particular, such that they often prefer a more charismatic or even Pentecostal style of church life. Many of the churches shaped to the needs of these people have

begun to struggle as their children have generally not bought into that expression of church life.

3. Baby boomers who have left the church, but who have an increasing interest in spirituality and religious questions. There are two groups of these. One is those who left as part of the drift out of church as young people in the 1960s and 1970s and who have remained outside of it, although they may be occasional visitors. The census data discussed in chapter 4 indicated that large numbers of these still identify with established churches, and often in midlife they become more concerned with religious or spiritual issues. A second group is those who have left church in midlife, the subject of research mentioned several times already by Jamieson on church leavers. Many of these have left strongly evangelical, charismatic, or Pentecostal churches, but have retained their faith and are seeking a more open understanding of faith. For both of these groups a more reflective and open-ended approach is helpful, using traditions eclectically, with a strong emphasis on relationships and a more liberal approach to ethical issues.

4. Young families who are often a mix of GenXers and some of the following generation, generally now called GenY.[28] The approach here is often a highly active participatory style. Many churches which are doing well have a strong emphasis on young families, and the provision of good children's and youth ministries is obviously important. The active, participatory, and somewhat chaotic style is often difficult to mix with a large percentage of older people, who desire a more structured and "reverent" approach. Another challenge is that highlighted by the McNair research[29] on young families, who were open to religious questions but did not attend churches and who found that Sunday morning was one of the most unlikely times for them to attend church, as for working parents Sunday was family interaction day, especially for fathers. These young families saw churches as dividing families' loyalties and being basically passive rather than interactive in style. For churches targeting this sector, a participatory style involving the whole family together is the key, and if separate children's activities are provided they are better done during the week after school.

28. Born after the early 1980s, sometimes called "millennials."
29. See the previous chapter for a description of this.

5. Young adults, a mixture of mainly GenXers and GenYers, who are in their mid-twenties and often up to the late thirties. A high proportion are unmarried, and indications are that many are likely to stay that way.[30] There is considerable evidence that, while they place a heavy emphasis on experience, they do not relate strongly to the charismatic style. Partly this is related to musical tastes, with their dislike of what is labeled "contemporary worship," partly to their desire for forms of communication other than the sermon-as-monologue, and partly to the use of images, involvement of the body, and desire to be creatively involved in designing their own worship. The Emerging Church movement fits well with many in this group.

6. The youth of today, GenYers. I am somewhat suspicious of those who assign a list of generational characteristics to cohorts who are still quite youthful, some even doing so for those who are only in their mid-teens. Generational characteristics only begin to really emerge or solidify in the late twenties, when what may be age effects of youth can be distinguished from cohort effects that will remain. With this group still being under thirty, we still need to be cautious, but it does appear there are significant differences from GenXers, with a more optimistic and less cynical outlook. Whatever the characteristics are, they are an emerging group who already need their own space to develop their own forms and style.

An important note at this point is that, while each group has been identified with a particular generation or age band, we should not primarily identify the group up front in that way, but rather in the style that is offered. While this style or attitude may be strongest in the age ranges mentioned above, there will be a number of people outside of that range who identify with it and would want to be part of a congregation that participates in worship and community in that way. Identity based solely on age becomes exclusionary and may prevent people who want to belong from doing so.

---

30. Robert Wuthnow, in *After the Baby Boomers*, shows how a whole raft of data comparing people of that age group in the early 1970s compared with those in the early 2000s demonstrate a significant postponing of the age at which they enter 'full' adulthood, indicated by finishing education, leaving home, becoming financially independent, being married and having children. In New Zealand the impact is likely to be even greater as he identifies for the church the key factors are marriage and children and the age for those here now is even later than it is in the US.

Generational characteristics are of course only one way of describing the diversity that now exists within society. Ethnicity and lifestyle are other ways which we will explore in the next chapters. As a consequence, many are arguing that while they might concede there is still a place for some "traditional churches" they will become less important, and the greatest imperative is to develop a variety of diverse, culturally and socially specific congregations. If society now consists of a mosaic of fragments or niches, then we must do church in fragments or niches. Australians Michael Frost and Alan Hirsch use the image of Vianne's *chocolaterie* from the film *Chocolat*, where her secret is that she is able to make a chocolate individually tailored for each person's specific taste—the analogy being that what postmoderns are drawn to is a "Chocolate Shop Church."

We are now witnessing such a dramatic fracturing of Western society, with even the suburbs splintering into a myriad of subcultures, that a "one size fits all" ecclesial paradigm is increasingly outmoded. Churches, like missionaries, will need to understand the cultural mores and folkways, and incarnate themselves into the rhythms of each specific people group or "tribe" to which they feel called.[31]

Marketing the Church

The issues highlighted over the last few pages raise the question of to what extent the shape of the church should be driven by market forces determined by social science findings. Two recent books raise this issue provocatively. In the Foreward to *Selling Out the Church: The Dangers of Church Marketing*, Stanley Hauerwas writes that "it never seems to occur to those who put forward marketing as a strategy for 'bringing people back to Christ' that the Christ to whom they are brought back has very little to do with the one who would require our very lives if we are to be faithful to his cross."[32]

In *Thieves in the Temple: The Christian Church and the Selling of the American Soul*,[33] Jeffrey MacDonald provides multiple examples of the latest consumer driven incarnation of the church, fueled by the latest social science findings on the needs and wants of potential custom-

---

31. Frost and Hirsch, *The Shape of Things to Come*, 65.
32. In Kenneson and Street, *Selling Out the Church*, 13.
33. MacDonald, *Thieves in the Temple*.

ers, and the ways in which church life is shaped to ensure these are met. This, he argues, raises the question as to whether the church's essential character has been overwhelmed, or at least seriously diluted, such that congregations have lost their larger life-transforming (rather than mere enhancing) character and reason for being.

Jackson Carroll wrote *God's Potters: Pastoral Leadership and the Shaping of Congregations* based on very comprehensive research, including a sample of over 1,200 senior ministers. They were asked this question: "When deciding on a new program or ministry," do you "discuss the theological rationale" or do you "primarily take into consideration how well it meets the desires and needs of members or prospective members?" Only 27 percent give priority to a theological rationale, compared with 73 percent prioritizing how well the program will meet the desires and needs of prospective members.[34]

Of course this cultural captivity of the church is nothing new. It was pointed out some almost 60 years ago in Winter's *The Suburban Captivity of the Churches*,[35] at a time when the church seemed to be ascendant in the culture. But one go can back even further, to the powerful cultural dynamics which captured the church when it became "the establishment" in the fourth century, or to the crusading interests of feudal kingdoms in the Middle Ages, or to the German Church of the Third Reich, which explains so much of Karl Barth's objection to anything cultural informing our faith.

The relationship of the church to culture is a central issue in theology and has already been discussed briefly, particularly in evaluating the charismatic movement, and will be discussed more fully in the next two chapters. Here I simply want to give a reminder that the church lives in the tension of, on the one hand, needing to incarnate its message and its life into the social and cultural situation in which it exists while, at the same time, needing to allow these to be distinct from and stand over against those norms when the gospel calls it in a different and transcendent direction. We have noted earlier in this chapter that even Karl Barth allowed for this in discussing the form of church that might take place. This is where social science becomes useful in helping us understand what these might be in any particular context, despite the protests of those who feel it has no place.[36]

34. Carroll, *God's Potters*, 145–46.

35. Winter, *Suburban Captivity of the Churches*.

36. A recent expression of this is Davidson and Millbank, *For the Parish*. Millbank states this view in most of his writing and is represent of radical orthodoxy which

Pope John Paul II wrote this in 1979:

> The church as a human society can of course be examined and described according to the categories used by the sciences with regard to human society. But these categories are not enough. For the whole of the human community of the People of God and for each member what is in question is not just a specific 'social membership'; rather, for each and everyone what is essential is a particular vocation. Indeed, the church as the People of God is also 'Christ's Mystical Body.' Membership in that body has for its source a particular call, united with the saving action of grace. Therefore, if we wish to keep in mind this community of the People of God, which is so vast and so extremely differentiated, we must see first and foremost Christ saying in a way to each member of the community, 'follow me.'[37]

This encapsulates the challenge for those of us who do believe the social sciences offer important insights into understanding the nature of the church as a human community, as well as to the forms by which the church might most fully give expression to its calling in our contemporary context. On the one hand, the use of the social sciences is possible and even necessary in ecclesiology because the church is a human society; on the other hand, it is not sufficient because the church is also a theological reality. So how can this tension be negotiated so that the social sciences can be employed to enrich ecclesiology and, at the same time, preserve the nature of the church as the mystical body of Christ called into being?

Until recently, ecclesiology, while acknowledging the church as a human society, scarcely made any use of the social sciences to understand how the human element functions in the life of the church. There was no attempt to study by means of empirical methods the concrete ways in which the church and its organizational structures should function so as to become a credible sign of God's presence. The method was strictly historical and theological. It is only more recently that theologians have turned to the social sciences to derive insights to help the church become an effective sign of the Kingdom of God for the world in its current contexts.

This shift is of course related to the much greater awareness of context as a factor to be taken into consideration in doing theology, and

---

tends to this position. Stanley Hauerwas also consistently articulates this position, although his writings do also offer much of which we need to take note.

37. Pope John Paul II, *Redemptor Hominis*.

being the church in a fragmented world 157

the recognition of many that all theology is, to some degree or another, contextual, whether recognized as such or not. As Kevin van Hoozer argues, in the light of the postmodern critique of universal reason, and the demographic shift of the centre of Christianity away from Europe and North America, "it is becoming increasingly apparent that theology is ineluctably tied to and rooted in particular social and cultural conditions," and so "context has become primary for the theological task. Do systems neutralize contexts or contexts explode systems?"[38]

Clare Watkin examines the work of a number of theologians and sociologists who have attempted to bring the social sciences and theology together in discussing the nature of the church.[39] After reviewing these she offers three conclusions:

1. In all of these authors a weakness has been "the simplicity and generality of the theological side of the conversation, compared with the concrete detail of the organizational side . . . which results in a dominance of the social sciences in the discussion."[40]

2. The way in which the social sciences are used in ecclesiology depends on the model of church adopted: If the Church institution is seen as a thoroughly human expression of a certain faith, then the organizational ecclesiologist may take a fairly adventurous approach to structural reform, in which, almost inevitably, the social science view will dominate in the actual conclusions drawn. A more sacramental ecclesiology, in which the relation of the divine or transcendent to the here-and-now church is not so clear, will feel more restrained in its consideration of concrete change, and will tend to emphasize the theological in its conclusion.[41]

3. Organizational ecclesiology must retain its theological character in its conversation with the social sciences. "The theologian cannot stop being properly theological but always needs to learn more about human realities, in which there are other experts."[42] Some believe this cannot be done, and warn about the "sociological reduction of theology," which it is feared reduces the church

---

38. van Hoozer, "On the Very Idea of a Theological System," 132.
39. Watkin, "Organizing the People of God," 689–711.
40. Ibid., 708.
41. Ibid., 709–10.
42. Ibid., 710.

to a merely human institution. As an institution of divine origin, the use of sociological categories is considered inappropriate, and only theological categories and language are deemed suitable for understanding the church. However, as Richard Roberts puts it, "a theology uninformed by engagement with the social sciences may well persist as a form of 'false consciousness,' but it will do so at a dangerous distance from what . . . Jürgen Motmann once referred to as the 'dialectic of the real.'"[43]

Despite these legitimate concerns, if we are to interpret what it means to be faithful to our calling in Christ in the contexts in which we find ourselves and confront the challenges they now provide, we must use sociological insights to elaborate an ecclesiology "in such a way that it retains its epistemological status as theology and does not become a kind of religious or ecclesiological sociology."[44]

So, What Kind of Church?

In a previous era, the denominational era, diversity in the church was expressed through different denominations. People belonged to particular denominations according to long-standing family identities, often based around cultural identities that may have been imported from the home country (English Anglicans or Methodists, Scottish Presbyterians, or Irish Catholics). These denominations offered the same menu at each outlet, which was located on the basis of geography, presupposing a reasonably homogenous society.

Prior to the 1960s this was true of New Zealand society, as in other Western societies. Today's context, however, demands a different kind of diversity, as local communities become more and more plural, fostered by increasing global migration trends, which impact New Zealand on a proportional basis as much as any other country. While keeping faithful to some of the core elements of its tradition, each needs to develop a diversity of styles at the local level, and these styles, rather than being determined solely by geography, need to be determined more by the culture of the network they are based around. This will naturally mean developing new congregations.

---

43. Roberts, "Theology and the Social Sciences," 711.
44. Phan, "Social Sciences and Ecclesiology," 61.

One may question the value of this when we already have too many churches, many of them rarely used. Robin Gill, who has argued that for a long time that Britain has been over-churched, establishes convincingly that this is a case of too many buildings rather than too many congregations.[45] Maintaining buildings saps far too much of the time, energy, and resources of the many small congregations that identify with them. In contrast, there is considerable evidence that new congregations have greater vitality and show more growth than older congregations.

In bringing these two concepts together the obvious way forward is for existing churches—whose style does not match with some of the niches identified above, particularly where the existing congregation is elderly and therefore largely homogenously European—to help with the birth of new and different congregations within existing buildings.[46] The challenge is to create new congregations, not new church buildings; in a sense we need more congregations but fewer buildings. Several different congregations based around different networked communities may all use the same buildings. A building complex where a congregation is associated with a particular building symbolizes the old paradigm of geographically based church communities.

Moynagh, in identifying the strong and probably growing interest in spirituality, asks whether it will remain largely unfocused as it is now, or whether it will be, once more, channeled into church:

> Much may depend on whether we can move away from standardized church which requires newcomers to worship in a uniform way ... [the] church may connect with our more spiritual age if it offers not only a spiritual map, but the freedom for people to select the route most helpful to them. Churches will draw the map a little differently; some will offer more routes than others, but both creating the map and allowing people to find their own paths on it will be essential if church is to resource the emerging generations.[47]

Earlier we enumerated four shifts which Moynagh suggested the church needed to make in its understanding. He also adds a fifth change, from "we'll do it on our own" to "we'll do it together." If our society is increasingly diverse and, in order to engage with it significantly, we

---

45. Gill, *A Vision for Growth*, Chapter 3.
46. See the discussion on pp. 33 and 34 on this.
47. Moynagh, *Changing World*, 87, 89.

need a variety of styles, then it is obvious that no one church can meet the needs of all, despite the claims made by some large churches. One size simply does not fit all as it did in a standardized culture, however large that size is.

It is therefore important for us to acknowledge that we need other expressions and styles of church which are working among people groups and networks different from ours, and that we seek to work with them in symbiotic relationships rather than seeing them as competitors. I believe there are also some important kingdom and gospel imperatives in this as well, which will be explored in the following chapters. Not only do we need to work together, but we also need to work on ways to express our togetherness. Cross-fertilization and contributions from those who are different from us—in age, ethnicity, lifestyle, family situation, and so on—are important. Larger churches need to work on ways in which the different congregations can come together at times, and smaller niche churches need to see themselves as part of a bigger whole ("the church") and do things from time to time with other churches.

These, then, are some of the challenges and opportunities that our very different social and cultural contexts bring to the church. It is obvious that if we are sensitive to these realities, and seek to adapt our forms and life to them, while at the same time being faithful to whatever the tradition is in which we stand, then the ways in which the life of the church expresses itself at both a congregational and denominational level will lead to significant changes. To try and change at one level and not the other would create destructive tensions, and indeed change in one will lead to change in the other. At the core is the issue of how we allow for a growing diversity but, at the same time, cultivate sufficient unity around an agreed-upon identity. The ways in which churches come to resolve these tensions will determine much of the future shape they take.

9

It Might be Emerging but is it Church?

AT A THEOLOGICAL CONFERENCE I was attending, one of the presenters, outlining some of the factors in the changing context for theological education, referred to "Fresh Expressions." He argued that this was a more appropriate term than the previously favored descriptor for experimental faith communities, "Emerging Church," since as it turned out most of what was emerging was not church. He was Anglican and the term "Fresh Expressions" is a phrase developed by the Church of England for some of the new forms of church it is seeking to foster. The term "emerging church" remains widespread, however, and gains much attention from younger church leaders in New Zealand.

At a Vision NZ Conference several years ago, one of the major presentations was entitled "A Kiwi Emerging Church: Yeah, Right!"[1] This was given by Steve Taylor, who had become the leading spokesperson for Emerging Church in New Zealand, and a significant global voice. Indeed, it is interesting in reading about the movement globally how prominent New Zealand is, along with Australia and the U.K., as a key initiator. Mike Riddell and Mark Pierson from New Zealand, and Michael Frost and Alan Hirsch from Australia, are seen as pioneers. I might add that, as well as being from "down under," they, along with Taylor, are Baptists, a heritage which I share myself[2]—a factor which is not irrelevant and to which I will return.

---

1. Taylor, "A Kiwi Emerging Church," 311.
2. Riddell is no longer Baptist and now identifies with the Catholic tradition.

A recent Google search of "Emerging Church" came up with about 17,200,000 entries.[3] So what are we to make of what Scot McKnight calls "the most controversial and misunderstood movement in the church today?"[4] One eye-catching article about this movement is entitled "Emerging Churches—Heroes or Heretics?" A clearly unambivalent answer to that question was contained in a brochure I received in the mail a few years ago. Its headings screamed out: "The last days. Apostasy. Coming to a church near you. The emergent church." It warned that, "With the move of the Church back to Rome through organizations like Evangelicals and Catholics Together, Alpha, Promise Keepers, and Interfaith dialogue, . . . Rick Warren's Purpose Driven Church and now the postmodern Emergent wave . . . believe that today's postmodern culture needs a more relevant and experiential approach to God, Church and Worship, e.g., Playing U2 as an expression of worship, using multi-sensory stimulation, candles, icons, art, images, stained glass, etc." And it warns, "The Emergent Church has taken hold in NZ and its teachings have been aired on Radio Rhema and are also being taught in the Bible College of New Zealand."[5]

We need of course to ask why this movement has arisen. The broad answer is fairly simple: it is part of a number of responses over the past half century to the increasingly obvious fact that the church in particular, and Christian faith in general, has been having a rather difficult time of it in Western societies like New Zealand. I have written in a number of places on this, as have many others, and have no intention of rehearsing the supporting information. It is simply a given, whatever figures one uses and however positive the spin one tries to put on them. There have been many responses to this post-Christian—or perhaps, more correctly, post-Christendom—reality, from the God is Dead theologies of the 1960s, to the Church Growth movement of the 1970s, the Cell Churches of the 1980s, and the Seeker Sensitive Churches of the 1990s. Despite all of these grand initiatives, the rot continues.

---

3. I note that five years ago I found 1,530,000, the rapid increase indicating that the term still has a lot of energy.

4. McKnight, "Five Streams of the Emerging Church."

5. This brochure gave no indication of who was responsible for it.

Emerging Emerging

What emerged in the 1990s was the realization among some that not only were our Western societies post-Christendom, but they were also postmodern, at least in part. That term is rather problematic, and it is not within the scope of this work to explore all of the issues surrounding postmodernism. However, in the broadest sense it is helpful to identify the fact that the cultural, social, and intellectual world we live in today is very different from that which existed in 1960, even if there may well be more continuities than discontinuities.

In this world all sorts of institutions that have existed for centuries have increasingly struggled. A number of Christian thinkers and leaders began arguing that the problem with the recent efforts to reorganize or reframe church for our post-Christendom world was that they were still based on the assumptions and thinking of a modern society and culture. As modernism was rapidly diminishing and being replaced by postmodern forms, so these attempts were simply short-term arrangements, much like rearranging the deck chairs on the Titanic. Something more fundamental was needed.

There have been many attempts to define the Emerging Church movement, some helpful and others not. Perhaps the simplest and most widely used is that by Eddie Gibbs and Ryan Bolger, in their study of the phenomenon, *Emerging Churches*.[6] They define the movement as "communities that practice the way of Jesus within postmodern cultures." Brian McLaren, who has emerged as the movement's main spokesperson, wrote in the first of his many books, "You see, if we have a new world, we will need a new church. We don't need a new religion *per se*, but a new framework for our theology. Not a new Spirit, but a new spirituality. Not a new Christ, but a new kind of Christian. Not a new denomination, but a new kind of church . . . The point is . . . you have a new world."[7]

Before raising a number of questions for consideration, I want to make clear that overall I would agree with the broad parameters of this argument. As Australian missiologist Randall Prior summarized it in an address to the General Assembly of the Presbyterian Church of Aotearoa New Zealand in 2010, "The form of the church which evolved in the era of Christendom and which served us well in that period is no longer sustainable. It is dying. It will die."

6. Gibbs and Bolger, *Emerging Churches*.
7. McLaren, *Reinventing Your Church*, 13–14.

One important cautionary note I want to raise initially is that often the people involved in the Emerging Church movement use rather hyperbolic language, as if the church has only ever existed in one form or shape since the inception of Christendom—often referred to as the "inherited church"—and that this traditional form now needs to be discarded and a brand new form developed. This is of course quite misleading. The form and shape of the church has constantly changed throughout its 2,000 year history. We see this even in the New Testament, and writers such as Hans Küng, David Bosch, and Andrew Walls have provided helpful ways of understanding this.

Using a provocative image, Andrew Walls invites us to imagine a long-living, scholarly visitor from space, a Professor of Comparative Inter-Planetary Religions, who is able to get periodic study grants to visit planet earth every few centuries in order to study the earth religion known as Christianity, on the principles of Baconian induction. He visits a group of Jerusalem Jewish Christians about 37 CE; his next visit is in around 325 CE, to a Church Council in Nicaea; then, around 650 CE he visits a group of monks on a rocky outcrop in Ireland; in the 1840s he visits a Christian assembly in Exeter Hall, London promoting mission to Africa; finally, in 1980 he visits Lagos, Nigeria, where a white robed group is dancing and chanting through the streets on the way to church. At first glance the groups visited might appear to have nothing in common at all, but on deeper analysis he finds an essential continuity about the significance of Jesus, the use of scriptures, of bread and wine and water. But, writes Walls, he recognizes that these continuities are "cloaked with such heavy veils belonging to their environment that Christians of different times and places must often be unrecognizable to others, or even to themselves, as manifestations of a single phenomenon."[8]

At the heart of this debate about these emerging new forms of church life is the question of the relationship between the historic faith and the environment in which it presently finds itself, the relationship of theology and context, Christ and culture. This question is actually at the heart of many of the disputes that go on in the church, at both the local and trans-local levels, as well as some significant debates within theological institutions.

---

8. Walls, *The Missionary Movement*, 3–7.

Church and Culture

When it comes to the relationship between the church and the culture that surrounds it, there are a number of different models used to explain the various orientations. The classic work, which has formed the basis for all following discussions, is that of H. Richard Niebuhr's *Christ and Culture*. He identifies five basic models: Christ against culture, Christ of culture, Christ above culture, Christ and culture in paradox, and Christ the transformer of culture.[9] I believe that the alternatives can be more simply discussed by reducing these to three.

1. An "anti-cultural" response—"Christ against culture." This is an orientation in which the church sets itself up in opposition to the prevailing culture. The difficulty with this position is that there is no such thing as a culture-free articulation of theology or understanding of the church. Consequently this position, while opposing contemporary culture, is in fact usually holding on to some culture of the past. The Amish, for example, hold on to the culture of early nineteenth century German settlers in Pennsylvania, traditional Anglicans to 1950s England, and many fundamentalists to the pre-1960s American south.

2. An "accommodationist" response—"Christ of culture." This is the opposite approach, where the church is so anxious to fit into the world that it becomes merely an extension of the culture and has lost any distinguishing particularity as a culture of its own. This response assumes a congruence between church and culture. It is assumed that the primary symbols of the church and of the culture are identical. The church sees itself in some way as representative of the culture at large, and prides itself on its shaping, transforming role. Churches in nations where the two grew up together often exhibit the most radical forms of this. This has been aligned with a strong tendency towards liberalism in Western countries and can be seen as a major factor in the decline of mainstream denominations. This view fails to recognize that there is a basic incompatibility between the church and whatever time or place in which it lives.

3. An "incarnational" response. This response recognizes a kind of tension between Christ and culture, as is found in all of Niebuhr's

---

9. Niebuhr, *Christ and Culture*.

final three categories. There is both continuity and discontinuity between Christ and culture. Lesslie Newbigin rightly insists that the gospel only retains "its proper strangeness, its power to question us . . . when we are faithful to its universal suprarational, supranational, supracultural nature."[10] Yet the gospel travels through time not in some ideal form, but from one inculturated form to another. Consequently, what missiologists call the "culturally indigenous church" is the aim of the incarnational approach.

Textuality and Contextuality

A number of different terms are used to describe this approach to culture. The one that I find most helpful is "contextualization," although heated debate over its precise meaning continues, with ecumenical and evangelical interpretations differing considerably. At the core is a recognition that many aspects of what humans believe, think, and do are contextually shaped. William Reiser defines contextualization from a Christian perspective as "the process of a deep, sympathetic adaptation to, and appropriation of, a local culture in which the Church finds itself, in a way that does not compromise its faith."[11]

At the heart of the process is the incarnation, when in Jesus God took on fully the particular human context into which he came, historically, culturally, and religiously. This principle was carried on by the early church as the gospel moved from the Jewish context into a Graeco-Roman one, and Paul especially understood fully what the implications of this meant. Since then the most effective missionary expansions of the church have occurred when those carrying the gospel have understood that any culture can be host to Christ.

At the same time, what is critical in an authentic contextual or incarnational approach is that there are limits to how far culture can set the agenda or determine the shape of our Christian life. While living within and by many of the norms of their cultural contexts, both Jesus and Paul stepped outside and challenged it in certain respects. We saw that Walls expressed this by holding together the "indigenizing principle"—that the gospel is at home in every culture—and the "pilgrim

---

10. Newbigin, "The Enduring Validity of Cross-Cultural Mission," 50.
11. As quoted in Sweet, *Aquachurch*, 81.

principle"—that it is never fully at home in any culture and will put us out of step with every society.

So there are two critical dimensions of the church, which Max Stackhouse defines as the "textuality" of the church—its faithfulness to the gospel—and its "contextuality"—its faithfulness to the world in which it finds itself.[12] Hans Küng contends that we should aim for a "critical correlation" between the biblical message and the paradigm of the culture, and that "the task today is to come to terms with a postmodern paradigm."[13] The Emerging Church movement is endeavoring to take that latter task seriously and is to be commended for that.

To bring a personal perspective to bear, this book is in a very real sense part of an ongoing and unfinished journey and conversation with myself over the past 25 years or so. It was that which led me into my doctoral research and has continued in the decade since. In that post-doctoral period I began to question whether the church in New Zealand had much of a future. Some of the content delivered in seminars and lectures is contained in chapter seven. Basically I was arguing, in line with the overall framework of this book, that while religious belonging continued to decline, religious believing showed ongoing resilience. Hence, while religion or spirituality seemed destined to continue, the church itself seemed to face a rather tenuous and uncertain future. I suggested that it would continue but needed to develop many more diverse forms, and these in essence would be "less church," in the sense of being much looser, less institutionalized, more eclectic, fluid rather than solid. This sounds much like Emerging Church!

A number of people, more theologically inclined than I am, have raised the question with me, "Where is the theology in all of this?" This is always a valid question. In this instance, it was a timely reminder that central to my own thesis was the proposition that churches which had thrived had not only shown an ability to adapt their life and message to their rapidly changing cultural and social situation, but had also held a strong commitment to the central tenets of orthodox Christian belief. My major focus has been on the first half of that proposition, aiming to help churches realize that the forms their life and message have taken have been wedded to a cultural and social context that has not existed for some time, and that if they continue in their current form they indeed

---

12. Stackhouse, "Contextualization, Contextuality and Contextualization," 6.
13. Küng, *Theology for the Third Millennium*, 166, 211.

have a rather limited future. They are no longer incarnating the gospel in their context and so are disconnected. As Phil Goff put it after taking on the leadership of the Labour Party in New Zealand following their heavy defeat in the 2009 election, they had "lost touch with their electorate" and "need to reconnect." Change is the essential challenge for the church, and I continue to be invited to help a broad range of churches understand the context in which they are embedded and how they might change to become culturally connected.

This is an essential task, and while some forms of theology, particularly that found in radical orthodoxy, continue to argue for some pure form of church derived solely from theological sources, this usually ends up being some reified ideal picture that never touches down into the realities of human existence. As we have noted, even Karl Barth, with his theology of the Word, recognized that there is no sacred sociology of the church, and that its "constitution and order" have been broadly determined by and adapted to its situation in history.

Marks of the Church—Does Anything Go?

There are, then, no sacred forms of church, however sacrosanct existing forms might appear to some. Of course those of us who identify with the Reformed tradition have always held this to be so, holding to the Reformation principle, *ecclesia reformata semper reformanda*. If the church's forms are determined by whatever the current "political, economic, and cultural models" of its historical situation are, does that mean that anything goes? If the answer to those who pose theological questions about changes in church life is that theology does not have a place in determining the form of church life, then the 73 percent of leaders who give priority to practical issues over theology are right, and there is no theology of the church, merely a praxis.

It is interesting to review literature on the church from a historical perspective. For centuries the basic question was "What are the marks of a true church?" From the 1970s onwards the nature of the question changed by one word. Instead of "What are the marks of a *true* church?" the question became "What are the marks of a *successful* church?" The word "successful" was sometimes interchanged with the word "growing," since to be successful was equated with growing.

Two factors likely lie behind this change. As the decline of churches in the West became increasingly evident, the overwhelming preoccupation became turning decline into growth. As the church splintered into greater and greater variety, as the culture became more and more diverse, it was seen as a hopeless task to try and presume there was any true form. This was reinforced by a developing culture that was suspicious of any insistence on adherence to one particular form or expression in any area of life. Indeed, ideology became the enemy, grammar was fascist, theory was irrelevant, praxis was what mattered. I might add that in New Zealand, which has always had a bent toward pragmatism and suspicion of intellectualism, all of this found fertile ground.

And so in the Emerging Church movement there is a sense of "anything goes." For those for whom tradition or inherited forms are in fact an obstacle to being effective churches and a barrier to the mission of Jesus, it is a waste of time to listen to what the past might have to say about how the church should form its life. Graham Redding, shortly before he took up the role as principal of the theological institution where I work, delivered his inaugural lecture, in which he asked the question, "Does John Calvin have any place in the Café Church?"[14] His question suggested that perhaps the Café Church was not allowing Calvin's theology to shape its practice; but, in fact, café church is relatively tame fare and rather orthodox when church can also apparently be a bunch of kids at a skateboard park or BMX track, a group of students gathering in a pub or dance club, or several midlife couples sharing wine and a movie together.

So when is a gathering of followers of Jesus actually a church? A few years ago I spent four months of my study leave in the U.K., devoting some of my time to looking at some of the new forms of church that were developing there. Many of those I met with were involved in resourcing Fresh Expressions or the Emerging Church movement, and I found that it was the question of ecclesiology that dominated their concerns. There was a growing realization that unless the movement is undergirded by solid ecclesiology it may well suffer the same fate as the failed alternative worship and church planting movements of the 1990s.[15]

---

14. Redding, inaugural lecture, School of Ministry, Knox College.

15. One person who was very strong on this was Michael Moynagh, who has recently published a book that seeks to go some way to addressing this issue. Moynagh, *Church for Every Context*. I found this both surprising and interesting, as Moynagh's writings, which are referred to several times in this book, had mainly focused on looking at the changing context of the church and some of the lines along which it needed to adapt if it was going to become connected.

Many of those engaged in experimental forms of church argue that because Jesus promised that "wherever two or three come together in my name, there am I with them," any such gathering is church. Within the Baptist tradition this is the primary definition that is used, as it is in the Pentecostal and charismatic streams. The presence of Jesus by the Spirit is all that matters. It is thus no coincidence that many of the initiators of the Emerging Church movement in New Zealand and Australia have been Baptists. Such a simple definition leaves them much freer to experiment with a diversity of forms, particularly when the focus on the autonomy of the local congregation means they do not have to get permission from some regional or national body.

I should add that in the past I would also have held that this was sufficient. It is interesting to observe, however, that the Baptist movement in New Zealand, after having being driven by a fairly pragmatic approach for the past couple of decades, is now acknowledging that it has significant problems and challenges. The immediate past leader of the movement said several years ago that "our first task is to get our ecclesiology sorted out." Over the past two years they have held conferences focusing on ecclesiology. In other words, even for Baptists, ecclesiology seems to matter in the long run, even if in the short-term pragmatism can appear to produce results.

Further reflection has made me realize that, even though I had moved from the Baptists to the Presbyterians some years ago, I was still at this stage more Baptist than I had imagined. In arguing in my doctoral work that effective churches had maintained a strong commitment to the central beliefs of orthodox Christian faith, I identified these as being beliefs about Jesus Christ, about God, about Scripture, and about mission, and used the Nicene Creed to define these. There was nothing about the church, however—no ecclesiology. Of course the Nicene Creed does include among its statements, "We believe in one holy catholic and apostolic church." If we use these *notae ecclesiae* as a measuring rod, how does the Emerging Church movement measure up? Is it in fact church?

One . . .

Everybody affirms the unity or oneness of the church, but ever since the Schism of 1054 that oneness has been somewhat difficult to locate, and since the splintering of the Reformation even more so. Daniel Migliore helpfully defines it as "a distinctive unity rooted in communion with God through Christ in the Spirit. The unity of the church is a fragmentary and provisional participation in the costly love of the triune God."[16] Recent trinitarian theology, with its focus on a plurality within an essential oneness, is helpful for us in understanding how the Christian gospel embraces both diversity and unity, and some of the best recent ecclesiology begins from this basis.

So Jürgen Moltmann argues that this kind of community creates "unity in diversity, while at the same time differentiating and making diversity possible . . . we call this the Trinitarian fellowship of the Spirit."[17] The unity of the church does not exist in either a controlling doctrinal conformity or a formal institutional structure, and I would resist all attempts to impose either of those kinds of unity on the church. Within the diversity of our expressions, unity is situated in the life in which we participate together with the triune God. As Hans Küng expresses it, "It is one and the same God who gathers the scattered from all places and all ages and makes them into one people of God."[18]

However, ever since the Reformers placed the focus on seeing the unity of the church in the invisible church rather than the visible church, that understanding has been used as a way of enabling churches and their leaders to do little about working to see unity as a visible mark of the church in its present reality. We have continued to be happily schismatic, tearing apart the fabric of church whenever we find something on which we differ. This "creeping congregationalism," which afflicts all varieties of church life in contemporary societies, heightens the tendency to focus on the local and the particular, as if that were all there was to being church.

Jesus left behind a visible community, not an invisible concept. This was a community he called to be one, and so it is incumbent on we who are as the church to continually work hard to find ways to express, even in our increasingly diverse cultures, that this oneness is a reality, not merely some ethereal and mystical entity. If the life of the Trinity is the model of our unity, then it does involve the diverse members working synergistically together for the glory of the one.

One of my concerns about the Emerging Church movement is that, with its brisk dismissal of inherited forms of church life, its distancing

---

16. Migliore, *Faith Seeking Understanding*, 201.
17. Moltmann, *The Spirit of Life*, 220.
18. Küng, *The Church*, 353.

itself from tradition, and its reluctance to work with the church as it is, it is magnifying the image of a divided church and failing to put energy into working hard at ways to give expression to and so maintain the unity of the church. While I admire the movement's willingness to engage with our cultures, and to seek to find new ways of incarnating the gospel and church within these, I believe it would be truer to being the church of Jesus Christ in the world today if it sought to do that by working with the church as it already is. Brian McLaren says we need "a new church." There is only one church, and it already is. The challenge is to continue to work within that church so that it might better be the faithful presence of God in Christ through the Spirit in the diverse communities it inhabits.

Holy . . .

The word "holy" and the concept of holiness is hardly popular in our contemporary context, whether inside or outside the church. It raises images of a "holier than thou" judgmentalism and an isolationist separatism, fearful of contamination by an evil world. A preoccupation with holiness, it is suggested, has been a major hindrance to the mission of the church in the world. Identification and engagement with the world is what the creator God is about. The word holy is of course the primary word used to name the essence of the nature of God. It is, if you like, what marks God as God, as distinctly different from everything else in creation. It is something that belongs essentially to God. For other things or persons to be described as holy, therefore, is to claim that they also are marked by the essence of the character of God, and in this way are to some extent different from the rest of creation.

But how do we know what God is like if we are meant to share in that character? The central claim of the New Testament and of Christian thought is that the fullest revelation of God is to be found in the human person of Jesus Christ. By looking at the life of Jesus, we see what it is like to live a human life marked by the character, or holiness, of God. But more than that, the New Testament makes the claim that, by his death, resurrection, and gift of the Holy Spirit, Christ mediates to us the very life of God so that we can share in the fellowship of the Trinity. Here is the essence of the holiness of the church. It can be identified by the degree to which it lives a life reflecting the glory of God seen in Christ, and this is made possible by the presence of the Spirit in its midst. When we do this we will demonstrate a distinctive quality to our life that will indeed mark us out as different, distinct from others—as Peter put it, a "peculiar people."[19] While this quality of holiness will be demonstrated in the church in an imperfect way, it is, as Calvin put it, the "measure toward which it is daily advancing."[20]

As previously argued, the church lives in a relationship of some tension with whatever culture it inhabits. It needs to both incarnate the gospel into that culture but also allow the gospel to transcend and judge every culture in which it is present. Part of the problem with Christendom, and the way of being church that developed in that context, is that it ended up identifying the culture of those societies as being Christian, and then simply became a reflection of these societies. The church was no longer a distinct or holy people.

As the societies and cultures in which the church existed changed rapidly, particularly in the post-World War II era, it ended up with nothing left to offer the new societies which emerged, and was seen as an antiquarian reminder of a world that once was. Dean William Inge said in the nineteenth century that "If you marry the spirit of the age you will find yourself a widow in the next."[21] Sadly, this has come to be true of much of mainline Protestantism in the West, including many of its evangelical expressions, which are shaped more by the values of the consumer market and business models than the gospel. The Emerging Church movement has been quite right in much of the critique it has offered on how traditional church life had been simply an expression of modern Western life and values.

While some of its analysis is invaluable, in its headlong rush to become relevant to the emerging culture of a postmodern world, it runs the risk of making the same mistake. It may end up wedding itself to the spirit of this age, just as firmly as the church it critiques may have to a previous age. When the wonders of this age begin to dissipate—and it may well be a phase in history that is much more short-lived than the previous—where will the Emerging Church be then? What will it have to offer and to say when all of its own inadequacies have been laid bare? The Emerging Church puts a heavy emphasis on an incarnational theology and understands Jesus almost solely in these terms. Yet any serious

19. 1 Peter 2:9, AV.

20. Calvin, *Institutes of the Christian Religion*, 3.1.5.

21. A much used quote found in many sources. Taken here from http://www.dictionary-quotes.com.

reading of the life and ministry of Jesus will identify that, while he did live incarnationally within the culture of first century Judaism, he also lived in considerable tension with much of that culture, at times spoke judgment on it, and ended up being rejected by it. If he were simply concerned with relevance to the culture, why was he strung up on a cross?

At times it is difficult to distinguish an emerging café or night club church from any other café or night club down the street. Postmodern culture is neither any better nor any worse than modern culture. Emerging Church leaders may celebrate the death of modernity and raise three cheers for the arrival of postmodernity, without recognizing the need to provide a proper critique of that which is problematic for living a Christ-shaped life. On the other hand, some critics of the Emerging Church movement, such as Don Carson and David Wells,[22] see only a culture antithetical to Christ in postmodernity, and fail to recognize that they are just as closely wedded to the culture of modernity. Whatever the culture in which we happen to find ourselves as the church of Jesus Christ, we need first to allow Christ by the Spirit to form us into a distinctive culture which preaches the unique holy life of our Trinitarian God in the language of the time and place in which it is set.

Catholic . . .

The affirmation of the catholicity of the church refers to its universality and inclusivity. It is the church that has existed everywhere, always, and for all. It guards the church against parochialism, sectarianism, racism, and chronological conceit. It is clear that both the unity and the catholicity of the church go together, that they are two interwoven dimensions of the one church. However, as with the church's oneness, we need to guard against catholicity being understood merely as an abstract kind of universalism hovering over the particularities of culture and history. Again, it is a mark that needs to be demonstrated in the life of the visible church, its expression being in the life of local congregations. Avery Dulles claims that catholicity "is not the accomplished fact of having many members or a wide geographical distribution, but rather the dynamic catholicity of a love reaching out to all and excluding no

---

22. See, for example, Carson, *Becoming Conversant with the Emerging Church*; and Wells, *The Courage to Be Protestant*.

one."²³ I would agree with Daniel Migliore that "the church today needs to interpret the meaning of catholic as inclusive of all kinds of people."²⁴ What might this mean for us today?

One of the major trends of the post-1960s world of the global village has been the growing pluralism of our societies. This is seen not just through the migration to societies such as New Zealand of markedly different cultural groups from overseas, but also by the breakup of the dominant white European culture into a multiplicity of subcultures. Not only is this across generations, but also within generations, so much so that since the beginning of the 1990s it has been pointless to even talk about youth culture. This pluralization has been heightened by the fact that increasingly people do not live their lives in one geographical place, where they might mix with people of a wide variety of ages and cultures, but rather are mobile and live their lives within communities of choice, usually consisting of people of the same culture as themselves.

Often these subgroups are quite exclusive, having their own distinctive language, symbols, and lifestyles. At a time in the past when people in a community lived their lives in that particular community, when generations shared many of the activities of life together, the local church embraced members from every walk and stage of life represented in that community. It was catholic and inclusive in that sense. This was the parish or family church, an increasingly rare bird in our pluralistic society. How do we reach people today within all these different cultural subgroups, when the culture of church, as presently configured, represents that culture of a bygone age?

The answer of much of the Emerging Church is that we need separate churches to incarnate the gospel into all those cultural subgroups. And so we have youth church, student church, young adults church, young marrieds church, breakfast church, café church, biker church—and so on, and so on. These churches become quite age- or culture-specific. One practical question to ponder becomes, "what happens to these churches when their particular niche finishes?" But there is a bigger issue. Murray Robertson completed 40 years of pastoral ministry at Spreydon Baptist Church in 2008 by serving as the President of the New Zealand Baptist Church. During that year he travelled widely throughout New Zealand, visiting many churches, and wrote a series of columns in the *NZ Baptist*

---

23. Dulles, *Models of the Church*, 122.
24. Migliore, *Faith Seeking Understanding*, 203.

on his observations. In one of these he noted that churches now "tend to divide along shared interest lines," and that there is "an age based apartheid;" he adds, "Maybe this is part of the phenomenon of people looking for a church in which they will feel comfortable, but . . . something quite precious is lost when you only meet and share with people who are pretty much identical to yourself."[25] Indeed, is it a church when its membership is so exclusively limited to some subgroup that others are in fact shut out?

The Emerging Church movement is to be commended for its recognition that in our multicultural world there is no one expression of the gospel that will incarnate it for "all," even within one community in New Zealand. They draw correctly on the missional principle which Paul spells out in 1 Corinthians 9, of becoming "all things to all peoples so that I might by all possible means save some." But that needs to be balanced by the ecclesial principle Paul spells out in Ephesians 2, where he addresses the major cultural divide of his world, that between Jew and Gentile—namely, that "Christ . . . has made the two one and has destroyed the barrier, the dividing wall . . . to create in himself one new humanity."

Perhaps what may be a legitimate mission group is not in fact a church. It needs to see itself as part of the church catholic, and commit itself to being part of that church, and share its life with the greater whole in its lived practices, so that in this fractured, divided, and tribalized world people may see that the gospel makes a difference, that estranged groups can be reconciled, that in Christ cultural separation might be transcended, and that the new community of God's people is inclusive of people of every race, tribe, and tongue, even here now on earth. Might these questions also be asked of ethnic specific churches? To quote David Bosch, "The new fellowship transcends every limit imposed by family, class or culture. We are not winning people like ourselves to ourselves but sharing the good news that in Christ God has shattered the barriers that divide the human race and has created a new community. The new people of God has no analogy; it is a "sociological impossibility" that has become possible."[26]

---

25. Robertson, "Presidential Ramblings," 5.
26. Bosch, *Transforming Mission*, 389.

Apostolic . . .

A number of those in the missional church movement define the apostolicity of the church as its essential missional nature—that before it is anything else apostolicity is missional. While it is true that the word "apostle" does embrace the idea of one who is sent, and while I agree fully with the sentiment being expressed, I do not believe that particular interpretation of apostolic as a mark of church is how it was understood historically in the church, or by those who created the Nicene Creed.

The word apostle came to be used in the early church as a kind of technical term for those who were originally sent out by Jesus after the resurrection to be his witnesses.[27] In confessing the apostolicity of the church we are acknowledging that the true church is founded on the apostles. The faith and life of the church must stand in continuity with their enduring witness. This continuity is ensured not by some physical link through the sacramental laying on of hands, but by our faithfulness to and reaffirmation of the gospel to which the early apostles gave witness in the writings of the New Testament. As Jürgen Moltmann puts it, "The apostolic succession is in fact and in truth the evangelical succession, the continuing and unadulterated proclamation of the gospel of the risen Christ."[28]

It is, of course, one thing to affirm that "our supreme rule of faith is the Word of God," as the Presbyterian Church does, or that "the Bible is the final authority in all matters of faith and practice," as a Baptist church might. It is quite another to interpret what those words actually mean for us today. One of the things postmodern hermeneutics has made us aware of is that there is no such thing as an un-interpreted word or act. There are two issues this raises in relation to our engagement with Emerging Church.

First, being faithful to the apostolic witness is not just mere repetition of phrases like the ones above, or repeating the way in which they might have been interpreted as being appropriate for another place and time. The apostolic word must be interpreted anew for every generation and every context. The Emerging Church is to be commended for its willingness, by and large, to take scripture seriously, and to seek to interpret

---

27. For Paul the authenticity of his apostleship is his encounter with and sending by the risen Christ on the road to Damascus. The word is used in a secondary sense for some other individuals in the New Testament, but this is its primary sense.

28. Moltmann, *The Church in the Power of the Spirit*, 177, 359.

afresh what it might mean for us today in our particular context, rather than simply repeating unthinkingly the formulas and answers of the past.

But, secondly, how do we know that a new appropriation or interpretation is faithful to the witness of the apostles? Calvin argued that interpretation of scripture must take place within the hermeneutical community of the church. Too often in Protestant and Evangelical circles the doctrine of the priesthood of all believers has been understood within the culture of Enlightenment individualism, to mean the right of every individual to interpret scripture for himself or herself, a tendency heightened in the radical individualism of late modernity. So much is this the case that Kevin van Hoozer asks in his hermeneutical tour de force, *Is there a Meaning in this Text?*[29]—or is there in fact just a never-ending possibility of meanings?

Listening to the voice of the church, the hermeneutical community, is one of the significant factors to take account of in discovering what "this text" means for us today. And by the church we mean the "one, holy, catholic, apostolic church," the church throughout time historically and throughout the world geographically. This means giving due weight, but not stifling weight, to the voice of tradition. G.K. Chesterton wrote: "Tradition means giving votes to the most obscure of all classes—our ancestors. It is the democracy of the dead. Tradition refuses to submit to the small and arrogant oligarchy of those who happen to walking around."[30]

The Emerging Church, with its ditching of traditional church, its giving up on traditions that may have developed and been passed on for centuries—apart from occasionally ransacking them and tearing out of any meaningful context some token that seems cute in the eclecticism of postmodern culture—runs the risk of missing the wisdom that has developed over the centuries, of listening to the caution that can come from previous misinterpretations. The result can be that, in the end, it can run outside the boundaries of where the Spirit might be willing to venture with them.

Sadly, this is a pattern that has happened all too often in the history of well-intentioned new movements. There is a misuse of scripture which is false teaching; there is heresy that is full of proof texts, although one needs to be cautious about making these kind of assertions. Less dramatically, there are also representations of the gospel that are unbalanced

---

29. van Hoozer, *Is There A Meaning In This Text?*
30. Chesterton, *Orthodoxy*, 73.

and therefore unhelpful. Maintaining conversation and community with the whole church, so that interpretation occurs within the checks and balances therein, will help ensure an ongoing, yet presently meaningful, faithfulness to the gospel within the emerging movement.

Word and Sacraments

Two further marks of the church have also been identified, particularly among Protestants. As Calvin put it, "Wherever we see the Word of God purely preached and heard, and the sacraments administered according to Christ's institution, there it is not to be doubted, a church of God exists."[31] Holding this definition central to its Reformed understanding of the church, the Presbyterian Church ordains those who complete the formational requirements as ministers of word and sacrament. This is so that it will have communities of believers where the "Word of God is purely preached" and "the sacraments are rightly administered."

The former is in some ways easier to assess than the latter. What does it mean to ensure that the sacraments are rightly administered? Orthodox theologian John Zizioulas has argued that it is the presence of the bishop that makes it so, obviously a problematic definition for many churches. For Catholics and Anglicans it is someone rightly appointed by the bishop who ensures faithful continuity with the apostolic tradition. We have argued here that being apostolic means faithfulness to the witness of the apostles as contained in the New Testament. Hence for Calvin it is as "as instituted by Christ." This is why the Reformed tradition has held word and sacrament together, because it is not just receiving the bread and the wine, but doing so in the context of hearing the gospel story of what makes them sacramental, a means of grace. A theologically informed and properly recognized ministry is important to ensure that the church remains apostolic—faithful to the scriptures in all aspects of its life, including the preaching of the Word and the sacraments.

Parts of the Emerging Church, as well as other experimental forms of church life, have often been critical of and resistant to theological training, preferring to have leaders and pastors who are more entrepreneurial and creative. Too much theology kills that, they argue. Many churches in New Zealand have followed this approach by appointing individuals as ministers who have no theological training but show

---

31. Calvin, *Institutes of the Christian Religion*, 4.1.9.

good entrepreneurial and managerial skills. And I have to say that at times I have been in churches and listened to sermons, witnessed baptisms, or experienced communion which, at best, have not been faithful to the Scriptures and, at worst, have bordered on the heretical. These may have been entertaining events but scarcely a sacrament. Sometimes Word and sacrament are missing completely, which again raises the question, "is it church?"

A central Reformation principle, as we have noted, is *ecclesia reformata semper reformanda*. This phrase is often quoted by those who want to "do church" in a different way. Are we being true to our tradition in doing this? In some senses, yes, but it is a misunderstanding of the Reformers' intent to see reform as giving us *carte blanche* to try whatever we want. The Reformers reformed the church in the light of the Scriptures. Luther did not just say "Here I stand, I can do no other," but "My conscience is bound to the Word of God, here I stand . . ."

This is why ministers in the Reformed tradition have been known as "teaching elders," and now "ministers of word and sacrament," so that by making the role of scripture central in the life of the church and the office of ministry, the church will be continually reformed in the light of scripture. As a 2000 Church of Scotland statement on ministry puts it, ministers are "to represent Christ in the faithful proclaiming of the Word and right administration of the Sacraments and so ensure the possibility of such reform and renewal."[32] The Emerging Church movement would do well to seek to ensure a theologically formed leadership, so that it too will experience the renewing presence of Christ that comes from faithful preaching of the gospel and administration of the sacraments.

In addition, it is worth reflecting briefly on what some of the Reformers considered a third mark, church discipline. Neither Luther nor Calvin regarded this as a mark, although Luther on occasion referred to "the power of the keys"—the power to absolve from sin and withhold absolution—and Calvin strongly advocated the practice of church discipline. Martin Bucer did in fact regard such discipline as a prime indicator, alongside word and sacrament, and both the Scottish Confession (1560) and the First Helvetic Confession name church discipline as a third mark of the church.

Discipline of course is a very unpopular word or concept in our postmodern Western world, and conjures up all kinds of negative images.

---

32. Quoted in Lyall, *Integrity of Pastoral Care*, 146.

Discipline of any kind is regarded as the enemy of personal freedom, creativity, and the ability of individuals to discover their true selves. I would certainly not want to advocate a return to the kind of restrictive and conforming discipline that many of my generation, raised in the conservative, fundamentalist, or Roman Catholic churches of even the 1950s experienced, and which has led to many being outside of and strongly opposed to church ever since. Many of those in the Emerging Church movement are in some sense also reacting against that kind of church culture, developing churches with very few restrictions.

Overall, however, we might question whether the pendulum has swung too far, both in the wider culture as well as in the church in general. If we examine the word "discipline" in a positive light, it is related to the words *disciple* and *discipleship*. It is the process of learning and being formed to take on a particular identity and lifestyle, to become like the teacher—in this case, Jesus. Without the practice of some kinds of discipline in community this is unlikely to happen. The highly motivated individual is able to achieve this, but for most people it is fostered much more readily in a community that keeps some disciplines central to its life, whether it is a sports community, a recovery group, or a church.

It is interesting to note that there is an increasing focus, in much of the more recent writing on the church, on the practice of "spiritual disciplines" and the concept of formation. This is a healthy sign, and I would suggest that for some parts of the Emerging Church movement a focus on this dimension, alongside the desire to incarnate the gospel in forms and practices that come out of the culture they seek to reach, would help move them toward being a church rather than just another club within that culture.

A Sociological Insight

I want to finish by drawing from a sociological insight, a discipline I believe is a very helpful conversation partner for theology. Many of the grand theories of the earlier sociologists are now viewed with much suspicion, particularly the grand modern metanarrative of secularization.[33] However, there is one theory which I believe continues to provide

---

33. A recent very readable book which summarizes much of the overwhelming evidence to refute this is Micklethwaite and Wooldridge, *God is Back*.

invaluable insight—Max Weber's theory of the routinization of charisma.[34] He argues that what happens in the evolution of religion is that a new group gathers around a charismatic leader and is a dynamic, free, loose charismatic movement. Over time it rationalizes, routinizes, and systemizes its life and so loses its charisma. Some adherents become frustrated with this and break away around the edges to form a new charismatic group, with new energy and dynamism. It is this that ensures the ongoing renewal of the religion.

Looking at the history of Christianity in the West, there is much that can be helpfully explained by Weber. There is no question that much of church life in the West has become routinized and rationalized, such that there is little dynamism or charisma. The Spirit has been routinized out of much of the Western church. I believe the Emerging Church movement can be understood in these terms, as can the Charismatic movement of the 1960s and 1970s.

What has happened often in the past is that the established religious institution de-churches the new movement and the action is reciprocated by the movement. My hope is that, in this instance, we can avoid repeating history and, by remaining in communion and continuing in conversation, the Emerging Church may be part of a wider movement for renewal and reformation of the church in the West, gaining from the wisdom and catholicity of the church to grow into a more faithful and dynamic communion of the triune God in our challenging Western context.

So . . . When is a Church a Church?

When is a church a church? I would probably, in the end, agree with Miroslav Volf's conclusion, that "where two or three are gathered in Christ's name, not only is Christ present among them, but a Christian church is there as well, perhaps a bad church, a church that may well transgress against love and truth, but a church nonetheless."[35] Many in the Emerging Church movement prefer to talk about the emerging conversation rather than the emerging church. My plea would be for those within the movement to include in the conversation all of those who with them are members of the "one, holy, catholic, apostolic church," so that they might come to more adequately share those marks. And to those who

---

34. Weber, *The Sociology of Religion*.
35. Volf, *After Our Likeness*, 136.

are sure that they are members of that church, but are suspicious as to whether these newcomers qualify, the hope would be that they might reach out in conversation with the Emerging Church movement and so help us all to more fully demonstrate the transforming presence of the risen Christ in our life together.

10

Migration and the Future of Christianity

HUMAN HABITATION OF NEW Zealand has always been by migrants who, for a variety of reasons, have made the decision to travel significant distances across oceans to settle here, until recently in often hazardous conditions. The first to arrive were people from the Pacific Islands to the north in the 14th century, who became the indigenous Maori population. Europeans discovered the islands in the 17th century, although the first Dutch explorer, Abel Tasman, had sailed down the eastern seaboard thinking it was part of a much larger continent. In the eighteenth century the great English explorer James Cook visited three times, and mapped the coastlines of the islands with remarkable accuracy. A few settlers from Europe began to arrive later that century, and increasing numbers from the early 19th century on, particularly with planned settlement after the signing of the Treaty of Waitangi between the British Crown and Maori chiefs in 1840.

For the following 130 years, the vast majority of settlers were European, more precisely, mainly from Britain. There were a few Chinese settlers from the nineteenth century, who came for the gold rush and chose to remain, and some from Pacific Island countries after World War II, who were allowed in because of New Zealand's relationship with some of these island nations following World War I. Samoa is the most populous of these islands, and in 2011 celebrated its 50th anniversary of independence from New Zealand.

Although there was no official "white" immigration policy as in Australia, the policy made it difficult for non-Europeans to gain entry, and those from Britain were particularly favored. In the later 1960s and

1970s significant numbers began migrating from the Pacific Islands, welcomed because they were willing to do the manual jobs New Zealanders did not want, but they were unwanted and sometimes sent home when unemployment levels began to increase.

In 1987 a major change in immigration policy was made and New Zealand began to diversify the countries represented in immigration numbers. An increasing number of migrants came to New Zealand from Korea, Hong Kong, Taiwan, Southeast Asia, India, and later the People's Republic of China, as well as continuing numbers from Pacific countries. There were also significant numbers of white immigrants from South Africa and Zimbabwe with the changing political situations there.

In looking at these trends it is important to remember that the highest number of immigrants continue to come from the United Kingdom, and many also immigrate from our closest neighbor, Australia. Nevertheless, there have been significant changes in the ethnic makeup of New Zealand's population, and they will lead to even bigger changes in the future. Figures from the United Nations show that currently the highest percentage of New Zealand's population consists of people who are immigrants from a broad range of countries (24 per cent), followed by Australia (23 per cent) and Canada (22 per cent).[1]

New Zealand, in other words, is no longer a country populated mainly by European New Zealanders (often called *Pakeha*—the Maori term—or *Palagi*—the Samoan term). It retains a significant minority of Maori, and one or two pockets of other ethnicities.

- In 1961 New Zealand was 92 percent European and 7 percent Maori, with Asian and Pacifica minorities sharing the remaining 1 per cent.

- In the 2006 census,[2] those who identified as European made up 68 per cent. By 2026 it is estimated they will be 62 percent and, in all probability, below 50 percent by 2050.

- Maori were the next largest group, with 14 per cent. By 2026 they will be 15 percent of the population.

- Asians grew the fastest between 2001 and 2006, growing to 9 per cent. By 2026 this will be 15 per cent.

---

1. http://esa.un.org/MigFlows/MigrationFlows.aspx.

2. There is normally a New Zealand census every five years. However, because it is operated out of Christchurch the impact of the February 2011 earthquake meant that it was postponed, and it has not yet been carried out. Figures here are from 2006.

- Pacifica people made up 7 percent of the population. By 2026 they will be 9 per cent.
- In addition, there were small numbers of Middle Eastern, Latin American, and African peoples.

As well as immigration, another significant factor fueling demographic changes is the aging profile of the European population and the much younger age profile and higher birth rates of other ethnicities. In 2006, 92 percent of the population over 65 were European, while 55 percent of babies born were of Maori, Pacifica, or Asian descent. In Auckland, by far New Zealand's largest city, 40 percent of inhabitants were born overseas in the last census, only 56 percent of the population is European (likely to be down to 50 percent by 2016), and over half of children enrolled in primary schools are non-European.

Similar patterns of demographic change are found in all Western societies which were previously dominated by those of European descent. Analyzing the situation in the U.S., Charles Van Engen writes:

> We are all being radically impacted by the largest redistribution of people the globe has ever seen. And the multiculturalness of our new reality is so staggering that we are reeling between rising new protectionist racism, rampant individualization and balkanization, and a radical postmodern embrace of cultural relativism that calls into question many of our most cherished values. In this new reality, all of us are being called on to find ways to affirm cultural relativity: tolerance, understanding, justice, equality, and coexistence within the new multiculturalism. The cities of our world are being especially impacted, and the church in the city knows very little, and seems to care even less, about how to present the gospel in this new reality.[3]

Commenting on this increasing ethnic diversity in New Zealand, and the failure of some established churches to connect in areas with a high concentration of ethnic minorities, Peter Lineham claims that "any religion that did not engage wider than the rich white middle-class will certainly not be growing in a city with Auckland's demographics today."[4]

---

3. Van Engen, *Mission on the Way*, 179.
4. "Christian Faith Losing Out to other Religions."

Immigrant Churches

The first significant arrival of Christianity in New Zealand was missionary-driven, with Samuel Marsden beginning mission activity in 1814 under the auspices of the Church Missionary Society. Wesleyan and Roman Catholic missions shortly followed. After a very slow beginning there was a significant embrace of Christianity, in some form, by Maori people, and estimates are that by the mid-1840s perhaps as many as 70 percent had become Christians.

From the beginning of formal settlement following the signing of the Treaty of Waitangi, in which the Maori chiefs granted sovereignty to the British Crown (greatly abetted by the missionaries, who had considerable *mana*[5] with a number of these chiefs), immigrants arrived in significant numbers, bringing their churches with them. Hence New Zealand came to have English Anglican and Methodist churches, Scottish Presbyterian churches, and Irish Catholic churches. For the first 100 years of its new history these four churches dominated the ecclesial landscape, with about 90 percent of the population identifying with one of them, even if only about 25 percent turned up at church on any given Sunday. This pattern of Christianity among New Zealand's European immigrant settlers continued with only minor variations until the mid–1960s. Other expressions of church life (sects, as they were commonly known) were very minor players.

The other significant event to occur in these early years was the sudden collapse of Maori Christianity as a consequence of the land wars in the 1850s and 1860s. When the Maori saw the church siding with the British forces who were seizing their lands, and many of the ministers and missionaries acting as military chaplains, they deserted the faith in droves. As one Maori chief expressed it to a missionary, "You taught us to turn our eyes to heaven to pray, and while we were looking up you took the land from under our feet."

A religious consequence was the springing up of many new forms of Maori faith, what would now be called New Religious Movements, combining Christianity, especially Old Testament stories and beliefs, with traditional Maori beliefs and culture. The most significant of these in the 19th century was Ringatu, founded by the charismatic warrior

---

5. The word *mana* is important in Polynesian cultures and is related to the concept of power. In Maori culture it refers to someone having considerable personal prestige, influence, and authority. It is now a commonly used term in New Zealand language.

chief Te Kooti, while in the 20th century a very important movement was the Ratana Church, founded by the Maori prophet and faith healer Ratana, the *mangai* or mouthpiece of God. Unfortunately, like all the earlier expressions, this was regarded by the European churches as being outside the fold of true Christianity, instead of being embraced as a local contextual adaptation.

The church landscape began to change significantly from the late 1960s, as we have seen, with the decline of the mainline churches and the growth of more independent evangelical, charismatic, and Pentecostal churches. A second factor bringing about change, slightly later, was the arrival of considerable numbers of Christians from non-European countries, who also brought with them their own versions of church from their homelands.

The first wave of these migrant Christians, as indicated, came from the Pacific Islands. With their churches having been established by Anglican, Presbyterian, Congregational, Methodist, and Roman Catholic churches, in a sense they brought with them churches that already existed in New Zealand. However, the culture, beliefs, and practices, as well as the languages of worship they brought with them, differed significantly. The role that religion and religious communities play in the settlement experience of migrants is well covered in the literature. Helen Ebaugh, comparing early patterns of immigrant religion with that of the "new immigrants" (the term employed in light of the new patterns which emerged from the mid-1960s on) found that "Then as now, ethnic places of worship served the dual purpose of reproducing the group's cultural and religious heritage, while assisting immigrants in the process of adapting to the new society."[6]

And so these new immigrants formed their own ethnic specific churches in the new country, retaining the practices and languages of their old identity rather than becoming members of existing churches of the same denomination. Over time they did become part of the national bodies of those denominations, but their local churches remained distinct. One notable shift in this identity is that many Pacific Islanders came from a Congregational heritage, the result of London Missionary Society activity. The Congregational Church was always very small in New Zealand, and even weaker after the post-1960s decline, and in 1969 most of their churches joined the Presbyterian

---

6. Ebaugh, "Religion and the New Immigrants," 228.

Church of Aotearoa New Zealand (PCANZ), bringing many Pacific Islander churches into the denomination. This historical fact helps to explain some of the issues that have emerged later for Presbyterians. The next significant wave came from Asian countries and, in church terms, Korean Presbyterians and Filipino Catholics were particularly strongly represented. Other more recent immigrants from Africa, Latin America, Eastern Europe, and the Middle East have brought an increasingly wide array of expressions of church life.

Throughout this book we have consistently noted the decline of mainline denominational churches and the growth of evangelical, charismatic, and Pentecostal churches since the 1960s. An additional factor, which has become clear from the 1990s, is that much of the recent growth of these growing churches has come from immigrants, and that if we took immigrant/ethnic figures out of the mainline church data, the decline would be even more catastrophic.[7] Certainly a considerably higher proportion of Pacifica people, Koreans, Filipinos, and South Africans attend church than do European New Zealanders. Particular churches have benefitted from different ethnic immigrants: Roman Catholics from Filipinos; Presbyterians from Pacifica and Koreans; Baptists from Chinese and South Africans; Pentecostals from Pacifica especially, but also Asians; Methodists from Pacifica.

With immigration from Asia and the Middle East, there has also been a very rapid increase in those who identify as Hindus, Buddhists, or Muslims, although the actual numbers are still very small, at a combined total of only 4 percent in the 2006 census, compared with 54 percent Christians, and 32 percent "no religion." The impact of this immigration into New Zealand from what might be regarded as the "new Christian heartlands" is similar to that identified by Jehu Hanciles for America.[8] This multicultural influx is changing the face of New Zealand Christianity by de-Europeanizing it. Immigrant congregations are the fastest growing segment across all traditions, and represent forms and expressions of faith that may seem as foreign to Pakeha/Palangi Christians as other religions. This immigration of non-Western Christians represents a new missionary encounter with New Zealand society.

---

7. While research data is difficult to find on this, partly because ethnic churches or ethnic members of mixed churches rarely fill in survey forms, it is clear from the data that can be found, and also from observing the changing ethnic mix of larger and more youthful churches.

8. Hanciles, *Beyond Christendom*, 379.

While South Africans have blended fairly easily into European congregations, most of the other groups have preferred their own congregations, and significant numbers of churches have targeted specific new congregations for them. It is estimated that 45 percent of the 1,100 churches in Auckland may be ethnic communities. Beyond the makeup of local congregations, there is the question of how these particular ethnic communities fit into the wider denominational structures of the church to which they belong. In this chapter, while exploring both sociological and theological issues, I will focus on Pacifica churches as they are the most long-term non-European immigrants in New Zealand, well into the third generation, and also because it is a particular issue for the Presbyterian Church to which I belong. The issues identified here are, I believe, true for all ethnic groups in their respective churches.

Pacifica people have the highest rates of Christian identity in New Zealand at 76 per cent, compared with 54 percent for the population overall, and 28 percent for Asians. Of these the largest group belong to the Presbyterian Church, and there are also significant numbers of Pacifica Methodists and Roman Catholics, as well as a growing number of Pentecostals among the younger generations raised in New Zealand.

As noted already, it is understandable that new immigrants form and are attracted to churches of their own kind. It provides a world of the familiar in a strange land, a stable base in a precarious new world, a "place to feel at home."[9] It is important to note that the islands from which these immigrants come had generally been completely Christianized in the 19th century and had, in effect, become little expressions of Christendom. The church was very much at the center of village life. When they left their islands, the church in the diaspora in many ways operated as a village community for these immigrants in a strange new land, providing much more than just religious services. This has been recognized by government and social agencies in New Zealand.

In terms of structure, when the Congregational Church joined the PCANZ a Pacific Islands Council was set up to work with their particular concerns within the church as a whole. Eventually this became a Synod, somewhat parallel to the Maori Synod (*Te Aka Puaho*), which was concerned with Maori affairs, although with limited powers. Over time, however, tensions have begun to develop within both the local congregations and the Synod itself, between the older immigrant leaders and

---

9. The title of a book on African immigrant churches. See Welbourn and Ogot, *A Place to Feel at Home*.

younger 1.5 and second generation members. The former want to retain the forms, practices, and languages they brought with them, while the latter increasingly want to adjust to the wider New Zealand cultural ways of doing things, but also become increasingly involved in multicultural or multiethnic settings.

At a national level these older leaders, dissatisfied with what they see as a lack of recognition of Pacific Island cultural concerns and practices by the wider church, seeing increasing integration as being simply assimilation into a Palagi church in which they have little power, and fearing losing their identity—all valid concerns—have increasingly wanted to set up a separate Pacific Island structure with full powers. This is the structure which the Anglican Church in New Zealand has taken, with a Tikanga Pakeha, Tikanga Maori and Tikanga Pasefika, each having the power of veto and so making cooperation and unity very difficult.[10]

For the PCANZ this issue is also fueled by Pacific Islanders' historic roots in the Congregational rather than the Presbyterian tradition, as the polity of the former gives more autonomy and authority to the local congregation. In addition, Pacific Islanders still have a sense of being newcomers rather than part of the establishment.[11] As a result of these tensions, and a considerable degree of intransigence among the leadership in a very hierarchical and age-oriented culture, many of the younger people have either begun attending Pentecostal churches or have left church completely.

It is important to recognize that this is not just a Pacific Islander issue, as distinct from a European issue, although it is that. It is also an issue of a Samoan way of doing things, as distinct from a Niuean way, a Tongan way, a Cook Islands way, or a Tokelauan way. Many of the Pacific Islands churches exist for a separate island group, and some current doctoral research being done on this issue within the PCANZ indicates that 83 percent of its churches are ethnically homogenous, defining ethnicity in the Pacifica context as being a separate ethnicity for each group. Other

---

10. *Tikanga* is a Maori word that translates as "correct procedure, custom, habit." The Anglican theological institution at St John's in Auckland incorporates separate Colleges, one for each *tikanga*, and it has been so rent by divisions that it has been barely functional and is currently being run by a commissioner, who is seeking to sort out some of these issues. The new Dean of the Tikanga Pakeha College, coming from overseas, notes that what she finds noticeably absent is "any language of the body of Christ."

11. Over the last decade or so there have also been "new" Congregational churches established, still governed from Samoa or the Cook Islands, complicating the relationship further.

Pacific Islander churches have several distinct worshipping congregations for each ethnic group. Attempts to merge these have usually been resisted, or at least to insist that everything should all be done in the language and culture of the dominant group, most often Samoan.

It should be noted that the Asian communities involved in the church, as they reach considerable numbers of 1.5 generation members, are showing a much greater degree of willingness to adapt, integrate, and become multicultural. It is interesting to discover that as the largest Korean church has begun an English-language service for its 1.5 generation, it has attracted Japanese and Chinese people, thus becoming pan-Asian, a first move toward becoming multicultural—a pattern also found in the U.S. There is some tension in that the Asian congregations do not have a Synod, merely a council, and likewise feel that they have little power, and that their concerns and particular issues do not receive adequate attention. Occasionally, as with the Pacific Islands churches, there are threats to withdraw completely and form their own denomination. Adding fuel to the fire of this conversation is the reality that the three largest churches in the PCANZ are now Korean churches.

Missiological Considerations

In the wider church scene many churches, particularly in the evangelical-charismatic-Pentecostal sector, with their concern for growth, have identified a market in this situation, and have begun planting ethnic specific churches, meaning effectively that the much discredited "homogenous unit principle" articulated by Donald McGavran and championed by Peter Wagner has re-emerged, although not of course called by the same name. I would add parenthetically that I believe this trend is also being uncritically embraced in some of the Fresh Expressions and Emerging Church forms discussed and critiqued in the previous chapter. An example of this trend emerged recently in a Presbyterian church with 13 different ethnic groups, when the Filipino group decided they wanted to leave and begin their own worship service so that they could attract more of their own people.

Of course, missiologically speaking, McGavran was right: "People like to become Christian without crossing racial/linguistic/class/cultural barriers. In other words, they prefer to remain who they are culturally while changing to become Christian. Culturally they remain the same and tend to gather with others from the same culture who share their faith."[12] Indeed, it could be argued that he was simply articulating in principle the practice of the apostle Paul expressed in 1 Corinthians 9 of becoming "all things to all people . . . that I might by any means save some." This led Wagner to declare, "He was the first century champion of the homogenous unit principle."[13]

Certainly almost every missionary knows this, and often a church never begins to really develop until mission is taken on by members of the local community. An example of this would be the rapid growth of Christianity among Maori in New Zealand, where most of the far-reaching mission was carried out by Maori "evangelists," and often European missionaries reached new tribes only to discover that the gospel was already present. This is also another illustration of the fact, as Hanciles reminds us, that "the spread of Christianity in the non-Western world has largely been the work of non-Western agency," with the work of the missionary being "more catalytic than comprehensive."[14] So there is clearly missiological truth in this principle, and the principle of the incarnation would seem to affirm it. Christ can be present in any and every culture.

Practically speaking, however, in the increasingly multicultural or multiethnic societies in which we live it becomes questionable as to whether this principle retains the same validity, particularly once an immigrant group moves beyond the first generation. When I was visiting the U.K. in 2000, Peter Brierley, Director of Christian Research, told me in an interview that he could describe where the church was growing in one word: "black." He noted that as one traced changes in the level of church attendance in those countries where it was increasing, this was where there was the greatest increase in the percentage of immigrants. Whereas in the 1970s and 1980s in the U.K. this was with those from the Caribbean, in the 1990s and into the 21st century, as those communities moved into the second generation, the greatest growth came from new immigrants from Africa. Now over 50 percent of church attenders in London are of either Caribbean or African ethnicity.

The point Brierley was making is well identified in sociological studies—that as the community moves through the generations in the new land, so people become more like the host community, especially the

---

12. McGavran, *Understanding Church Growth*, 198.
13. Wagner, *Our Kind of People*, 136.
14. Hanciles, *Beyond Christendom*, 368–69.

young people.[15] In the U.K., as in New Zealand, regular church involvement is not one of their characteristics. This shows up in statistics on church involvement among young Pacifica people raised in New Zealand (the 1.5 generation) and increasingly those born here. This was discovered in a study by Jemaima Tiatia;[16] and a further study of Cook Islands churches[17] found that a significant proportion had left those churches for similar reasons as those identified in Alan Jamieson's research on European (Pakeha) church-leavers in New Zealand.[18] Cluny MacPherson's study of Samoan adolescents and young adults found that they became increasingly impatient with "the adherence to traditional forms and styles of worship and a gerontocratic principle of leadership that denied them a voice in the church's decision making process."[19]

As well as those who left church altogether, what is also evident is that many others who have left Pacific Islander ethnic churches have moved to multiethnic churches, particularly Pentecostal and Charismatic churches. Yannick Fer, a French sociologist, has been researching religious change among young Pacifica people for over a decade, and has found that in New Zealand many had moved to Pentecostal churches, which provided a way for them to remain within their traditional faith (Christianity) and yet express that in cultural forms appropriate to their belonging within a contemporary Western society.[20] In visiting the most significant Pacifica church in New Zealand, Newton PIC in Auckland (the church around which a significant New Zealand film, *Sione's Wedding*, was based), the aging leadership, still strongly committed to their Samoan cultural way of doing things, acknowledged that they now had only small numbers of young people, and that most of their children who were still going to church were attending Pentecostal churches. "But they are still our young people," they hastily added.

While acknowledging that ethnic-specific churches play a critical role in the adjustment to a new world for first generation immigrants, it is a dubious question as to whether pursuing such churches is the most effective missional strategy for the church in the long term, once immigrant

15. Ebaugh, "Religion and New Immigrants," 235.
16. Tiatia, *Caught Between Cultures*.
17. Joseph, "Cracked Coconuts."
18. Jamieson, *A Churchless Faith*.
19. Macpherson and Macpherson, "Evangelical Religion among Pacific Island Migrants," 31.
20. Fer, unpublished paper.

communities move beyond the first generation. Adding further to this question is interesting research in the U.K. which indicates that churches with an ethnic mix are more likely to grow than those of one ethnicity, and that the richer the ethnic mix the more likely they are to grow.[21] A report on church growth in the U.S. claims that one of the major characteristics of the fastest growing churches is that they are multiracial.[22]

Similarly, research among Baptist Churches in New Zealand, which over recent years have begun to experience decline, found that the most rapid rate of decline was among ethnic-specific churches (meaning in this instance non-Pakeha ethnicity), and the least decline was among multicultural churches.[23] Hence, to argue for maintaining ethnically homogenous churches as a critical mission strategy in societies which are becoming increasingly multiethnic, such as New Zealand, seems to be, in light of the findings of an increasing array of research data, a policy which is difficult to support on empirical grounds.

Ecclesiological Perspectives

The main issue I want to raise here is that, even if ethnic-specific churches could be justified on those grounds, they are difficult to defend ecclesiologically, when the nature of the church is examined from a biblical or theological perspective. There is no question that the "new immigration" is changing the demographic makeup of Western societies such as New Zealand. While migration has always been a fact of history, the unprecedented numbers of recent decades, and the spread from almost everywhere to anywhere, have significant implications for the nature of religion in those societies.

For most of human history, the religion to which one belonged was determined by the geography of where one lived. One was born into faith, and religion formed the "sacred canopy" helping to bind societies together, which is why heretics were generally dealt with so harshly. Religious communities were generally ethnically homogenous. Religions only clashed when one "region" moved into another, and the conflict was eventually settled when one side won against the other and

---

21. Jackson, *Hope for the Church*, 86–93.
22. MacDonald, "From US Churches That Are Growing," 1–10.
23. An unpublished report from Lynne Taylor, statistician for the Baptist Union of New Zealand, 2010.

became the ruling power. As secularization occurred in societies this ended, leading to the pluralization of religion in those societies, as Peter Berger noted in *The Heretical Imperative*. Still, in Western societies this was mainly the pluralization of Christianity, and of European denominational forms at that.

All that has changed in the last few decades, with the arrival not only of significant numbers from non-Christian religions, but also greater numbers of Christians from non-European ethnicities, bringing their own ethnic forms of Christianity and church with them. We now have pluralistic societies, often called multicultural, a term now being somewhat contested.[24] Regardless of how we label it, we now have societies in which people of a wider variety of ethnicities, religious identities, and cultural practices are living alongside each other, particularly in large cities.

Many scholars have pointed out the parallels between this reality and the world in which Christianity spread in the first few centuries. "The region around the Mediterranean Sea was multilingual, multiracial and multiethnic, with many different religions and philosophies. The Jewish groups and Gentile nations comprised the multiplicity of cultures that Christianity sought to address and to embrace. In this multicultural arena, the diversity of early Christianity took shape."[25] A significant theme running through the New Testament, particularly in Paul's epistles, was that the unity which people from all of these different ethnicities and cultures had in Christ was primary and their ethnic or cultural identity was secondary.

There has been much debate over the centuries about what was central to Paul's theology, and those of us in the Reformed tradition have been sure it is justification. However, over recent decades that has been increasingly challenged. N.T. Wright now argues that it is "the unity of the church," the "united family" of God. "When we read Paul on his own terms, we find that for him the one, single community is absolutely central. The community of Christ, in Christ, by the Spirit, is at the very heart of it all."[26]

---

24. Some prefer either "cross-cultural" or "intercultural," as in multiculturalism different groups can exist alongside each other without any significant engagement or interaction.

25. Rhoads, *The Challenge of Diversity*, 2.

26. Wright, "Whence and Whither Pauline Studies," 266.

I believe that Wright is right, and that this is a theme which runs through all of Paul's writing. We only have space here to deal briefly with a small number of texts. The letter to the Ephesians is generally regarded as being where Paul's ecclesiology is most fully developed. Markus Barth sees Ephesians 2:11–22 as "the key and high point of the whole Epistle,"[27] and Klyne Snodgrass views it as "perhaps the most significant ecclesiological text in the New Testament."[28] What Paul is saying here is that in Christ the identity marker of circumcision, and all the other aspects of keeping the law that made the Jewish people ethnically and culturally distinct, no longer act as the marker for the people of God. The wall that divided them and kept them aliens has been broken down. There is a new identity marker, "Jesus Christ." Being in Christ marks us out as belonging to the people of God, the new humanity.

Those old identity markers may be appropriate to indicate one's human identity as Jew or Gentile, but they are no longer of any relevance in identifying those who are God's people and who have access to God. Only one thing counts; that is Christ. Through his death he has made it possible for all people, whatever their cultural or ethnic identity, to become part of the "one new humanity" who are reconciled to God. Thus Christ is "our peace," peace not only in our relationship with God but also peace with all of those who are in Christ, whatever our previous relationship with them might have been This now is our primary identity and all other identities are secondary. As James Earl Massey puts it, "The fence that once stood between them is now down. Because believers are reconciled to God, they are also related to one another. A new set of criteria applies now for human relations in the Church. In church life social distance must no longer be the order, and a sense of oneness and equality must prevail when previously-honored differences seek to intrude themselves."[29]

Paul develops this theme in other places also, such as Romans 10:12, 1 Corinthians 12:13, Colossians 3:11, and most famously in Galatians 3:28, where he broadens it to include the cultural and social divisions that demarcated slave and free, male and female. The early church struggled to keep this unity in Christ in the midst of its diversity, and much of Paul's writing deals with such episodes. A very

27. Barth, *Ephesians 1–3*, 275.
28. Snodgrass, *Ephesians*, 123.
29. Massey, "Reconciliation: Two Biblical Studies," 208.

significant occasion is the setting in Galatia, which leads into 3:28. Peter has been persuaded not to share in table fellowship with the Gentiles in the church (2:11–14) after some of the hardliners from Jerusalem arrived, and this leads to other Jewish Christians following suit. Paul's response was swift and strong. He "never wavered in his conviction that God was making a new creation by drawing into one church both Jews and Gentiles."[30] He believed it was not enough merely to maintain a spiritual unity in the universal church; it needed to be seen and experienced in the local congregation as well. The break in sharing meals together would end "the social unity of the church."[31]

This unity of all in Christ, across whatever ethnic, cultural, or social divisions, is a central theme running through Paul's longest letters, those to the churches in Rome and Corinth. It is not only a central theme of Paul's ecclesiology, but also finds profound expression in 1 Peter. In 1 Peter 2:9–10 the church (most probably in Rome) is described as "a chosen race, a royal priesthood, a holy nation, God's own people . . . Once you were not a people, but now you are God's own people." David Horrell points out that this is the only text where three central words for ethnic identity in 1st century Greek, *genos*, *ethnos*, and *laos*, are all applied to the church. The implication is that the church is a new "ethnic form of identity" that draws into it all other identities.[32]

An ecclesiology that takes seriously the parameters and implications of the New Testament, then, compels us to work for multiethnic rather than homogenous churches in our current ethnically and culturally diverse contexts. It is no wonder that, as the early church developed its theology, it came to understand that the church must be "one, holy, catholic, and apostolic"—what have become known as the "marks" of the church. We have seen in the previous chapter how they provide an interesting lens through which to examine many of our contemporary forms and practices. Developing Paul's theme of our identity in Christ, Thomas Torrance notes that these marks "do not denote independent qualities inhering in the church, but are affirmations of the nature of the church as it participates in Jesus Christ . . . They are first of all attributes of Christ himself, but attributes in which the church shares through its union and communion with him. Therefore in the unity, holiness,

---

30. Martyn, *Galatians*, 236.
31. Meeks, *The First Urban Christians*, 161.
32. Horrell, "'Race,' 'Nation,' 'People,'" 123–43.

catholicity, and apostolicity of the church it is the image and face of Christ himself that comes to view."[33]

Bearing in mind the subject of this chapter, the critical marks for us to consider are its oneness and its catholicity, and the comments made on these in the previous chapter, in relation to the Emerging Church movement, apply here also. While people of different ethnicities used to be "over there," and thus not so much an issue of everyday life and faith, today they are "over here." The church's catholicity (universality and inclusivity) and its oneness are marks that need to be demonstrated in the life of the visible church, in local congregations and denominational structures, as well as in its ecumenical arrangements. Tyron Inbody goes so far as to assert that "any church, including a local congregation, which does not intend to be catholic in the sense that it invites all manner of people . . . is not the church."[34]

This is not at all easy or natural for many of us, so deeply enculturated in our own particular ways, and often feeling uncomfortable and out of our depth with those who do not operate within those cultural norms. Jürgen Moltmann, noting the tendency for churches to be made up of "our kind of people," comments: "Birds of a feather stick together. But why? People who are like us, who think the same thoughts, who have the same things, and who want the same things confirm us. However, people who are different from us . . . make us feel insecure."[35] Consequently, even after becoming Christian we still tend to operate largely within the cultural and ethnic worlds into which we were born.

The doctoral research noted previously on PCANZ churches found that this ethnic homogeneity was reflected in the friendship of members inside as well as outside of the congregation. For others raised within in a particular cultural and ethnic form of Christianity, like the frog in the kettle, we simply live that way without thinking there might be some cultural ways of being that are not necessarily in step with being Christian and may need to be transformed, or indeed discarded, if we were to move toward a more faithful living out of our new primary identity in Christ.

---

33. Torrance, *Atonement*, 381.
34. Inbody, *Faith of the Christian Church*, 261.
35. Moltmann, *Church in the Power of the Spirit*, 30.

Gospel and Culture Considerations

The relationship of gospel and culture, as we have noted several times, has become a very significant and often hotly debated question. While many see this as arising from the rapid changes in Western societies and culture, the main factor that has led to it has been the rapid growth of new indigenous expressions and forms of faith and church that emerged in post-colonial non-Western societies. It is in this context that Andrew Walls developed his helpful description of the tension between the "indigenizing principle" and the "pilgrim principle." This is a tension which runs through the pages of the New Testament, and indeed lies at the heart of the reason many of the epistles where written. What the writers of these letters seem to insist upon is that, whenever our cultural practice is clearly in conflict with the essence of the gospel, the call of the gospel must have priority in our cultural habitus.

In the debate over single-ethnic vs. multi-ethnic churches, where our natural tendencies have pulled us toward churches of "our kind of people," the gospel impels us to challenge that predisposition, both within ourselves and others. As Paul Hiebert expresses it, "the gospel must be contextualized, but it must also be prophetic."[36] This is a difficult calling, but as the church demonstrates that in Christ God has shattered the barriers that divide the human race and created a new community, so it becomes, in Lesslie Newbigin's words, a "sign, foretaste and instrument" of the reign of God.[37] As local congregations live out a way of life that is in contrast to the wider communities in which they are located, they become, to use another Newbigin phrase, the "hermeneutic of the gospel," interpreting to the world what God is on about.[38] Ross Hastings argues that the church is intended to represent what God is like and what God is doing, and since the Godhead is characterized by unity and diversity, "the unity and catholicity of the church is so important for mission."[39]

There is a growing realization among scholars that, rather than the Roman Empire being simply the political and cultural locale in which early Christians lived, having little to do with how they shaped their ideas and actions, an essential key to understanding the New Testament is to see the Christian movement as a self-conscious alternative to the empire

---

36. Hiebert, *Anthropological Reflections*, 86.
37. Newbigin, *A Word in Season*, 60–63.
38. Newbigin, *The Gospel in a Pluralist Society*, 223–33.
39. Hastings, *Missional God, Missional Church*, 115.

which often tyrannized them. If we read Ephesians in this light, picking up from where Paul finished in chapter two with a multiethnic, multicultural, multi-tongued family of God, it this new community which in chapter three declares to Caesar that he doesn't run things any longer because in fact Jesus Christ is Lord, and that in him God is gathering all things together. Reflecting on the implications of this affirmation, N.T. Wright comments:

> As long as we continue to collude with things that no Paulinist should ever collude with—fragmentation, petty squabbles, divisions over this or that small point of doctrine—the powers can fold their arms and watch us having our little fun while they really run the show. But when there actually is one body, one Spirit, one hope, one Lord, one faith, one baptism (Eph. 4) then the powers are called to account and they will know it. Something new has happened.[40]

Forming communities like this in a society such as New Zealand, divided as it is into all kinds of fragments on all kinds of grounds—ethnicity, culture, socio-economic status, generations, lifestyle, gender—so that there are very few comprehensive communities that embrace all kinds of people, may indeed be the most profound witness to the gospel we can give. Indeed, such witness is a foretaste of what will be when God does in fact reign. As Bosch puts it, "The church can only be missionary if its being-in-the-world is, at the same time, a being-different-from-the-world."[41]

In a similar vein, John Howard Yoder writes, "The political novelty that God brings into the world is a community of those . . . whose fellowship crosses lines instead of reinforcing them. This new Christian community in which the walls are broken down . . . by the work of Christ is not only a vehicle of the gospel or only a fruit of the gospel; it is the good news. It is not merely the agent of mission or the constituency of a mission agency. This is the mission."[42]

The book of Revelation imagines a time when those who are gathered together before the Lamb are made up of a multitude of peoples from "all tribes and peoples and languages" (Rev. 7:9). They are apparently still distinguishable in their ethnicity, culture, and language, but nevertheless they are united together in worship. Of course that is an eschatological

---

40. Wright, "Whence and Whither," 267.
41. Bosch, *Transforming Mission*, 387.
42. Yoder, *Essays Ecumenical and Ecclesiological*, 91.

picture of what things will be like when all things are perfected in Christ. But living as we do in the eschatological tension of the "now" and the "not yet," we must not be content with arrangements the way they are, in our sin-marred and alienated existence; rather, we must work in the power of the eschatological Spirit toward the way things will one day be.

In considering the marks of the church, missiologist Charles Van Engen helpfully suggests that it is better if they are read as adverbs rather than adjectives, so that they capture the dynamic character of the church's faithfulness to its missional calling. This means that rather than these being standards by which we may be marked, but which we will inevitably fail to fully meet in our fractured and estranged human contexts, they are the ideal to which we are being called by Christ and pulled toward by the Spirit. The question we need to ask, then, is "are we acting as a unifying and reconciling community, rather than simply reinforcing the fragmentation and alienations of the contexts in which we exist?" Are we actively participating in God's mission in the world?

The gospel does not call us to leave our ethnicity and our cultures. Paul makes it clear that Jews can still remain Jews and follow many of their cultural practices, provided they do not try to impose them on others. Likewise, he tells different groups of Gentiles they can still practice many of their differing cultural practices (see Romans, Corinthians, Colossians). Clearly there is still a need for us to associate at times with those of our own group, to work out what it means to be Christian as Samoan, Korean, or Filipino in a strange land, and support each other in that. Likewise, at times European New Zealanders (Pakeha) may need to gather together to deal with some of our particular social and cultural practices. Some of these occasions may be helpful in introducing others from the same ethnic group to Christian community.

But at the same time the gospel clearly calls us into a new community in which those ethnic and cultural identities are not primary. Our fundamental identity is in Christ and in Christ we are baptized into a new people, a new nation, a new race, what some of the early Christian Fathers called the "third race." If this is what we are baptized into in our initiating sacrament, then it is critical that we express that reality in our other sacrament, when we share in bread and wine together. Sadly, many of the churches which have separate ethnic congregations within them cannot even agree, if they in fact acknowledge the need to, work together on a way to worship as one on the occasions when they celebrate communion. Yet, as Moltmann reminds us,

> Because the fellowship of the table unites believers with the triune God though Christ, it also causes [persons] to unite with one another in messianic fellowship. The common bread and the common cup point to the oneness of the people who partake in the one Christ, and in him with participants at all times and in all places . . . The open invitation of the crucified one to his supper is what fundamentally overcomes all tendencies toward alienation, separation and segregation. For through giving himself up to death for the fellowship of [people] with God and with one another, the godless and inhuman divisions and enmities between races, nations, civilization and classes are overcome. Churches which permit these deadly divisions in themselves are making the cross of Christ a mockery.[43]

What I believe is critical for the future of Christianity in societies like New Zealand, as immigration trends move us toward becoming an increasingly multicultural society, is that we who are God's people are committed to forming churches that are intercultural communities. In that way we may be a sign to an increasingly fragmented world of what God in Christ is able to do.

---

43. Moltmann, *Church in the Power of the Spirit*, 257–58.

11

Sport and Religion
Lens or Threat?

SPORT, LIKE MANY INSTITUTIONS, has been challenged by a shift in public tastes and perceptions over recent decades. Once sacred traditions must compete with relative upstarts and, for younger generations, team sports controlled by rigid rules are increasingly abandoned for more individualistic pursuits that allow greater freedom and creativity. The changing nature of sport parallels changes in our relationship with the religious and with God. This chapter examines the relationship between religion and sport in two ways. The first uses changes in the way people participate in sport, particularly in New Zealand, as a window through which to understand the changes that have been taking place in the way people participate in religion. The second examines how sport might function in contemporary Western societies to fulfill some of the functions that were previously fulfilled by organized religions.

Viewing Religious Change through the Lens of Sport

It has often been observed that the true religion of New Zealanders is the game of rugby. The Rugby World Cup was held in New Zealand in 2011. On the morning of the final, between the New Zealand All Blacks and France, one of the leading media commentators wrote, "Rugby is more than our national sport. It is our religion, our soul." The section covering rugby in the major newspapers is called "Rugby Heaven," and the lift-out on the Monday morning after New Zealand had finally won the World

Cup again, after more than two decades of national mourning, began: "This is . . . Rugby Heaven. Thank you, Lord, at long last!"

While the place of rugby in New Zealand society is less dominant than it was thirty years ago,[1] the way in which New Zealanders engaged with the World Cup festival in a comprehensive way, and the state of national euphoria which followed the victory, suggest that it is still commands a strong enough presence that changes in people's involvement in rugby may provide some helpful insights into changes in society as they affect people's involvement in organized forms of religion, such as the Christian church.

Forty-plus years ago, when I was a young evangelical Christian, I had two major passions in life—the church and rugby. I was not involved with fundamentalist or Pentecostal religion, which regarded sports as worldly and therefore to be avoided altogether, however, for me the church and rugby seemed to occupy very different worlds. It was clear that sport was regarded as being of limited value and importance compared to religion.

As I became more and more involved in the world of rugby, playing at senior club level, coaching a High School 1st XV and representative team, and being in the local Rugby Union, it often became difficult to reconcile the two, and for a period the world of rugby won out, particularly as it was increasingly played on Sunday. My difficulties did not relate merely to the issue of playing and practicing on the Sabbath, although that was an issue. It was that rugby and religion seemed to represent two very different cultural worlds. The argument I want to make here is that, in fact, they have a considerable amount in common and today are struggling to come to grips with similar issues, as a consequence of the significant social and cultural changes that have occurred over the past several decades.

We have constantly referred to research which has found conclusively that in most Western societies, like New Zealand, there has been declining involvement in organized religion, yet also considerable resilience, and even signs of an upswing in other kinds of religious involvement. We have also noted that this loss of belonging is something that is happening in many sectors of society, especially in the voluntary sector.

---

1. Sociologist Geoff Fougere notes that "the place of rugby in New Zealand society has changed. Increasingly it is just another sport, important, but no longer central. In a more sophisticated, more diverse society, it no longer serves as a mirror, reflecting its particular image of New Zealand society." Fougere, "Sport, Culture and Identity," 120.

One of the great characters of New Zealand in the period since the 1960s has been Tim Shadbolt, who first became prominent as one of the leading counter-culture dissidents and protestors in the student movement. In later life he has been mayor of two cities in New Zealand, the second in the southernmost city, Invercargill, where he is now in his sixth term and seems so popular that he could have the job for as long as he wants. In a recent address given to a ratepayers' association in Christchurch, he spoke on the topic of social changes in New Zealand over the past thirty years and identified, with various illustrations, the marked decline in the numbers of people wanting to be involved in voluntary organizations, whether this be the Rotary club, the squash club, political parties, or ratepayers' associations. In relation to sport, he made the remark that in playing the game of squash, for example, people only want to pay ten bucks, play a game, have a shower and a beer, and go on their way. They do not want to belong to a club that involves them in fundraising, working bees, organizing afternoon teas, management committees, or other tasks required to keep such voluntary organizations operating.

An article in *Metro* magazine in March 2006 outlined the decline in all kinds of voluntary organizations in New Zealand. Over the past decade or so this has been a recurring theme in many articles in local and national media, as clubs of all kinds have struggled to find new members and many have either merged or closed. We have previously referred to Robert Putnam's research in *Bowling Alone*, which examines the decline in the commitment of people to organized social structures. The title comes from the sport of ten pin bowling, which Putnam uses to illustrate his argument. In the U.S. more people are bowling than ever before, but the numbers in organized bowling leagues have plummeted to their lowest level ever. Putnam shows similar figures for other types of sports.

There is clear evidence, then, that sport retains a significant, perhaps even increasing value in New Zealand and other Western societies, but that across the board organized sports clubs and organizations are in decline and struggling for survival. A report on a research project by the Christchurch City Council found that "Christchurch sports clubs are struggling to stay afloat . . . [71 per cent] had a shortage of volunteers—particularly those aged under forty."[2] I already knew this from personal experience. When I was coaching a high school rugby team in Auckland which played on Saturday afternoons, I was also coaching

2. "Sports Clubs Struggling," A-4.

my son's junior soccer team on Saturday mornings because, had I not stepped in, there would not have been a team since no one else was volunteering to coach. Then, when I moved to Christchurch, I ended up coaching my other son's rugby team, despite another Saturday commitment, because the same situation arose.

Because it has been so central an element in New Zealand's cultural and social life, rugby is an interesting area of study. While the decline of church "belonging" can bring on great despair among church-goers, the figures presented elsewhere in this book look fairly healthy alongside those for rugby. Although no annual figures were kept in the 1970s, the number of those playing rugby in that decade is estimated at 400,000. This number had plummeted to below 100,000 in the early 1990s. The decline was arrested and the figure now sits at about 125,000, with the last three years showing a slight decline again.[3]

As with other sports, this has led to many clubs closing and others merging. Joseph Romanos wrote a significant book analyzing trends that confirm the declining involvement in rugby in New Zealand. One of the main indicators, he claimed, was what was happening to local rugby clubs: "Clubs are struggling all over New Zealand. Saturday evenings used to be big money spinners for the clubs. Clubrooms would be packed, full of members, and members' wives and girlfriends . . . Now many clubs no longer have clubrooms as such . . . The cost of keeping clubrooms running outweighs the financial benefits of opening them."[4]

While over this period of time the involvement of people watching major rugby games held up reasonably well, signs of a decline even in this level of involvement have been indicated over the past few years. Crowds at Super Rugby[5] games have been down in recent years, even at Hurricanes and Crusaders games, where fan loyalty had kept the number ups while they have declined elsewhere.

The South Island province of Otago has traditionally been one of the most powerful centers of rugby in New Zealand, but toward the end of the 2004 season an article was written in the *Otago Daily Times* bemoaning the small crowds at a sparsely populated Carisbrook Stadium.[6]

---

3. "State of the Union: Part II."

4. Romanos, *The Judas Game*, 130.

5. This is a competition involving teams from New Zealand, Australia, and South Africa. Originally this included 12 teams (Super 12), then 14, and now 15 (Super 15). There are five New Zealand teams.

6. *Otago Daily Times*, April 5, 2004.

Then in 2005 the unthinkable happened, when a critical test between the national team, the All Blacks, and their old enemy, South Africa, was not sold out. There was a lift in crowd numbers at Super rugby games last year in the post-World Cup euphoria, but these have dropped off this year. It was particularly concerning that the Christchurch-based Crusaders team, usually the team with the most loyal supporters, had several thousand empty seats at a home semi-final game, and that was in a temporary stadium which only seated half the number of their previous stadium (made unusable by the 2011 earthquake). Season passes sold for the 2013 season were down by 25 percent on the 2012 season.[7]

Empty seats of course mean less income, in church as in sport, and a number of provincial rugby unions have teetered on a financial knife edge. Finally, in February 2012, the Otago Rugby Union, once one of the power houses of the game, was declared bankrupt. In a remarkable parallel, in June that year the Bishop of the Anglican Church in Dunedin announced that if they continued operating in the same way as in the past they would be in the same position of collapse within two years.

A number of reports have consistently indicated that even the numbers of those watching rugby games on television have been in decline for some time. The Canterbury rugby union reported that television viewership in 2012 was down by 5 percent from 2011, and 21 percent from 2010. All Black test matches used to attract over 1 million viewers, but now if this reaches 800,000 the officials are well pleased. Television is a major source of income for rugby organizations, and this is also a concern for television companies unwilling to chase high figures to gain broadcasting contracts.

As with church-going, the future of the game of rugby depends significantly on the participation of children and young people. Numbers have held up reasonably well at primary schools, but at secondary schools there is a concerning drop-off in participation. The numbers at two of New Zealand's leading boys' schools, who have produced a significant number of All Blacks, tell the story. Auckland Grammar School in 1970 had around 1,200 students and 17 rugby teams. By 2000 student enrolment had almost doubled, to 2,000, but the number of rugby teams had remained at 17. In other words, participation on a percentage basis had almost halved. By comparison, the number of soccer teams had risen from 11 to 32. Christ's College in Christchurch had around 600 students

---

7. "Fan Fatigue Poses a Concern."

in 1970 and 21 rugby teams. By 2000, student numbers had risen slightly but the number of rugby teams had fallen to 13. In contrast, soccer teams had gone from 0 to 6.[8] It is not surprising that soccer is already the most popular sport for children between 5 and 17, with 114,000 participants, compared with 100,000 playing rugby. When young people leave school there is even further drop-off. 60 percent of those playing rugby when they were aged 15 have stopped playing at 19.[9]

A few years ago, I spent some time talking with a researcher who had been employed by the Canterbury Rugby Union to try and find out why this is happening. This, plus my own anecdotal research and general reading of cultural changes, indicate a combination of factors: rugby's hierarchical structure and organization; the authoritarian and controlling environment of clubs; rigid codes of protocol, dress, and obligation; a very conformist and highly structured culture; high institutional costs; high demands on time, over which the individual has no say; lack of choices over which teams are played, or even which position one plays; lack of choice about when one plays or practices; a culture that demands loyalty instead of individual freedom; and a repression of individual expression for the good of the team.

These are values that are increasingly at odds with the more permissive, individualistic, personal choice orientation of the wider culture. While they are seen as good values for children to learn, and hence they are encouraged into team sports like rugby by parents and educators, as soon as they get to the age of personal choice (15 onwards), if they wish to remain involved in sport they tend to do so through playing more individualistic sports. Sociologist Geoff Fougere claims that: "Its [rugby's] new vulnerability stemmed from changes in the social context which meant that, for increasing numbers of New Zealanders, the values and practices embodied in rugby were felt to be at odds with patterns newly emerging in NZ culture."[10] With an increasingly wide variety of other options available for leisure activities, rugby participation is becoming increasingly less desirable, as indeed are other highly structured team sports.

What interests me is my suspicion that these are similar to the reasons that increasing numbers of the younger generations of New

---

8. Romanos, *The Judas Game*, 212–14.
9. "A Man for a Crisis," 98.
10. Fougere, "Sport, Culture and Identity," 120.

Zealanders are turned off by organized religion. They see it as hierarchical, authoritarian, controlling, conformist, highly structured, time-consuming, lacking in variety and choices, and demanding exclusive loyalty. There are some even closer parallels between the two. The first is that while many parents encourage their children into church, Sunday School, and youth group, as places where they can learn good values and make good friends, the drop-out rate when they are able to make their own choices (from about 15 years old on) appears to be similar. The age composition of churches in New Zealand, discussed in the previous two chapters, and the findings from youth ministry surveys, confirm the huge absence from church of those aged 15 and over.

A second factor shows an even more remarkable similarity. Several reports recently have talked about a "white flight" from rugby. In Auckland in 2002, of 445 senior rugby players only 30 were of European descent. The Blues Super 12 squad that year had only 5 players of European descent, two of them imports from overseas. That ratio has improved somewhat, but this year the Chiefs, who won the Super 15 title, had only 9 players of European descent out of a squad of 34. Many High School 1st XVs are almost completely dominated by players from Polynesian ethnic groups, even in communities where they are not an especially high percentage of the population.

A spectator at an inter-school match in Auckland was overheard saying to a parent from the opposing team, "We will win because our Samoans are better than your Samoans."[11] Schools wishing to have strong rugby teams offer scholarships to attract students of Pacific Islander descent, who could not otherwise attend.[12] In the provincial district in which I grew up, the MacKenzie Club (located in cold, inland high country farming territory—especially cold in winter when rugby is played) won the local championship for the first time in 2004. The reason was that they had managed to attract six players from tropical Fiji, despite the climatic disincentive, by offering financial rewards. If not for the continuing attraction of rugby amongst Pacific Islanders, the situation in the rugby kingdom would certainly be even more alarming than it already is.

If we dig below the surface of New Zealand church figures, a similar picture exists. If it were not for the large number of new Pacific Islander and Asian congregations, the figures for church-going would have

---

11. Laidlaw, *Somebody Stole My Game*, 163.

12. This was the basis of series of articles in *The New Zealand Herald* in 2013. For the first of these, see "Two Worlds of School Rugby."

declined even more dramatically, as we identified in the previous chapter. In addition to the new ethnic congregations, there are the considerable number who worship in already existing congregations, often predominantly European in character. The common factor in this attraction to rugby and to the church is that these are cultures that still value those qualities mentioned above: hierarchical organization, leadership with strong authority figures, conformity, group loyalty above individual freedoms, structured environments, personal identity devolving from group involvement. It seems that both the traditional game of rugby and its organization, as well as the traditional approach to church life and its organization, lack much appeal for the under-forties in mainstream European New Zealand (Pakeha) culture.

Referring again to Putnam's work, his basic thesis is that traditional structures that depend on broad-based, long-term exclusive loyalties are giving way to single-stranded, less formal, smaller groups that engage only part of one's life and are easy to come into and out of. Following from this research, Robert Wuthnow examined trends in American civic involvement. He found a shift to "porous social institutions" with permeable structures, and a society marked by "loose connections," where people have much greater flexibility and limited commitments in a wider variety of networks. He quotes from a follow-up study of the "organization men" of the 1950s, which found that their "children utterly lack their father's loyalty to a specific organization, [and] are more inclined to join many ever-shifting networks than to seek a niche in one immortal hierarchy."[13]

I believe an interesting phenomenon to place alongside rugby which illustrates this is the game of "touch."[14] This only began in an organized sense in 1990, but by 2000 it had 272,000 registered participants, and it has continued to sustain similar levels of participation. This represents an increase that is quite phenomenal, especially alongside the decline in rugby. Among 18–24 year olds it is the most popular form of sporting involvement, and among 25–34 year-olds second.[15]

13. Wuthnow, *Loose Connections*, 49.

14. Touch is a game played with a rugby ball between teams, but with no tackling or kicking allowed. When one is touched by a member of the opposition one has to stop and play the ball from the ground to another player. It was mainly played by rugby players warming up before 'real' training began, but has more recently evolved into an organized sport.

15. Statistics from www.hillarysport.org.nz.

What are the contrasting qualities that make it so attractive? These are fairly self-evident. It is minimalist in terms of structure and cost. Individuals choose their own teams and their opposing teams. They choose their own name and uniforms, as well as competitions. The sport entails a limited time commitment (for a period, and then this is evaluated). Individuals can be involved in multiple teams and competitions. It is gender-inclusive. There is usually a high value placed on socializing and fun. No one minds too much if one misses a game or two. There is often a close connection between workplace and involvement, with teams frequently being fellow employees, although open to others being included. Commitment is much looser. Rather than being focused on one block of time each week, such as Saturday afternoon, it takes place at a wide variety of times, as much during the week as the weekend. In other words, "touch" is not just another form of rugby, a repackaging of the same product. Although some of the same skills are involved, it is a game whose characteristics have evolved.

One final observation on the way rugby has evolved entails looking at how those who are not playing participate. In a previous age, people used to go to the game of rugby to watch, usually as individuals, or with a mate or family member. This was either at the local club or at the stadium, where spectators merged indistinguishably into the mass crowd. Now very few people come to watch club games, and spectators at representative games are declining all around the country.

This is not a phenomenon unique to rugby in New Zealand. Grace Davie notes that "the fall in attendance at professional football matches in Britain . . . more or less mirrors the decline in religious practice."[16] Most people watch games in small groups with their friends, either in the comfort of the lounge or a bar somewhere. Occasionally they might go along to the big game, but when they do, especially among the under-forties, they tend to go as a group, often costumed and face-painted to indicate their group identity. In other words, the small group is primary, the mass crowd is secondary.

We could examine other sports and other Western countries and find similar trends. In the U.S. the big four sports are football, baseball, basketball, and ice hockey—and one only has to travel there to realize they have as big a hold on the general populace as rugby in New Zealand

---

16. Davie, *Religion in Modern Europe*, 112. She also notes that "in both activities what might be called the top divisions continue to flourish; the lower divisions (or average parish church) very much less so."

or soccer in the U.K. Yet a whole raft of recent articles chronicle their demise, and those I speak with in Australia point to similar trends.

Even beyond team sports, comparable trends are occurring. A good example in New Zealand is the very different sport (or perhaps more accurately, recreational activity) of "tramping"—or hiking, as it is known in most other countries. At some points the activity passes over into medium-level climbing or "scrambling." Again, this is something in which I have been involved for most of my life. Back in the 1960s when I was first participating, most of it was organized through tramping clubs, which often owned huts at strategic points. It was the activity of the devoted few, and one could often tramp all day and meet no one outside of one's group.

Since then tramping has increased tremendously, and the more popular tracks at times appear more like busy urban footpaths. Huts often need to be booked in advance, sometimes a year ahead. However, membership in tramping clubs has declined considerably; many have closed, some have amalgamated, and membership is largely for the over-fifties. Very few younger people join these clubs, yet the walks and tracks are full of young people from all over the world. The huts, now provided in increasing numbers and sizes, are no longer the domain of clubs for members, but are publicly provided and open to all (at a cost). It would be a mistake to see the decline of the old tramping and climbing clubs as a signal that the activity itself is on the way out. Rather, the increasing numbers who are involved are engaging in this activity in different ways. These changes are very similar to those I observed in relation to running in chapter seven. Commenting on the scene in the U.S., Barry Taylor, an astute observer of popular culture, writes:

> Like many institutions, sports have been challenged by a shift in public tastes and perceptions. Once sacred traditions must compete with relative upstarts that defy gravity. While team owners have been trying to find new ways to squeeze water from a rock, the emerging generation has moved on, creating new sports that reflect its desperate need for risk-taking, solitude, and group identity. Bored by established sports and old rules, this bored generation has taken its activity to the streets, to the mountains, to the waves, anywhere but well-defined, clearly lined fields. Kids no longer join teams and wear uniforms. They simply grab a board and start grinding. The changing nature of sports parallels our evolving relationship with God. Worship is no longer a spectator sport but an active, engaging practice.

> People consider themselves spiritual yet often have little or no connection to organised religion.[17]

The implications of this shift for religious institutions are obviously significant. It is not that people are no longer interested in sport. However, the way they want to participate in it with other people in an organized form that has changed significantly. Likewise, it is not that people are no longer interested in spirituality or religion, but the way they want to experience it, and participate in it with others in an organized form, has changed.

As we have seen, many are suggesting that we are moving away from an era of rampant individualism into a new communitarian era. However, it will be a very different form of communitarianism than what existed in a previous era, where it was marked by conformity, control, and hierarchies. In contrast, it will be one into which people bring a strong sense of individuality, and therefore it will be marked by a high degree of diversity and variety. With the democratization of everything, people want to have the freedom to make their own choices about how to participate. Yet they still seek to participate as a community, as the gang who gather at the skateboard park or the half-pipe show.

Here I believe is the challenge for organized religion: to find social forms that resemble much more a community of "touch" teams or the skateboarders at the local park than the local rugby club. This will mean a community which is much less tightly controlled, more eclectic and varied in the ways it expresses itself, greatly de-centralized in terms of organizational structure, more tolerant of diversity, offering more choices in which people make their own rules, run at a much lower cost, less demanding of people's loyalty and time, and more connected to their places of work. This will mean that the small, self-defining group is the primary form of religious belonging and the large gathering is secondary and, for many, occasional.

This presents an interesting challenge for already existing religious groups. "Touch" was originally called "touch rugby." It was a relatively informal game played by rugby players as a warm-up or between seasons to practice skills and keep fit, without the risk of injury from contact. However, it eventually developed into an officially organized game with its own competitions. At this point the New Zealand Rugby Union decided it was a game too different from that from which it had evolved to be

---

17. Detweiler and Taylor, *A Matrix of Meanings*, 244–45.

incorporated within its orbit, and so it become just "touch," with its own organization. The history of the church indicates that existing churches tend to treat new expressions of church that emerge in their midst in a similar way. I wonder if at this time in history, as the new forms and trends described throughout this book emerge, the established church might for once be able to accept them as authentic new expressions of the Christian church.

Sport as Functional Religion?

In the film *Bull Durham*, the opening sequence features photographs from the collection of Annie Savoy, whose "wall gallery serves as a sort of shrine to bygone baseball superheroes and their seemingly cosmic feats."[18] To the background of a gospel melody, Annie confesses, I believe in the church of Baseball. I've tried all of the major religions, and most of the minor ones. I've worshipped Buddha, Allah, Brahma, Vishnu, Siva, trees, mushrooms and Isadora Duncan.

I know things. For instance, there are 108 beads in a Catholic rosary and there are 108 stitches in a baseball. When I learned that I gave Jesus a chance. But it just didn't seem to work between us. The Lord laid too much guilt on me. I prefer metaphysics to theology. You see, there's no guilt in baseball, and it's never boring.

I've tried 'em all, I really have. And, the only church that truly feeds the soul day in and day out is the Church of Baseball.[19]

For Annie baseball functions like a grand myth that gives meaning and makes sense out of life. Being in the U.S. for the opening of the baseball season while working on this book, I can understand the religious devotion to which baseball gives rise. For many in New Zealand the same could be said of rugby and, to a lesser extent, for some other sports. For many in Britain, Italy, or Brazil, the object of devotion would be soccer, and for Australians and Indians it would be cricket. The well-known Australian sociologist Hugh MacKay suggests that, "If you really want to hear Australians—especially Australian men—getting excited about ritual, doctrine and tradition; if you really want to see a congregation of Australians standing and singing with passion and commitment; if you

18. Price, "An American Apotheosis," 212.
19. *Bull Durham*, Ron Sheldon (Director), Orion Pictures, 1988.

really want to understand how intensely Australians can debate a moral issue . . . listen to them talking about sport, or go and watch a major sporting contest."[20]

I first reflected seriously on this religious function of sport some years ago, while reading an article in the *Economist*, where the writer suggested that if Karl Marx had visited a contemporary Western society instead of Victorian England, he would have declared that sport and the mass entertainment culture were the opiates of the people rather than religion. It was these cultural forms that were now providing relief from the misery of their daily lives, through a vicarious form of participation and an often delayed form of gratification. Joyce Carol Oates has noted that "The decline of religion as a source of significant meaning in modern industrialized societies has been extravagantly compensated by the rise of popular culture in general, of which the billion dollar sports mania is the most visible manifestation."[21]

In the 2002 soccer World Cup, England's first game kicked off at 10.30 a.m. on a Sunday morning. The Church of England, realizing that soccer is a religion unto itself, sent an email to dioceses advising that they arrange to televise the game for parishioners and approved changing the time for services. In New Zealand, a similar occurrence happened in 1995 during the America's Cup sailing regatta in San Diego, when it was realized that what was anticipated as the final race of the series (when Team New Zealand would ultimately win the Cup) clashed with the normal start of Sunday morning worship services. Many churches provided televised coverage and delayed the start of worship. In 2013 New Zealand was once again endeavouring to win the America's Cup, this time in San Francisco. As New Zealand stretched out to an early lead in the series, and looked like winning comfortably, the television news coverage began with the words, "Its Sunday morning and the church of sport is full," as the camera zoomed into a yacht club packed full of people focussed on the big screen. The theme was picked up the following Sunday when anticipation was high that this was the day we would finally clinch the cup, with the major online news outlet running the headline: "Televangelism rife as Kiwis sold on Cup hype." The writer claimed, "we are in quasi-religious waters as Aotearoa skips over the surface of San Francisco Bay" and likened the coverage to television evangelism. The article traced

20. MacKay, *Turning Point*, 232.
21. Oates, "Lives of the Latter-day Saints," 9.

this development back to the 1980s when Rupert Murdoch decided that "sport was the religion of the masses."

Of course, as soon as one begins to talk about sport as religion one must confront questions of definition. The philosopher George Santayana thought of religion as "another world to live in," having doubtless no idea that what he thought of as religion would for many be displaced in the most immediate, existential, and emotional sense by sport. For millions of devoted fans, sports certainly do constitute a popular form of religion by shaping their world and sustaining their ways of engaging in it. Paul Tillich defined religion as "the state of being grasped by an ultimate concern, a concern which qualifies all other concerns as preliminary, and which itself contains the answer to the question of meaning and of our life."[22] Again, for millions their favourite sport is their ultimate concern, and many are willing, as Tillich goes on to say, to "sacrifice any finite concern which is in conflict with it"—a reality to which many wives, as well as not a few others, can testify.[23]

Functional definitions of religion do not see religion as being defined by core elements, but rather by its ability to perform certain functions for society. Emile Durkheim, for instance, defined religion as "a unified system of beliefs and practices relative to sacred things . . . which unite into a single moral community called a Church, all those who adhere to them."[24] He saw religion as the point of integration of values, providing ultimate reference points for society. Clifford Geertz has provided one of the most widely used definitions of religion: "Religion is (1) a system of symbols which acts to (2) establish powerful, pervasive and long-lasting moods and motivations in men, by (3) formulating conceptions of a general order of existence and (4) clothing these conceptions with such an aura of factuality that the (5) moods and motivations seem uniquely realistic."[25]

Clearly, if we use functional definitions like these, sport can function at least as a surrogate religion. The sense of national or community identification with sports teams and their successes and failures can lead either to euphoric celebration or to despair and sometimes even violence.[26]

22. Tillich, *The Shaking of the Foundations*, 6.
23. Ibid.
24. Durkheim, *Elementary Forms of the Religious Life*, 62.
25. Geertz, "Religion as a Cultural System," 4.
26. In 1999 when the All Blacks lost a Rugby World Cup semi-final to France, the leader of the Labour Opposition Party, Helen Clark, famously commented that,

Certainly for many individuals, who participate either as players or fans, sport provides a center of personal meaning and identity. If this is true for many individually, then it could be argued that, from a functionalist perspective, the symbolic place of sport in societies like New Zealand is not dissimilar to that occupied by religion in the past.

Throughout history, of course, and across multiple cultures in today's world, mythic and ritual significance has often been recognized in a number of sports and play activities. In ancient Greece, the Olympic Games were only one set of games performed in honor of the gods. In Japan, in the football game of *kemari*, ritual is far more important than the actual competition, and sumo wrestling tournaments still utilize Shinto purification rituals. In Central America, Mayans played ball games officiated by priests, on courts attached to temples, with victory perhaps demanding the sacrifice of the team captain. Amongst New Zealand Maori, the leisure activity of *poi*, the performance of the *haka*, and serving in the *waka*[27] were actions which involved ritual preparations and brought people into the sacred orbit of the gods.

In the United States sport has been identified as a form of civil religion by Michael Novak,[28] and a form of cultural religion by Catherine Albanese.[29] Other commentators have refrained from making that kind of judgment. Robert Higgs contends that "sports are like religion in many ways just as they are like war in some ways, but they are not equitable with either."[30] One of the most helpful writers on the subject is Harry Edwards, who suggests that sport is "essentially a secular, quasi-religious institution."[31] He outlines the following characteristics which the two phenomena have in common:

---

with the National Party in office, this would be good for her in the upcoming general election. She became Prime Minister. Conversely, in 2011 when the election followed shortly after the All Blacks victory, one political commentator observed that the country was in too much of a state of "post-World Cup euphoria" to be concerned about the real issues which the country faced. The governing National Party and John Key retained power very comfortably. Women's refuge centers report that when the All Blacks lose there is an increase in domestic violence.

27. *Poi* is a rhythmic activity, engaged in by women, swinging balls on the end of a rope. The *haka* is a war dance in which men participate. The *waka* is a traditional war canoe. All of these became part of Maori ceremonial activity.

28. Novak, *The Joy of Sports*, 18–34.

29. Albanese, *America: Religions and Religion*, 332.

30. Higgs, *God in the Stadium*, 15.

31. Edwards, *Sociology of Sport*, 261–62.

- Superstar athletes correspond to religion's gods and deceased players serve as saints.
- The coaches and executives who sit on boards and commissions and make and interpret the rules are like religious patriarchs and high councils.
- The reporters and broadcasters who chronicle sports events and tabulate their statistics are like the scribes of the religious traditions.
- Sports trophies and memorabilia are like religious icons.
- The formally stated beliefs that are commonly accepted about a sport are like religious dogmas.
- Sports stadiums and arenas are like houses of worship where millions of fans congregate each week to bear witness to the manifestation of their faith.
- Halls of fame as well as the most local of "shrines," trophy cases, are like religious shrines.
- The faithful or devoted fans can be identified with the "true believers" of the religious tradition.

Novak is even blunter, asserting that "sport is, somehow, a religion."[32] He notes that the joy of victory in an athletic contest often prompts a religious response, for winning generates a feeling that "the gods are on one's side."[33] Novak interprets the rituals of sport as providing a kind of mythic structure in which participants repeatedly experience death and resurrection. In this way sports, it can be argued, provide a sense of transcendence.

Where I think Novak is most helpful is in discussing the third way we suggested sport may fulfill the functions of a religion, by providing a sense of identity. Novak notes that religions normally create a sense of belonging by focusing initially on the bonding of local communities. This sense of affiliation then becomes a paradigm for the germination and nurture of larger commitments—from local to national, from earthly to universal. Sports similarly generate a sense of identity with "the home team" and the loyalty that such a self-understanding entails. One of the means for generating this group identity is through rituals that are common to both religions and sports: even as religions use chants, songs, and

32. Novak, *The Joy of Sports*, 19.
33. Ibid., 26.

certain gestures, so too do sports bond teammates and fans together by using cheers, songs, and bodily movement. While Novak's analysis is in the United States context, Desmond Morris,[34] writing about soccer in the U.K., has a similar perspective, seeing it as a type of quasi-religion which fulfills powerful psycho-social needs: to be together in significant groups, to voice support, to experience catharsis.

In New Zealand, Hans Mol, writing about religion and identity, labeled rugby a national religion. He argued that at a group level it engenders a team consciousness and "ritualizes the hug and the champagne dousing of victory."[35] He saw the game as representing the solidarity of the community or tribe against other such groups. Here the game shares with with traditional religions "emotional commitment, the strict ritual of time and rule, the legends of the past, and the stable, orderly context, the antidote of chaos."[36] Sport, then, can certainly perform the social function of religion in binding people into a community formed around certain beliefs and values.

As a new minister at a Presbyterian church in Kansas City, Brian Ellison learned a hard lesson one Sunday when the church was almost empty. A colleague told him, "Don't ever, *ever* again schedule anything at the same time as a Chiefs game." Deciding to investigate this phenomenon further, Ellison found the tailgate parties in the parking lot before a game to be a model of religious fellowship. "Speaking and listening together. Breaking bread and offering the cup. [Being] part of a group that is diverse and inclusive. United with a shared sense of purpose. All in all, it's not a bad way to spend a Sunday . . . What have we been doing—and not doing—that leaves people looking to football for fellowship, service opportunities, pastoral care and identity formation?"[37]

Interestingly, the etymology of the word "religion" is from the Latin *religare*, which simply means "to bind." This binding comes about through conflations of "ordinary" and "transcendent" qualities such as order, hope, and charisma, and reaches its ultimate context in the form of celebration, whether of a religious nature or simply a famous win in a local derby. Followers are transformed into "fans," a word which comes from *fanticus*, meaning "inspired by a deity, frenzied," which in turn comes from the Latin word for temple, *fanum*.

34. Morris, *The Soccer Tribe*.
35. Mol, *The Fixed and the Fickle*, 91.
36. Ibid., 92.
37. Quoted in Detweiler and Taylor, *A Matrix of Meanings*, 246.

Finally, I want to suggest three other connections which indicate a strong relationship between religion and sport, and which also suggest ways in which sport increasingly fulfills some of the functions previously provided by formal religions. The first is in providing an experience of transcendence or ecstasy for people. Runners, myself included, often speak of the "runners' high." I used to do my long run, of about two and a half hours, early on a Sunday morning. In Christchurch, this would be along the top of the Port Hills, with the glistening harbor and sea on one side and the plains stretching out to the snow-capped Southern Alps on the other. The experience was a real "high." I would then go to church, and I often remarked to people that I went to church twice on Sunday; guess which was the most transcendent or religious experience?

Some commentators have noted that one can find a direct correlation between the decline in institutional religious participation and the increase in "nature" recreation, with people tramping, climbing, boating, or doing whatever they can to get out into "the great outdoors" during the weekend. Connection with nature has always provided a feeling of a sacred world. My brother is a keen hiker, climber, and skier who has lived for over thirty years on the edge of the Canadian Rockies. He is one of the many who were keenly involved in church life into his early twenties, but now very rarely goes. We climb or hike together whenever we can, and he often remarks, looking across some beautiful sacred landscape, "this is my church now, this is where I experience God."

The high days and holy days of a former society have been transferred in contemporary society from religion to sport. Joseph Price writes that "the Super Bowl functions as a major religious festival for American culture,"[38] as I have witnessed. Evidence of this was seen in the reaction to Janet Jackson's exposure of a nipple in the half-time show during the 2004 Super Bowl, something that would be scarcely noticed normally, but on this occasion was seen as defiling a holy day. John Carroll points out that in Britain the national events that could be called rites are usually sporting ones, like the FA Cup final: "I mean rite in the powerful sociological sense of an activity full of sacred resonances, with an elaborate mythology, celebrated on a grand scale with strictly prescribed uniforms, rules of practice, and methods of celebration and lamentation . . . providing a common attraction for a population that for the rest of the year has extremely diverse and often incompatible interests."[39]

38. Price, "The Super Bowl as Religious Festival," 13–15.
39. Carroll, *Ego and Soul*, 29.

Note the concept of "binding together" again. The scenes in Manchester when United returned home in 1999, after winning the sacred treble of FA Cup, League Championship, and European Cup, were certainly of fanatical religious fervor. In Sydney it would be the NRL (National Rugby League) Grand Final, and Melbourne is blessed with both "Cup Day"[40] and the AFL (Australian Football League) Grand Final. In New Zealand the All Blacks in a World Cup Final is the nearest, and the scenes of euphoria and celebration that erupted immediately after the victory on home turf in 2011, and the ongoing victory parades in a number of cities in the following week, were the greatest festivals seen in the country for decades. The opening ceremony of the Olympic Games in Sydney in 2000 was a religious festival in a profoundly mythic sense, full of sacred symbols and ritual. Likewise, the opening ceremony for the Rugby World Cup in New Zealand had clear religious symbolism. Peter Lineham wrote: "You could see this clearly from each of the steps—from the opening call (*karanga*), and the sharks' heads coming together. Jonah Lomu became the symbol of the ultimate dream to be a rugby hero. He was the savior figure, and the little boy the searcher for salvation."[41] Meaning, identity, and transcendence are all provided by such events.

A final way in which I want to suggest that sport fulfills functions previously reserved for religions is in the idea of pilgrimage. In most world religions, including Christianity for most of its history, the idea of pilgrimage is an important element. Many see it as re-emerging in postmodern Western culture, in a variety of ways. Certainly it is evident that sporting pilgrimage is a dimension of this. I first began to think about this while watching the Soccer World Cup in Japan and Korea in 2002, and observing the fans following their teams from all around the world. Another experience that reinforced this for me was running the Boston Marathon in 2006—not only the event itself, but meeting runners from all over the world, along with their "support crews," in the days before and after. It really was a sacred pilgrimage for them, as it was for me.

But it became most clear at the Rugby World Cup in Australia in 2003, especially in the huge band of pilgrims following the English team. While the followers of all teams turned up at games and in the streets dressed and painted in the appropriate religious garb, those from England, festooned with red crosses on white shirts, made the religious

---

40. The Melbourne Cup, the most prestigious horse race in the Southern Hemisphere.

41. Lineham, "World Cup Shows Rugby is our 'Surrogate Religion.'"

function abundantly obvious. Clearly it provided meaning for these followers, who must have sacrificed much for their pilgrimage in search of the Holy Grail. The sense of transcendence and the experience of ecstasy was gained from participation in the events both at and around the games, let alone the worship of the demi-gods when they returned home in London. Finally, there was the sense of identity and belonging provided through such a self-identified community as they shared stories, food, and drink with fellow pilgrims. I was able to experience all of these dimensions first-hand with the tournament being held in New Zealand in 2011, and the opening game between England and Argentina in Dunedin where I live. The singing was some of the most wonderful mass singing I have experienced. All of these are functions previously provided by religious pilgrimages and religion in general.

In conclusion, what I am suggesting here is part of a wider argument. That institutional forms of religion have declined considerably in Western countries like New Zealand is indisputable. One of the mistakes of earlier versions of secularization theory was to assume that this meant that religion itself, in its deeper sense, was disappearing and would one day do so completely. However, it seems that most people are fundamentally religious, and where those needs are no longer met through specifically religious institutions, then other cultural forms are taking on some of the functions they previously performed.

This is an important issue in the debate about secularization, because if we focus merely on counting as religious what is happening with some traditional religious groups in a specific cultural milieu, then we may be blind to other religious realities. William Cavanagh, in *Migrations of the Holy*, writes that "Whether one thinks that religion continues to fade or has made a comeback, defenders and attackers of the secularization thesis tend to agree that religion, for a time, went away somewhere, at least in the West." He makes an argument that "a third option is more plausible: the kind of public devotion formerly associated with Christianity in the West never did go away, but largely migrated to a new realm."[42] Cavanagh sees this realm as being "defined by the nation-state." I would not want to deny the significance of this, and some dimensions of the "sport religion" we have identified would fit into this realm, but others would not. I would suggest, therefore, that it has become pluralized, as have so many things in our contemporary world, and migrated to many

---

42. Cavanagh, *Migrations of the Holy*, 1.

different realms, of which sport is one. Some of these others will be examined in the final chapter.

Many are suggesting today that popular culture is a significant carrier of religion and spirituality. Gordon Lynch, for example, argues that there is "a reasonable case for examining whether popular culture is now replacing more traditional forms of religion as a source of community and meaning and a medium for encountering transcendence."[43] Many have written about film as being especially important in this regard. Others see music, art, and even tourism as significant elements. I am suggesting here that sport is also another important channel. Perhaps this shift in values is illustrated by a 2004 BBC poll which asked British people aged 16–24 to name the person they admired most. David Beckham came first and Jesus came in at number 123.[44] In New Zealand a 2013 poll asked which New Zealander to name the person they trusted the most. First was John Kirwan, a knighted All Black great who has recently returned home to New Zealand to coach the Blues Super 15 rugby side; and third was Richie McCaw, the current All Black captain. Indeed, four of the first ten were sports heroes. There was no religious leader in the one hundred persons named.[45]

While sport may not be a religion in some of the traditionally established (and I would maintain critical) dimensions of the term—such as explaining where we came from, where we are going, how to behave, or how to deal with pain and suffering—I would suggest that sport does now function to carry out some of the tasks previously carried out by religions. For millions of deeply devoted fans, sport constitutes "a form of popular religion" in shaping and engaging the world, providing meaning, identity, and the experience of transcendence. If people no longer find these needs met through religious institutions, it appears that they will seek to have them fulfilled through other "secular religions," and sport has come to play an important role in this regard in "post-traditional" Western societies.

---

43. Lynch, *Understanding Religion and Popular Culture*, 30.

44. Perhaps this changing reality was reflected in the controversial decision of Madam Tussaud's Wax Museum in London to display David and Victoria Beckham as Joseph and Mary in 2004.

45. "New Zealand's Most Trusted People."

12

Religion Beyond the Boundaries

A WRITER WHO DID his most significant work decades ago has begun to gain considerable attention once again in helping us to understand the place of religion in our postmodern and post-Christendom Western world. Writing in the early 1970s, Michael de Certau shared the assumption that secularization was a *fait accompli*. His understanding of secularization, however, directly anticipated the later refinements which we have been considering throughout this work. What he believed had declined was not the presence of Christian belief or language, but the power of the church as an organized social body to control religious belief and behavior, or "to organize operations" in the broader culture. It had ceased to function as a place of strategic control.[1]

In 2007 the International Society for the Sociology of Religion Conference in Leipzig had as its theme, "Secularity and Religious Vitality." Increasingly scholars have come to accept that both of these things have been happening at the same time. That secularization has been happening, in the sense of a lessening of the control of the public spheres by religious institutions and, concurrently, the decline of involvement in institutional expressions of religion, is beyond dispute. However, as we have seen, it is a mistake to necessarily equate these processes with the loss of religion itself, and it is clear that alongside secularization there has been considerable religious vitality in these societies. As some forms of religious expression have declined, so others have risen to take their

---

1. de Certau, "The Weakness of Believing," 218.

place; or it may be, rather, that forms which have always existed have become more prominent. Charles Taylor writes:

> Now if we don't accept the view that the human aspiration to religion will flag, and I do not, then where will the access lie to practice of and deeper engagement with religion? The answer is the various forms of spiritual practice to which each is drawn in his/her own spiritual life. These may include meditation, or some charitable work, or a study group, or a pilgrimage, or some special form of prayer, or a host of other things.[2]

In exploring these shifts in the location and forms of religion, the term used by a number of scholars of so-called "latent religion" is helpful. Sometimes referred to as "folk religion" or "immanent religion," it describes the range of religious impulses latent in a population which are only manifested in response to some kind of event or crisis beyond the normal routine of life. These religious responses are latent within a large sector of the population who do not regularly attend churches, and do not have regular means of expressing their religious impulses, but they come to the surface at times of national crisis or celebration, at significant communal events, or on important occasions in the life journey of an individual or a community.

Recognition of the degree to which religion was still latent in the population emerged in Britain with the response to the Hillsborough Football Stadium disaster in Sheffield in 1989, when 95 supporters of the visiting Liverpool team were crushed to death. Within hours, Anfield, the home ground of the Liverpool team, became the sight of a massive pilgrimage and around a million people made their way to lay flowers and scarves. At the same time, the two cathedrals in Liverpool also became centers of mourning.

This awareness erupted even more dramatically with the public response to the death of Princess Diana in 1997, a massive and spontaneous outpouring of grief set within a religious framework of shrines, candles, vigils, flowers, prayers, and pilgrimage. Bryan Appleyard wrote at the time, "She [Diana] has given expression to a basic form of religious fervor that most of us thought had vanished."[3] An editorial in *The Telegraph* reflected that "The spiritual yearning which Diana's death has awoken is impossible to explain . . . But the spirituality her death has

2. Taylor, *A Secular Age*, 515.
3. *The Sunday Times*, September 7, 1997.

unleashed has shown that the yearnings of the soul are as strong as they have always been."

Many of us in New Zealand thought that, with an established church and over a thousand years of Christianity built into its culture, such expressions through religious forms were part of being British, and something that would not happen here. Princess Diana's funeral, so wrapped in that tradition, reinforced this view as we reflected on the absence of such symbolism and rhetoric in similar large-scale public funerals in New Zealand. But we are also now seeing in New Zealand, beginning with the role of the church in helping people to mourn following Diana's death, an increasing use of religious belief and ritual, mainly Christian, to process grief on a national and communal scale.

Some of the most public examples of this were noted in chapter seven, with the clearest example being the public outpourings following the Christchurch earthquake. One of the interesting aspects of this was the call by the Mayor of the city, himself not a Christian, urging people in the days after the earthquake to go to the churches to find support and help in their grief. For a few months after the earthquake, churches did report increased attendance, but this eventually returned to pre-quake levels, the pattern which usually occurs in these events.[4] Another indication that this kind of response was not just a phenomenon unique to Britain and her former colonies was the massacre which occurred at Erfurt in Germany in 2002. Here, in what had been East Germany, where the level of church attendance was as low as anywhere in the world, people rushed to normally empty churches to process their grief.

Beyond these communal occasions are its more private dimensions. If one attends the funeral of any young person whose life has been terminated prematurely, such religious sensibilities abound, although often expressed more through popular music or film than in specifically Christian forms. Or, away from the funeral itself, there is the increasing practice of placing Christian crosses with flowers as shrines on the sites where a fatal motor accident has occurred. At the other end of the age scale is the increasing trend of World War II widows to visit the graves of their dead husbands, a trend noted by Tony Walter in Britain, but also

---

4. A survey done by the combined churches of Christchurch 18 months after the earthquake found 10 percent of the population in church on any given Sunday, a level of attendance consistent with New Zealand church attendance statistics since 2000.

evident in New Zealand. Walter notes the many parallels between these and traditional religious pilgrimages.[5]

This was something I experienced first-hand during the eight years my mother lived after my father's death. He was a war veteran, and my taking her to the military section of the cemetery where his ashes were buried became a regular ritual, particularly at Christmas, Easter, and Anzac Day. This was always an occasion to bring flowers, and for her to meditate and pray. One of the things that interested me was the degree to which there was ample evidence, in the way of fresh flowers or other symbols, that other graves were also regularly visited, especially on the occasions mentioned above.

All this makes it clear that religion—and, in the case of most Western societies like New Zealand, the Christian expression of it—is much more resilient than had been assumed a few decades ago. The remaining high levels of religious believing clearly indicate this, as well as the continuing significant levels of Christian identification in census returns, even among the young. We have observed, however, that the longer these beliefs and identities are separated from attachment to specifically religious communities the more they evolve, and so it is important not to assume that the content of belief and identity conforms to previous understandings. Often the symbols, rituals, and language have been divorced from the story in which they had their meaning and so become, as it were, free floating signs that can be filled with almost meaning people like to assign.

This is the significance of the work of Daniéle Hervieu-Leger in *Religion as a Chain of Memory*. She argues that religious believers become part of a community that links past, present, and future members and passes on the tradition (or collective memory) which becomes the basis of their existence. The challenge for religion today is that one of "the chief characteristics of modern societies is that they are no longer societies of memory, and as such ordered with a view to reproducing what is inherited."[6] Hence she describes European societies as "amnesiac societies," where a memory of Christianity remains while the meaning carried by the tradition has been lost. Callum Brown's work describes similar processes in Britain. Nonetheless, the fact that these sensibilities remain, and are possibly even being heightened, means that it is important to consider what some of the means are by which these are transmit-

---

5. Walter, "War Grave Pilgrimage," 63–91.
6. Hervieu-Léger, *Religion as a Chain of Memory*, 124.

ted if they are less sustained by "the continuity of the lineage of believers" gathering together in community to sustain the memory.

Christmas and Easter

Playing a more important role than is often recognized is the place of Christmas and Easter in our culture. There has been considerable critique of these holidays, particularly by conservative Christian leaders, for their growing commercialism, replacement of essentially Christian symbols with others (such as Santa for Jesus), their drawing on "pagan" mid-winter and fertility festival rites, and the fact that they are regarded more as an excuse for a holiday and partying than as a religious festival. However, they may still serve a much greater religious function than these critics recognize.

While Christian symbols and messages are increasingly mixed with other purely secular symbols in some carriers of the festive season, such as cards, street decorations, and shop displays, other expressions such as the playing and singing of Christmas carols remain essentially traditional. In New Zealand, major carol singing occasions have in fact moved away from being held in churches, and are now outdoor public events, attended by significant numbers and organized and sponsored by "secular" groups or organizations. "Carols by Candlelight" can be a significant religious experience for many. Large "Christmas in the Park" festivals in the three major urban centers are organized by national television companies, and combine high-profile entertainment figures and a mix of contemporary commercial and traditional Christian songs and images.

Then there are the ways in which Christmas events are broadcast by television and radio programs, again usually combining commercial with religious portrayals. Many schools in New Zealand still acknowledge some recognition of the Christmas story in their end-of-year activities, despite the protest of some secularists. Finally, it is clear that attendance at church during the Christmas season is increasing. I have noted this anecdotally with friends who have not gone for years but are now attending, often persuaded by their children.

To some extent, this is the result of a move to offer Christmas services at a multiplicity of times, rather than the New Zealand tradition of Christmas morning services, a time which interferes significantly with family celebrations. The church I now attend is one of the most traditional Presbyterian churches in the country in terms of its liturgical worship and choir music. On an average Sunday there might be 120 in attendance, but for the Christmas Eve carol service last year the church was packed with over 800 people, something that did not occur five years earlier. Anglican Church figures in New Zealand also indicate an increase in attendance at Christmas services over recent years. It does seem, then, that even in the midst of a commercially driven "consumer Christmas," it still represents some form of "deep, nascent residual Christianity."[7]

The religious dimension of Easter has a less clearly defined Christian dimension in public culture than does Christmas. Easter eggs and the Easter bunny do not evoke any Christian connection at all, and the symbolism of even the cross, let alone the spices and fruit,[8] have lost any direct relationship to the faith. However, Easter still has a strong religious connection and this dimension is still portrayed in special television, newspaper, magazine, and radio programs devoted to it.

I was rather surprised when a national television poll in 2005 indicated that 31 percent of the population would attend church at Easter,[9] about three times the average weekly figure. This is even more surprising given the fact that a good number of regular church-goers use the opportunity (provided by the fact that Easter is the last long holiday weekend before winter) to escape into the great outdoors. Previously many ministers in New Zealand accepted that Easter was a time of low church attendance; but, again, the clear indications are that Easter attendance is increasing. At public events people are also setting up activities associated with Easter, such as Stations of the Cross, with reports of considerable numbers going on the "pilgrimage" through them. Clearly Easter still functions to keep alive something of the Christian tradition within the broader culture of New Zealand, as it does in other Western societies.

The ways in which religious institutions play a role in connecting with these events in the wider culture, and the fact that considerable numbers of New Zealanders are still willing to occasionally visit churches for such events, indicates that many are not as far removed from the

---

7. Percy, *Engaging with Contemporary Culture*, 58.

8. Hot cross buns are an Easter tradition in New Zealand, Australia, and the U.K. The buns are marked with a cross on the top representing the crucifixion. They are flavoured with spices, representing the spices (mainly cinnamon) laid in the cloth in which Jesus' body was wrapped. The fruit (currants or raisins) are seen as representing new life following the resurrection.

9. TV3/Colmar Brunton Poll, March 24, 2005.

church as we might often assume. Many still use the church for rites of passage such as weddings and funerals ("to hatch, match, and dispatch"), and even where these are held outside of churches they are often performed by "religious" persons who bring some religious dimension into the ritual. Often this is at the request of those involved, who may start out saying they do not want anything "religious." When I attend a wedding performed by a secular celebrant, it is also interesting to observe how frequently some spiritual or religious element is included—a reading, a blessing, a song. Somehow, in developing the service, the absence of anything spiritual or religious makes it seem rather empty and incomplete.

As indicated previously, a number of polls have found that almost half of the population attend church at least once during the year. Part of the challenge for churches in the future is determining who they count as belonging, if weekly or even fortnightly attendance is not the pattern for most. I was reminded of this at the celebration of the 125th jubilee of my high school, held in 2005 over Easter weekend, at which I had the privilege of preaching at the church service. There were 2,000 attending the reunion, and I thought that perhaps 300 or so might turn up for the service. However, 800 indicated in their returns that they intended to attend, creating some accommodation problems in a church with a capacity of about 600, and some had to be turned away. In addition, there were numbers who took the opportunity of returning "home" to attend the church in which they grew up.

Endless conversations with people whom I never thought of as "religious" or "spiritual," before and after the service, indicated that while they might not be regular church-goers, they have remained occasional attenders over the years and clearly identify themselves as Christian. They also placed considerable importance on the value of the Christian message for the good of both society and individual lives, and part of their concern had been about how their children would attain the values associated with the Christian faith. In addition to seeing the church as a place to turn in times of national or community crisis, many still see the church as a place to turn in times of personal crisis or transitions in their lives. Given then that they are "Christian vicariously,"[10] how do churches act "to build bridges of inclusion, rather than to shut them out?"[11]

---

10. Building on Daniel Hervieu-Leger's work, "vicarious religion" is the main theme which Grace Davie develops for her work in *Religion in Modern Europe*.

11. McLaren, *Mission Implausible*, 71.

Anzac in New Zealand

An interesting phenomenon in New Zealand over recent years has been the growing participation in and value placed on Anzac Day. This commemorates the day that Australian and New Zealand troops landed at Anzac Cove in Turkey on April 25, 1915, at the start of the Gallipoli Campaign in World War I. The percentage of New Zealand and Australian troops killed or wounded was very high, and on the first anniversary of that landing services were held throughout the country in remembrance of the 2,721 New Zealand soldiers who died during the eight-month campaign. Since the end of that war it has become a day when New Zealanders remember all those who died or suffered in the wars in which the country has been involved. It is something like Veterans Day in the U.S. or Armistice Day in Britain.

My earliest memories of Anzac Day are of a sacred day of commemoration of heroism and sacrifice. As mentioned earlier, my father had fought in World War II, along with three of his brothers. One was killed, my father spent over two years as a prisoner of war in Italy, and the other two returned home after battling their way up the Italian peninsula. Dad was also an amateur historian, especially of military history, and so war stories from both his own experiences and the overall story, were a significant part of our growing years. A highlight of our childhood was the regular visits with him to the movies whenever a new war film came out, along with a correction of the story on the screen with what had actually happened. We used to love dressing up in the military gear that dad had around the home, using home-made weapons to relive the battles of those heroic soldiers, always reminded that we too might one day be called upon to do the same for the freedom of our families and friends in the face of oppression. When we got to high school, military training in the Cadets, where we dressed in real uniforms and used real (if dated) weapons to learn the basics of military discipline and drills, reinforced this possibility. In this context, Anzac Day was a solemn remembrance of past sacrifices, a sacred communal ritual that bound together local communities and the nation, and also a sober reminder that our turn might also come to perform our sacred duty.

Then came a real war in which New Zealand was involved—Vietnam. The call-up for compulsory military training by ballot, on the date of one's twentieth birthday, made that a real possibility for me. In 1968 I went off from provincial Timaru to University in Christchurch at the height of the anti-war movement. Like many of my peers, I became a protestor against the war and any U.S. military presence in New Zealand. It was also at this time that I embraced the Christian faith. The possibility of military action became real as my twentieth birthday neared, and I decided that I would become a conscientious objector, the only way one could be excused if one's date came up.

Fortunately the ballot before mine was the last, as the government decided to end compulsory military training. But by then I had moved to a committed pacifist position, from which I have never departed. A consequence of this was that I came to object to Anzac Day celebrations, which I saw as glorifying war and killing, and never attended any of the Anzac Day events from the time I arrived at University. It simply became a day off from work. As a history teacher, I became committed to the argument that New Zealand's best foreign policy was one of non-aligned neutrality. During this period, Anzac Day became a rather contested holiday, and while I never took part in the anti-war demonstrations that disrupted many of them, I certainly sympathized with those who did, although they tended to divide communities rather than bind them together.

Over this period Anzac Day attendance, as well as its coverage in the media, continued to decline, becoming increasingly irrelevant to New Zealand, with some believing that Anzac Day would (fortunately) eventually disappear. This seemed to be a view shared by increasing numbers of New Zealanders, who celebrated and supported the line taken by the Lange Labour government in the 1980s, opposing nuclear weapons testing and eventually withdrawing from ANZUS, the defence alliance between Australia, New Zealand, and the U.S.[12]

In the late 1990s I began to discover how wrong I was. Reports began to appear in the media about the increasing numbers of New Zealanders, especially young people, who were attending Anzac celebrations, and a bit later about the growing crowds of young New Zealanders (and Australians) making a sacred pilgrimage to Gallipoli for Anzac Day.[13] What was going on? Being a keen cultural observer,

---

12. This lead to a strain in New Zealand's relationship with the U.S., particularly since this has been followed by an independent foreign policy which has meant that, unlike Australia, we have not joined any U.S. military action that has not been a joint U.N. action.

13. In 1996 it is estimated there were over 4,000 visitors. In 2000 the number was estimated at between 10,000 and 15,000. Brad West refers to this as "civil religious

I decided to start attending Anzac Day commemorations to find out for myself. I decided that if I were to do this, then I should make the journey to Timaru to go with my aging father on his annual solemn pilgrimage. I knew this would mean so much to him since my siblings had all lived overseas for over twenty years.

So began an annual ritual on April 25, until my father's death, of attending the dawn parade with him (or on my own when dad became too frail to brave the early morning cold), then taking him down for the veterans' parade, carefully walking along the footpath beside him as he became increasingly unsteady on his feet while he marched. Then followed the civil service and a rich time spent in the Returned Services Association (RSA) rooms talking with some of his old "cobbers." I discovered that what was being reported about increasing attendance, especially by young people, was true.

One final point of personal observation, before reflecting on what might be happening, is associated with my father's death. I had the privilege of leading his funeral. My own children, along with some of my nephews and nieces (now all in their twenties) also attended. The point in the service that really impacted them, bringing tears to their eyes, was the RSA tribute with the "ode of remembrance" and the few remaining old cobbers, including his very frail remaining brother, struggling to the front to lay their poppies on the coffin. Clearly something very deep was connecting with those in attendance, both young and old.

Grace Davie, commenting on war memorials, war cemeteries, and public anniversaries in Europe, argues that they are "crucial for a proper grasp of European religion in that they bring together a sense of national identity and some sort of religious (usually, but not exclusively Christian) teaching. In the vast majority of cases, for example, the inscription implies that the individual died for God as well as their country; war graves are marked with religious symbols and the cemeteries themselves are sacred."[14]

These words are equally relevant in New Zealand, particularly when the search for a national identity is a question that is being discussed and written about with increasing frequency. What is it that gives us a sense of being unique among the global multiplicity of communities, now that

---

pilgrimage." West, *Down the Road*, 10.

14. Davie, *Religion in Modern Europe*, 162. These words are equally relevant for New Zealand, and the latter part applies also to the visits to war graves by widows mentioned earlier in this chapter.

we no longer see ourselves as an extension of mother England or wish to be part of the American empire? Part of this quest is the search for some uniquely New Zealand rituals and perhaps, above all, for a home-grown festival that asserts our identity, a festival that does for us what Thanksgiving does for Americans, Bastille Day for the French, St Patrick's Day for the Irish, and Trafalgar Day for the English. It is in the context of this search that I believe the rising interest in and celebration of Anzac Day can best be understood.

This raises the question of how is it that this has been happening during a time when New Zealand has become clearly committed to a non-militaristic and anti-war stance. Part of the answer lies in our need to rediscover ourselves, to acknowledge who we are in this part of the world, a foundation on which to understand what it means to be "New Zealand," and for a festival to celebrate what that is. New Zealanders are desperately short of festivals. Like every human society, we crave occasions that mark and define us in some way. Ritual observations are as important to societies as they are to families and individuals. Our participation in such occasions is part of what actually constitutes our sense of self. These are not merely symbols but acts of affirmation.

Increasingly, especially among the young, we are developing grander rituals to celebrate births, significant birthdays, weddings, graduations, retirements, and funerals. On a societal scale we do make something of Christmas, and as we have seen it does retain something of its religious significance, but that can easily be swamped by all the commercial activity that surrounds it. However, Christmas is someone else's festival, imported from Europe, where most of the rituals make sense in the midst of a cold dark winter; we still have not quite worked out how best to celebrate Christmas in the warmth of a southern summer. Likewise, some of the religious symbolism of Easter, having to do with new life in spring, is lost in a southern autumn. Christmas and Easter will persist, of course, partly because they have intense religious significance for at least a significant group of people. They will also persist because the commercial drives now loaded onto them are irresistible in a consumer culture, and because any festival is better than none. However, in an increasingly pluralistic society they will not become festivals of national identity.

But the longing for a national festival will not go away. The only other alternative is Waitangi Day, which commemorates the signing of the Treaty of Waitangi between many Maori Chiefs and the British Crown, allowing New Zealand to become a British colony. An attempt to make it a national festival was made when it was briefly renamed New Zealand Day. However, Waitangi Day is too divisive and contested, an opportunity for debate and protest more than celebration. Besides, festivals need heroes and Waitangi mostly throws up villains rather than heroes. While Captain Cook, the first Britain to land on New Zealand soil, appeals to many, Governor Hobson, who signed the Treaty, is difficult to frame in heroic terms.

The search is still going on, and there is such a dearth of suitable occasions in our cultural calendar that even a grand rugby final, the Bledisloe Cup,[15] a Super 15 Final, or above all a World Cup, are becoming increasingly ritualized to provide the sense of ritual and excitement that communities and individuals crave. Yet despite the deep hold of sport and especially rugby on our psyche, these cannot provide the ongoing sense of national identity for which we long, however much the mood of the nation may temporarily fluctuate in response to results.

Festivals need two things to work: a symbolic hero—or a symbolic group of heroic figures—and a powerful sense of relevance to the lives of ordinary people. Sacrifice on behalf of others is also a powerful theme. This is where Anzac Day comes in. While there is no one hero who stands out in the national psyche (although increasingly Captain William Malone seems to be granted that status for his heroic deeds at Chunuk Bair), the collective group of New Zealanders who fought, were injured, maimed, or killed clearly qualify for the role of heroes. This is particularly so when the story is seen as one of heroic failure, in which victory could possibly have been won if it had been left to the Kiwis and "Diggers"[16] to run the show, and if they had not been needlessly sacrificed by incompetent British officers, who incidentally believed that colonial blood was worth less than good British blood, as they sent yet another wave over the top to certain death.

Clearly these men qualify as heroes, especially when the stories are told of the mutual respect that developed between the Anzacs and the Turks. Colonel Mustafa Kemal (Ataturk), the Turkish commander who went on to become the first the first President of Turkey, said this of the Anzacs: "Those heroes who shed their blood and lost their lives, you are now lying in the soil of a friendly country. Therefore rest in peace. There is no difference between the Johnnies and the Mehmets to us where they

---

15. A cup played for each year in a three-game series between New Zealand and Australia.

16. The nickname given to Australian soldiers..

lie side by side in this country of ours. You, the mothers who sent their sons from far away countries wipe away your tears, your sons are now lying in our bosoms and are in peace. After having lost their lives on this land they become our sons as well."[17] A memorial to Ataturk stands alongside the New Zealand Memorial at Chunuk Bair, and there is now a memorial to him as well in Wellington, New Zealand. Each year on Anzac Day the Turkish ambassador reads the words which Ataturk spoke nearly a century ago.

There also remains a very strong personal connection between contemporary New Zealanders and the events which Anzac Day commemorate. Such a high proportion of young New Zealanders fought at Gallipoli that almost every family has a story of a grandfather or great-grandfather, a great-uncle or some other relative who was part of that epic venture, and whose story is part of the family's folklore, usually along with some treasured artefacts. If not directly linked to Gallipoli, then somewhere in the family story there is a connection with at least one of the one-in-seventeen New Zealanders who were killed or maimed on one of the battlefields of World War I. My connection is with a great uncle who landed at Gallipoli, but was taken away wounded, and wrote a last letter home before leaving for France to be killed at the Battle of the Somme.

Not only is there a personal connection, but the story is told in such a way that we are reminded that the freedoms we have today in New Zealand are a consequence of the sacrifices these heroes paid to keep us free from tyrannical foes who would have overrun us if they could (even if that is a bit difficult to really justify from World War I). A young female New Zealander, writing on her blog about the increasing attraction which Anzac Day has for her, commented, "They made the ultimate sacrifice, with their lives, for our freedom. We hold up the All Blacks, sporting heroes, scientists, men who climbed mountains, and yet we should remember that the reason we can do this is because of the actions of men and women who fought for us and died for us." The significance which this tradition is given in New Zealand is evident in the fact that, in the poll of most trusted New Zealanders mentioned in the last chapter, the person who came second, between two sporting heroes, was Willie Apiata, who in 2007 became the first New Zealander to be awarded the Victoria Cross since World War II.[18]

17. http://www.mch.govt.nz/nz-identity-heritage/national-monuments-war-graves/ataturk-memorial.

18. Awarded for heroic bravery under fire in Afghanistan in 2004, carrying a badly

Finally, sacrifice in itself has considerable appeal, and there is no doubt that the death of these men has been couched in the terms of sacrifice for a greater cause—the freedom of others—even if, in the initial flood of volunteers, the chance to go on a grand overseas adventure and see some real action may have been a greater motivation. The idea that anyone would be prepared to die to ensure the freedom of the rest of us is such an astonishing and inspiring concept that, even when it is linked to what we now regard as the horror and futility of war, it becomes noble.

Historian and poet Keith Sinclair saw in Gallipoli the beginnings of our national identity. Those who produce television programs continue to support that line. The Prime Minister Helen Clark, in her address at the dawn service at Anzac Cove, Gallipoli in 2005, said, "It was here that our young nations [New Zealand and Australia] began to come of age. It was from here that we began to think of ourselves as not just servants of the British Empire, but as distinct national entities. Thus out of catastrophe, each of our nations emerged with a new sense of certainty about our own destiny and place in the world."

In fact, neither Sinclair, nor the Prime Minister, nor popular media presentations are entirely correct. New Zealand troops continued to serve under British command (despite Deputy Prime Minister Jim Anderton's claim to the contrary while unveiling the memorial to Captain William Malone in 2005). In 1932 New Zealand rejected Britain's invitation in the Statute of Westminster to take its independence (this was left until 1947), and when World War II commenced Prime Minister Michael Joseph Savage declared, "Where Britain goes we go, where she stands we stand." New Zealand actually declared war on Germany before Britain did. This loyal attitude meant that we kept troops in Europe to fight the Germans at Winston Churchill's request, while Australia withdrew from the European war to defend her own territory from the much more present threat provided to both countries by Japan.

However, as is often said, "What people think happened in history is more important than what actually happened." It is the former that becomes part of mythic history, and it is this that takes the form of myth and shapes our behaviors and identities, both corporately and individually. Durkheim saw the function of religion as being to integrate individuals into "one single moral community." He argued that an individual's religious faith is ultimately derived from the faith of the

---

wounded soldier across a battlefield.

community, and that this is generated as people signal to each other through symbols and ritual activity that they hold the same things sacred. Kelton Cobb writes that "When religious myths are on the wane, other myths appear to take their place . . . Identifying them is a matter of determining which of our cultural stories are performing this function of providing the plots and exemplary figures and actions around which we form our identities, measure the dignity of our actions, and derive the sense of meaning we grant to the world."[19]

There is little doubt that the Anzac story is developing this mythic function, and that Anzac Day is increasingly taking on this symbolic and ritual role. It is being increasingly sacralized so that the memory becomes sacred. There is a greater chance of shops being free to open on Good Friday and Christmas Day than on Anzac Day. As the interest in Anzac Day increases, along with the growing volume of television programs, films, new memorials, and sacred sights, and as growing numbers of young people make the religious pilgrimage to Gallipoli, so it takes on an increasingly mythic and therefore religious role in our culture.

It is true that this event did not shape our nation at the time, but a sense of nationhood and identity needs stories of mythic dimensions that can be remembered symbolically, and celebrated through ritual and festival, and young New Zealanders are increasingly joining with the remaining older New Zealanders in doing this. As they do so they are developing a sense of national identity which will continue to shape us into the future, one to which perhaps all New Zealanders can feel they belong. As this develops and grows, it will fulfill some of the deep and fundamentally religious needs for festivals, symbols, and rituals that help to define us as a people.

As the appeal of Anzac Day continues to grow, we seem to be creating a festival that combines solemnity and celebration. It is no longer, as people like myself once thought, anything to do with the glorification of war. It is about sacrifice and hope. It has come to celebrate values that many New Zealanders consider either distinctive or admirable about our country: mateship, unity, courage, self-sacrifice, loyalty. More than any other day in our calendar, it calls on us to answer some challenging questions. Who are we, these people for whom so many others gave up their lives? What are we making of this way of life for which people were once prepared to die? How do we measure up against those values? Are

19. Cobb, *Blackwell Guide to Theology and Popular Culture*, 123.

we building the kind of society that justifies the sacrifice of so many, not only those who died but those who thought our ideals were worth fighting for? We are reminded of these challenges by those leading services of celebration and remembrance and speaking on the media. Facing us with these questions is a fundamental function of religion, and answering them helps to fulfill our spiritual needs.

The experience known as Anzac, then, sits alongside many other signs of growing interest in forms of religious or spiritual ritual, symbols, festivals, or pilgrimages within New Zealand society. While in the case of Anzac this is not primarily perpetuating the Christian story, or myth, one only has to attend an Anzac Day service to realize how intertwined it has become with Christian concepts and rituals, both historically and in the present, to see that it has become an important national event with which the Christian church can continue to identify.

It could be argued that in New Zealand, as in other Western societies, the Christian religion's concept of laying down one's life for a greater cause has been used to "sanctify the sacrifice" of those who died for their friends and country. This says something not only about our national identity but also about the role which Christianity has played in shaping our culture. The church is often significantly involved in these ongoing remembrances, and as it does so it can continue to shape it, thereby not only serving the needs of a developing national identity, but also fostering the symbols and values of the Christian faith within the culture.

Popular Religion

I should make it clear that I am not suggesting that New Zealand has had a civil religion, or urging that it needs to develop one. An attempt to argue this for New Zealand was made by Hans Mol in a 1982 work on religion and identity in New Zealand.[20] I do not believe such an attempt will work here, and I agree with Michael Hill's assessment that in Western societies the concept remains "particular to the United States where its resilience is underpinned by a millennial-utopian ideology."[21]

Likewise, efforts to develop a civil religion by conservative religious groups in New Zealand since the campaign against the homosexual law reform bill in the mid-1980s, modeled on the success of the "religious

---

20. Mol, *The Fixed and the Fickle*.
21. Hill and Zwaga, "Civil and Civic Engineering," 25–35.

right" in the U.S., have met with abject failure. New Zealanders by a considerable majority have avoided buying into such an agenda, and the Christian political parties which have been formed since have never won more than a small handful of the 120 seats in parliament—indeed, in the two most recent elections they have won none. At the same time, the concept being explored here—of prevalent folk or latent religion, outside of religious institutions and carried by the kind of forms we are considering—is significantly more widespread than either academics or the media have been willing to acknowledge, at least until very recently.

Thus far we have examined the way in which popular cultural rituals or festivals with a historic religious base serve this function. But what about what might be more properly called "popular culture" itself? As we have seen, Gordon Lynch argues that with declining church-going, popular culture may now be "replacing more traditional forms of religion as a source of community and meaning, and a medium for encountering transcendence."[22] We have already seen how sport functions to provide both community and an experience of transcendence for participants, although we have suggested it falls short in providing meaning. Clearly, though, other forms of popular culture such as music (Bob Dylan, U2, Reggae, Hip Hop, Gothic) do provide meaning, as well as creating community and the experience of transcendence for devotees. Conrad Ostwalt outlines this growing sacralization of secularized societies.

> Yet even when this secularization and the loss of mystery occur, the religious sensibility does not disappear, and the need for mystery is dispersed through areas of life besides traditional religions. As religious beings, we desperately search for myths in other places, in art, in literature, film and a variety of cultural forms. If secularization has demythologized our religion, then it has also re-mythologized our culture, and we find ourselves needing mystery, needing to think in some other way than empirically, needing to visualize in some other way than literally – we need and nurture this re-mythologization . . . we want to continue to believe things are not always as we see them and hear them. If institutional religions no longer allow that belief, the religious sensibility will search for it elsewhere . . . As the secularization of society continues, so does the dissipation of functions formerly reserved for religious institutions. We find popular culture functioning in some of the same ways as institutionalized religious ritual, so that popular culture is the entity

22. Lynch, *Understanding Religion and Popular Culture*, 30.

that provides the context for understanding values, belief systems and myths.[23]

One particular cultural form, to which many are now paying attention, which provides all three dimensions for large numbers of people is film. Joseph Lyden[24] argues that film represents an important source of myth within contemporary society. The experience of watching a film is that of being temporarily drawn into an alternative experience of reality in which we are exposed to particular stories about basic issues of human existence. The myths portrayed on the screen may offer idealized stories of how life might be lived or dilemmas resolved, and so can serve as a challenge as to how we might live in the real worlds we inhabit. In offering an image of how we can live and act well, they can become a resource for reflecting on our own existence. Among the themes which can be readily identified in popular films are the search for identity; alienation and redemption; the sacredness of the universe; grace and forgiveness; the nature of friendship and love; what it means to be human; the nature of evil and the cause of suffering. Nor does it seem that this is merely accidental. The great film director, Martin Scorsese, has said:

> When I was younger . . . I wanted to be a priest. However, I soon realised that my real vocation, my real calling, was the movies. I don't really see a conflict between the church and the movies, the sacred and the profane. Obviously there are major differences. But I can also see great similarities between a church and a movie-house. Both are places for people to come together and share a common experience. And I believe there's a spirituality in films, even if it's not one which can supplant faith . . . It's as if movies answer an ancient quest for the common unconscious. They fulfill a spiritual need that people have: to share a common memory.[25]

The religious or spiritual dimension of George Lucas' *Star Wars* saga has been widely dissected, and in New Zealand some 51,000 individuals in the 2001 census identified their religion as "Jedi" (as did considerable numbers in the U.K.). Lucas himself was quite explicit about the religious dimension of his films. In an interview with Bill Moyers, he claimed that it was unfortunate that younger people no

---

23. Ostwalt, *Secular Steeples*, 26.
24. Lyden, *Film as Religion*.
25. Wernblad, *The Passion of Martin Scorcese*, 21.

longer affiliated religious institutions as they had in the past, learning there the myths from which they gained their values and beliefs. He felt this was a great loss for society, and hence what he was attempting to do in *Star Wars* was to create a new myth, around which people could gain a religious perspective to provide values and beliefs. He hoped that this would not be tied to any one particular religion, but a myth by which any religion could be carried.[26] As one commentator has summarized this view, "In an era in which Americans have lost heroes in whom to believe, Lucas has created a myth for our times, fashioned out of bits and pieces of twentieth century U.S. popular mythology . . . but held together at its most basic level by the standard pattern of the adventures of the mythic hero . . . Lucas has raided the junkyards of our popular culture and rigged a working myth out of scrap."[27]

Since then other sagas such as *Star Wars, Harry Potter, Matrix, Lord of the Rings* and now *The Chronicles of Narnia* have clearly performed a similar function. However, as was mentioned in chapter seven, many more popular and not so obviously spiritual films, such as *Forest Gump, Shawshank Redemption, As it is in Heaven, Doubt,* and *Whale Rider* also function in similar ways. Geoffrey Hills writes that

> As ironic modern worshippers we congregate in cinematic temple. We pay our votive offering at the box office. We buy ritual corn. We hush in reverent anticipation as the lights go down and the celluloid magic begins. Throughout the filmic narrative we identify the hero. Vilify the antihero. We vicariously exult in the victories of the drama. And we are spiritually inspired by the moral of the story, all the while believing we are modern techno-people, devoid of religion. Yet the depths and intensity of our participation reveal a religious fervour that is not much different from that of religious zealots.[28]

Lest it be imagined that all of this still simply fits within the realm of entertainment, and is only a kind of pseudo-religion providing a substitute for real transcendence and meaning-making that actually changes the way people think and act—as does "real" religion—Robert Johnson cites particular examples of people who have had significant religious

---

26. Moyers, "Joseph Campbell and the Power of Myth." See also Moyers and Campbell, *The Power of Myth*.

27. A. Gordon, cited in Martin and Ostwalt, eds., *Screening the Sacred*, 73.

28. Hill, *Illuminating Shadows*, 8.

experience in the context of watching film.[29] I am sure that those who, like myself, are reasonably regular film-goers can all identify moments when our thinking or behavior has been modified as a consequence of watching a particular film. In addition, there are the unconscious changes in our thinking and therefore behavior, which conservative religious critics of Hollywood's "agenda" assure us are happening, while those in the industry reassure us are not.

One final reflection on the role of film as a carrier of religion in contemporary culture is the particular genre of "Jesus films." Earlier films, such as *King of Kings* (both 1927 and 1961 versions) and *The Greatest Story Ever Told* (1965), tried to be "faithful" to traditional understandings of the gospels and understandings of Jesus, and the strict censorship codes ensured this. The last popular film of this type was Zefferelli's *Jesus of Nazareth* (1977), and most since have followed the interpretive licence shown by the more popular *Jesus Christ Superstar* (1973). In this genre are *Monty Python's Life of Brian* (1979), *The Last Temptation of Christ* (1988), and *Jesus of Montreal* (1989). Mel Gibson's controversial *The Passion of the Christ* (2004) was a return in some ways to the former although, given its own interpretive slant, it is highly disputed as to how "true" to the text it was.

There are two relevant observations on all of this. Frist, the popularity and tremendous box office success of *The Passion of the Christ* was a surprise to most, and a further reminder of the great interest in religion in general, and Jesus in particular, that still remains in the culture. But secondly, I would suggest that this kind of film performs another significant function. We have seen that one of the issues for a Christian memory in societies like New Zealand is that, while the symbols and images may remain, they have been removed from the story and are therefore devoid of meaning. If the young are no longer hearing the story in our Sunday Schools, then at least they are hearing a form of it through these films; and that, I would argue, is considerably more important than getting the exact details correct.

I would also suggest that perhaps the dominant image of Jesus and the gospel story for baby boomers is that provided by *Jesus Christ Superstar* (either on stage or film, or both); and for GenerationX it may be *The Passion of the Christ*.[30] These films are probably more significant shapers

---

29. Johnston, *Reel Spirituality*, 19ff.

30. Some might wonder why I have not included *The Jesus Film*, which some have claimed is the most widely viewed film in history, and which has been translated into

of the image of Jesus for these generations than are Matthew, Mark, Luke, or John. Personally I have no question as to which is the image and story to be preferred, but would argue that any story is better than no story. At least film images of Jesus might begin to get people thinking about and reflecting on the story and what it might mean for them. I would also suggest that the same is true for the even more controversial and speculative version of the Jesus story portrayed by *The Da Vinci Code*.

Consumerism and Religion

One of the things that all of these forms of religion we have been considering have in common is a degree of consumerism. Clearly film fits into that category; but also at Christmas and Easter, alongside the religious dimension there is the opportunity to consume by purchasing items and also buying gifts for others. Indeed, in both of these events the giving and receiving of gifts and cards is central to the rituals. This is true to a much lesser extent of Anzac Day, but there is the traditional commercial activity of purchasing poppies to wear. In addition, the production of books, magazines, films, and television programs that are available for purchase for oneself or as gifts is increasingly associated with Anzac Day in New Zealand.

It seems, then, that in contemporary culture the association of religion with the consumer impulse that is now so strongly culturally embedded does seem to be helpful for religion. We found in chapter two, when examining the cultural and social changes that have impacted on religion, that one of the dominant themes was a shift from religious commitment to religious consumption, noting the analysis of this theme by Marler and Roozen, and also by Bibby. Others have also identified this shift, including Davie's description of the shift from obligation to consumption in Europe.[31] David Lyon uses the metaphor of Disneyland in interpreting much of contemporary religion, and writes, "Consumerism has become central to the social and cultural life of the technologically advanced societies in the later twentieth century. Meaning is sought as a

---

many different languages. However, it is used by a specifically Christian organization, Campus Crusade, for specific purposes, and I do not think it could be regarded as part of popular culture.

31. Davie, *Europe: the Exceptional Case*, 174ff.

'redemptive gospel' in consumption. And cultural identities are formed through processes of selective consumption."[32]

Consumerism is generally viewed negatively by Christian leaders. Partly this is because of the shift from commitment to consumption, which has led to a lessening of the sense of duty to religious institutions, a loyalty from which they benefited for so long but now only receive from their more elderly members. Duncan McLaren writes that "As people come to view religious outlets not as objects of loyalty and commitment, but as service providers there to meet their spiritual needs and wants, they will tend to make the same ideological assumptions about such outlets as they make about the market."[33]

Many Christian leaders identify this as an expression of the materialism so rampant in our culture. Those more to the left see it as being part of the economic injustice of our society that leads to the poor being exploited and ripped off, while those to the right tend to see it as part of the preoccupation with the material that leads away from concern for the spiritual. Rather ironically, many in the latter group have been superbly successful at using the very marketing and merchandising techniques of consumerism to sell their particular brand of Christianity. I would argue that the critique of both, in seeing consumerism as primarily about materialism, is to misinterpret what it is about at a deeper level, and therefore to identify how it might be positively embraced by religion, as a number of authors are now suggesting.

We noted in chapter 2 how Robert Inglehart argues that, in the conditions of economic affluence and security that prevailed in most Western countries immediately after World War II, there was a gradual shift in which the "material needs" for physiological sustenance and safety became less dominant and needs for belonging, esteem, and intellectual and aesthetic satisfaction became more prominent. This prolonged period of high prosperity encouraged the spread of "post-materialist" values.[34]

This is a very important point that many of the critiques of consumerism fail to see. While an older generation may have accumulated material goods for their economic value, increasingly for baby boomers, and even more so for the generations following, they are purchased for something other than utilitarian gain. They are valued because of the

---

32. Lyon, *Jesus in Disneyland*, 74.

33. McLaren, *Mission Implausible*, 177.

34. Inglehart, *Modernization and Postmodernization*, 33–35.

meanings they communicate, and the meanings conveyed enable the construction of individual identity. The slogan "you are what you buy" has become profoundly true—or, as a tee shirt popular a few years ago put it, "I shop, therefore I am."

I was deeply aware of this while, along with many thousands of others, I was busy purchasing heavily over-priced goods at the fair preceding the Boston Marathon in which we were competing. The value was not in the quality of the tee shirt or jacket itself, but in being able to wear the all-important Boston Marathon 2006 logo as part of one's identity. It is still a symbol I wear proudly on certain occasions, a signifier of part of who I am. So the consumption of religious goods helps to give meaning to the consumers' lives and to give them a particular religious identity over against other identities. "Consumption is therefore more about meaning than acquisition; consumerism is more about identity than materialism. Strictly speaking, then, the threat posed to Christianity is not the material verses the spiritual. It is, rather, a competition between systems of meaning and identification.[35]" If this is so, then it stands to follow that it is important for Christianity to engage positively with consumerism, in ways in which individuals in the act of consumption are helping to find Christian meaning and therefore build a Christian identity.

A third thing about consumerism is that at its core lies the primacy of individual choice. It could be argued that consumerism actually empowers the individual and gives the greatest freedom to the individual. This is the argument of the advocates of the rational choice theory of religion, such as Rodney Stark and his associates, who claim that a free market and competition actually increase religion participation.[36] The argument is largely dismissed by most academics, especially outside of the U.S., and in the form presented it undeniably has enough significant counter-arguments to prevent it from being accepted as a universally applicable theory to explain religious vitality or stagnation.

However, I would suggest there is some merit in the concept, and it helps to go some way toward explaining why sectarian and more conservative forms of Christianity have done better since the 1960s. These have never relied on a privileged place in society, and so have to some extent always operated in a religious market seeking to win over new customers. Certainly since the 1970s and 1980s, these forms

---

35. Percy, *Engaging with Contemporary Culture*, 52.

36. A good introduction to this can be found in Young, ed., *Rational Choice Theory and Religion*.

of Christianity have become very sophisticated and unabashed about adapting their religion to the mores of a consumer culture, so as to compete in the "spiritual marketplace."

Televangelism and *Alpha* are two examples of this which have been widely commented upon, generally in a critical manner. Another is the mega-church phenomenon in the U.S., with churches developing very consciously like shopping malls, making a variety of experiences, services, and goods available for customers to choose from. Still another is the whole production of a Christian media sector: Christian music, Christian films and videos, Christian radio and television programs, billboards and television advertising, tee shirts, jewellery, posters, and so on. Nearly all are produced from the more conservative sector of the church.

Likewise, it has been largely more conservative churches who have sought to engage, either critically or positively, with such media phenomena as *Harry Potter*, *The Passion of the Christ*, *The Chronicles of Narnia*, and *The Da Vinci Code*. It is no wonder that overall they have shown considerably more vitality in this kind of culture than have more mainstream churches, who have often been critical of this approach and have felt that to engage in it themselves would be "lowering" themselves to the same level as these more populist forms of religion. "There is a conversation about God going on in popular culture that the church is not engaged in and is often unaware of. If the Christian world continues in its scholastic mode, viewing popular culture as degraded and superficial, then the gap between church and culture will continue to widen."[37]

There are many other forms that could be explored here. The internet is a significant carrier of every form of religious view that can be imagined. Type almost any word to do with religion into Google and the number of websites that appear is staggering. Clearly there is a significant amount of religious exchange and consumption taking place in the virtual world. Then there is the sale of books. The tremendously high sale figures for books such as *The Da Vinci Code*, Tim LaHay's *Left Behind* series, *Chicken Soup for the Soul*, Rick Warren's *The Purpose Driven Life*, Scott Peck's *The Road Less Travelled*, Paul Young's *The Shack*, or Marrilynne Robinson's *Gilead*—to mention only a few—indicates that this is a significant form of religious communication. Books on spirituality and self-improvement, the latter usually having a significant spiritual dimension, have often been identified as the most rapidly growing sector in the book market.

---

37. Detweiler and Taylor, *A Matrix of Meanings*, 23.

Wandering around any market indicates that there is a considerable market for religious symbols, images, and icons, and these kinds of signs appear all over the place in our culture. Apparently in Russia the post-communist era has seen the emergence of large religious fairs or markets at which all kinds of "Orthodox" religious goods are for sale, quite detached from the Russian Orthodox Church itself. A trip to England or Europe makes it very clear that pilgrimages to cathedrals and other significant religious sites, such as Iona in Scotland, Lourdes in France, the Vatican in Italy, or Santiago de Compostela in Spain, are big business also.

It is also obvious that people at these sites are not just doing a "tourist" thing; for many a significant religious experience itself is taking place as they meditate, pray, or reflect. In addition, the purchasing of prayers, sayings by significant religious figures or saints associated with the sites, pictures or paintings, statues, icons, and other religious items indicates that this it is regarded as not just a momentary activity, but as something they hope to sustain into the future.

In other words, it appears that some of these things suggest that more is going on in this kind of religious consumption in the wider culture than just some tenuous religious acknowledgement which a simple "yes" to a poll question "Do you believe in God?" reveals. As we have seen, polls in New Zealand consistently indicate that 70 percent of people believe in God, and a similar number say that they pray often. This suggests that the cultural religious consumption is about more than merely consuming goods. These items are then used by significant numbers of people for establishing a religious identity, and also as a means to be involved in one of the most foundational of all religious activities, praying to the religious or spiritual reality in which they believe. Religious items are not just signs that help to give the purchaser some kind of religious identity; they can also help people to engage in religious activities and rituals. The widespread nature of this activity also suggests that latent or folk religion may not only be used by people in times of crisis or transition, but more frequently than may be imagined in the ordinary course of daily life.

Conclusion

To conclude, it seems clear that despite apparently declining levels of regular involvement with and commitment to religious institutions, there is little evidence that religion is becoming less of a feature within contemporary Western societies, including New Zealand. It is clear that religion is considerably more important than people thought it was two decades or so ago, and there are many indications that it may even be increasing in importance, not just in the number of public issues in which it is a factor but also as a contributor to how people construct their identities.

One of the dangers of this kind of popular or folk religiosity is that it could just descend into a pure individualism, the kind of personal religion or faith constructed by the self for each individual from the wide cafeteria spread of options available in the marketplace, put together in a way that suits the individual alone. This is one of the criticisms made of it by conservatives in particular. We have mentioned several times that historically the root of the word "religion" comes from "to bind together," and that sociologists have tended to see this as the function of religion in communities. If religion today is carried more in forms found in the wider culture outside of institutions, and less by the institutions that previously performed this function in communal settings, then it is obvious that if religion is to continue to perform this important social function, then religious institutions need to affirm and engage positively with these cultural forms of religion. By doing this they can help them move toward valuing the collective and communal, rather than simply being consumed to meet the personal needs of the individual.

This is an area of contemporary religion that I suggest needs to exercise considerably more thought and energy of religious leaders, beyond their current preoccupation with the future of the institution itself that is so all-consuming for many. Religion has historically been a significant resource for the social good of communities. That role was significantly diminished by the trends that first emerged in the 1960s. However, since the 1990s, rather than continuing to decline as was expected, there are many signs that religion may be increasing in its significance for individuals. It can play an important role once again as a resource for social and communal good, but for that to occur religious organizations and groups will need to significantly alter what they value and where they place their energy, turning more to the wider culture and less to the institution itself.

Bibliography

"Age of Rockers Sustains Mega-Church." *The Evening Post*, June 5, 2000, 5.

Albanese, Catherine. *America: Religions and Religion*. Independence, MO: Cengage Learning, 2012.

"Altars of Intimacy." *The Press*, January 27, 2004, B–5.

"A Man for a Crisis." *New Zealand Rugby World* (February, 2004) 98.

Ammermann, Nancy. *Congregation and Community*. New Brunswick: Rutgers University Press, 1997.

———. "SBC Moderates and the Making of a Postmodern Denomination." *The Christian Century* (September 22–29, 1993) 896–99.

———. J.W. Carroll, C.S. Dudley, and W. McKinney, eds. *Studying Congregations: A New Handbook*. Nashville: Abingdon Press, 1998.

———. and W.C. Roof, eds. *Work, Family and Religion in Contemporary Society*. New York: Routledge, 1995.

"Are we Losing our Religion to Modern Life?" *The Press*, April 28, 2013, 24.

Attracting New Zealanders to Spiritual Life. Report prepared for the Presbyterian Church of Aotearoa New Zealand by A.C. Neilsen (NZ) Ltd., November, 2002.

Bacher, Robert, and Kenneth Inskeep. *Chasing Down a Rumor: The Death of Mainline Denominations*. Minneapolis: Augsburg, 2005.

Bandura, A. *Social Learning Theory*. Upper Saddle River: Prentice Hall, 1977. Translated by G. Bromiley. Edinburgh: T&T Clark, 1962.

Barth, Marcus. *Ephesians 1–3: The Anchor Bible*. New York: Doubleday, 1974.

Bass, Diana Butler. *Christianity after Religion*. New York: Harper Collins, 2012.

Bauman, Zygmunt. *Liquid Modernity*. Cambridge: Polity Press, 2000.

———. *Postmodernity and its Discontents*. Cambridge: Polity Press, 1997.

Beckford, J.A. *Religion in Advanced Industrial Societies*. London: Unwin Hyman, 1989.

Belich, James. *Paradise Reforged: A History of the New Zealanders*. London: Penguin Books, 2001.

Bellah, Robert N., et al. *Habits of the Heart: Individualism and Commitment in American Life*. Berkeley: University of California Press, 1985.

Bellamy, John, and Keith Castle. *Church Attendance Estimates: NCLS Occasional Paper 3*. Sydney: NCLS Research, 2004.

Bentley, P., T. Blombery, and P. Hughes. *Faith without the Church: Nominalism in Australian Culture*. Kew: Christian Research Association, 1992.

Berger, Peter L. *A Far Glory: The Quest for Faith in an Age of Credulity.* New York: Anchor Books, 1992.

―――. *A Rumour of Angels: Modern Society and the Rediscovery of the Supernatural.* New York: Doubleday & Co, 1969.

―――. *Invitation to Sociology.* Harmondsworth: Penguin, 1965.

―――. "Protestantism and the Quest for Certainty." *Christian Century* (August, 1998) 782–96.

―――. "Sociology: A Disinvitation." *Society* Vol. 30, No. 1 (November/December, 1992) 12–18.

―――. "The Desecularization of the World: A Global Overview." In *The Desecularization of the World: Resurgent Religion and World Politics*, ed. Peter L. Berger, 1–18. Grand Rapids: Eerdmans, 2001.

―――. *The Heretical Imperative.* New York: Anchor-Doubleday, 1979.

―――. B. Berger, and H. Kellner. *The Homeless Mind: Modernization and Consciousness.* New York: Random House, 1974.

"Beyond Belief—Why are we Turning Away from Religion?" *Sunday Star Times*, April 13, 2003, C-4.

Bibby, Reginald W. *Fragmented Gods: The Poverty and Potential of Religion in Canada.* Toronto: Stoddard Publishing, 1987.

―――. "Going, Going, Gone: The Impact of Geographical Mobility on Religious Involvement." *Review of Religious Research* Vol. 38, No. 4 (1997) 289–307.

―――. "Religion in the Canadian 1990s: The Paradox of Poverty and Potential." In *Church and Denominational Growth*, ed. D.A. Roozen and C.K. Hadaway, 278–92. Nashville: Abingdon, 1993.

―――. "Restless Gods and Restless Youth." Paper presented at the Canadian Sociological Association, Ottawa, May, 2009.

―――. *Restless Gods: The Renaissance of Religion in Canada.* Toronto: Stoddart, 2002.

―――. *There's Got to be More! Connecting Churches and Canadians.* Winfield: Wood Lake, 1995.

―――. and M.B. Brinkerhoff. "The Circulation of the Saints: A Study of People who Join Conservative Churches." *Journal for the Scientific Study of Religion* Vol. 12, No. 2 (1973) 273–82.

Black, A.W. "Australian Pentecostalism in Comparative Perspective." in *Religion in Australia: Sociological Perspectives*, ed. A.W. Black, 106–20. Sydney: Allen & Unwin, 1991.

Blockmuehl, Klaas. "Secularization and Secularism: Some Christian Considerations." *Evangelical Review of Theology* Vol. 10, No. 1 (1986) 50–73.

Bolitho, Elaine. *Meet the Baptists: Post-war Personalities and Perspectives.* Auckland: Christian Research Association, 1993.

―――. "In This World: Baptist and Methodist Churches in New Zealand 1948-1988." PhD thesis, Victoria University, 1992.

Bosch, David. *Transforming Mission.* Maryknoll: Orbis, 1991.

Bouma, Gary D. "Mapping Religious Contours." In P.H. Bayliss and Gary Bouma, *Religion in an Age of Change*, 5–11. Kew: CRA, 1999.

―――. and B.R. Dixon. *The Religious Factor in Australian Life.* Melbourne: MARC Australia, 1986.

Boyes, Nicola. "Most Avoid Church but still Believe." *New Zealand Herald*, January 7, 2006.

Bradley, R.L. "Who's in the Pews? An Interpretation of New Zealand Religious Census, Church Attendance and Survey Data, 1901 to 1991." MTh thesis, Australian College of Theology, 1992.

Breward, Ian. *A History of the Churches in Australasia.* Oxford: University Press, 2001.

Brierley, Peter. *A Global Analysis of the Christian Community to the Year 2010.* London: Monarch Books, 1998.

———. *Future Church: A Global Analysis of the Christian Community to the Year 2010.* Toronto: Monarch Books, 1998.

———. *Pulling out of the Nose Dive: A Contemporary Picture of Church Going—What the 2005 English Church Census Reveals.* London: Christian Research, 2006.

———. *The Tide is Running Out.* London: Christian Research, 2000.

———. ed. *UK Christian Handbook: Religious Trends 6.* London: Christian Research, 2006.

Brooks, N., and S. Currow. "Lifting the Lid on the New Zealand Church." In *Shaping a Future*, ed. Peter Kaldor, John Bellamy and Ruth Powell, A-1. Adelaide: Openbook Publishers, 1998.

Brown, Callum. *The Death of Christian Britain: Understanding Secularization, 1800–2000.* London: Routledge, 2009.

Brown, Colin. "The Charismatic Contribution." In *Religion in New Zealand Society*, ed. Peter Donovan and Brian Colless, 99–114. London: Continuum, 2006.

Bruce, S. *God is Dead: Secularization in the West.* Oxford: Blackwell Publishing, 2002.

———. *Religion in Modern Britain.* Oxford: Oxford University Press, 1995.

Brueggemann, Walter. *Texts under Negotiation: The Bible and Postmodern Imagination.* Minneapolis: Fortress, 1993.

Calvin, John. *Institutes of the Christian Religion.* Grand Rapids: Baker Academic, 1987.

Carroll, Jackson. *God's Potters: Pastoral Leadership and the Shaping of Congregations.* Grand Rapids: Eerdmans, 2006.

———. *Mainline to the Future: Congregations for the 21st Century.* Louisville: Westminster John Knox, 2000.

Carroll, John. *Ego and Soul: The Modern West and the Search for Meaning.* Sydney: Harper Collins, 1998.

Carson, D.A. *Becoming Conversant with the Emerging Church.* Grand Rapids: Zondervan, 2005.

Casanova, J. *Public Religions in the Modern World.* Chicago: Chicago University Press, 1994.

Castells, M. "Materials for an Exploration of the Network Society." *British Journal of Sociology* Vol. 51, No. 1 (January/March, 2000) 5–24.

———. ed. *The Rise of the Network Society: The Information Age—Economy, Society and Culture.* Vol. 1. Oxford: Blackwell, 1996.

Cavanagh, William T. *Migrations of the Holy: God, State and the Political Meaning of the Church.* Grand Rapids: Eerdmans, 2011.

Census of Population and Dwellings. NZ Department of Statistics, Wellington, New Zealand. 1926, 1961, 1996, 2006.

Chadwick, William. *Stealing Sheep: The Church's Hidden Problem of Transfer Growth.* Downers Grove: IVP, 2001.

Chaves, Mark. "Secularization as Declining Religious Authority." *Social Forces* Vol. 72, No. 3 (1994) 749–74.

———. "The Decline of American Religion?" (ARDA Guiding Paper Series). The Association of Religion Data Archives at Pennsylvania State University. Available at www.thearda.com/rrh/papers/guidingpapers.asp. 2011.

Chesterton, G.K. *Orthodoxy*. San Francisco: Ignatius Press, 1908, 1995.

"Christian Faith Losing out to other Religions." *The New Zealand Herald*, October 2, 2012.

Climmo, R., and D. Lattin. "Choosing My Religion." *American Demographics*. Available at http://www.demographics.com. April, 1999.

Cobb, Kelton. *The Blackwell Guide to Theology and Popular Culture*. Malden: Blackwell, 2005.

Coggins, Jim. "The State of the Canadian Church." Available at http://canadianchristianity.com /nationalupdates/2007/071213state.html. December, 2007.

"Conservative Churches Grew Fastest in 1990's." *New York Times*, September 18, 2002.

Cox, Harvey. *Fire from Heaven*. New York: Addison-Wesley, 1994.

———. "The Myth of the Twentieth Century: The Rise and Fall of 'Secularization.'" In *The Twentieth Century: A Theological Overview*, ed. G. Baum, 135–43. Maryknoll: Orbis, 1999.

Cray, Graham. *Youth Congregations and the Emerging Church*. Cambridge: Grove, 2002.

Davidson, Alan K. "Christianity and National Identity: The Role of the Churches in 'the Construction of Nationhood.'" In *The Future of Christianity*, ed. John Stenhouse and Brett Knowles, 16–38. Adelaide: ATF Press, 2004.

———. *Christianity in Aotearoa: A History of Church and Society in New Zealand*. Wellington: EFM, 1991.

———. and John Millbank. *For the Parish: A Critique of Fresh Expressions*. London: SCM, 2010.

———. and P.J. Lineham. *Transplanted Christianity: Documents Illustrating Aspects of New Zealand Church History*. Auckland: College Communications, 1987.

Davie, Grace. *Europe: the Exceptional Case*. London: Darton, Longman & Todd, 2002.

———. "From Obligation to Consumption." Paper delivered at the Joint Ecumenical Diocesan Schools Conference, South Wales, October 2003. Available at www.ctbi.org.uk/assembly/Davie.doc. October, 2003.

———. *Religion in Britain since 1945: Believing without Belonging*. Oxford: Blackwell Publishing, 1994.

———. *Religion in Modern Europe: A Memory Mutates*. Oxford: Blackwell, 2000.

"Death of the Samaritans." *Metro* (March 2001) 24–28.

de Certau, Michel. "The Weakness of Believing: From the Body to Writing, a Christian Transit." In *The Certau Reader*, ed. Graham Ward, 214–43. London: Routledge, 2000.

Detweiler, C., and B. Taylor. *A Matrix of Meanings: Finding God in Pop Culture*. Grand Rapids: Baker, 2003.

de Vaus, David. "Work, Sex and Religion." Paper presented at the Australian Values Study Seminar, Zadok Centre, Victoria, July 5, 1985, published by the Zadok Centre, August 1985.

Dickey, H. *What's Happening to the Children? A Nationwide Stocktake of the Church's Ministry to Children in 1991*. Auckland: Author, 1991.

"Diocese Near Collapse." *Otago Daily Times*, June 12, 2012, 1.

Donovan, Peter, and Brian Colless, eds. *Religion in New Zealand Society*. London: Continuum, 2006.

Drane, J. *The McDonaldization of the Church*. London: Darton, Longman & Todd, 2000.
Dulles, Avery. *Models of the Church*. New York, NY: Doubleday, 1974.
Durkheim, Emile. *The Elementary Forms of the Religious Life*. London: George Allen & Unwin, 1915.
Ebaugh, Helen. "Religion and the New Immigrants." In *Handbook of the Sociology of Religion*, ed. M. Dillon, 171–92. Cambridge: Cambridge University Press, 2003.
Edwards, Harry. *Sociology of Sport*. Homeward: Dorsey Press, 1973.
"Evangelism." *Barna Research Online*. Available at www.barna.org. 2013.
"Fan Fatigue Poses a Concern for Rugby Unions." Available at http://www.stuff.co.nz/sport/rugby/opinion/9037493. August 14, 2013.
Fer, Yannick. Unpublished paper presented at the International Society for the Sociology of Religion, Leipzig, July, 2007.
Fiddes, Paul. "The Theology of the Charismatic Movement." In *Strange Gifts*, ed. David Martin and Peter Mullin, 19–40. Oxford: Blackwell, 1984.
Finke, Roger, and Rodney Stark. *The Churching of America 1776–1990: Winners and Losers in our Religious Economy*. New York: Rutgers University Press, 1982.
———. *The Churching of America 1776–2005: Winners and Losers in our Religious Economy*. New York: Rutgers University Press, 2005.
Finney, J. *Finding Faith Today*. Swindon: British and Foreign Bible Society, 1992.
Flory, R.W., and D.E. Miller. "Expressive Communalism: The Embodied Spirituality of the Post-boomer Generations." *Congregations* (Fall, 2004) 31–35.
———. *GenX Religion*. New York: Routledge, 2000.
Fougere, Geoff. "Sport, Culture and Identity." In *Culture and Identity in New Zealand*, ed. D. Novitz and B. Willmott, 118–31. Wellington: Government Printing, 1989.
Frost, Michael. *Eyes Wide Open*. Sutherland: Albatross Books, 1998.
———. and Alan Hirsch. *The Shape of Things to Come*. Peabody: Hendrickson, 2003.
Gallup, George Jr., and J. Castelli. *The People's Religion: American Faith in the 90s*. New York: Macmillan Publishing Company, 1989.
Garrett, W.R. "Maligned Mysticism: The Maledicted Career of Troeltsch's Third Type." *Sociological Analysis* Vol. 36, No. 3 (1975) 205–23.
Geertz, Clifford. "Religion as a Cultural System." In *Anthropological Approaches to the Study of Religion*, ed. Michael Banton, 1–46. London: Tavistock, 1966.
"Generational Differences." *Barna Research Online*. Available at www.barna.org. 2013.
Gibbs, Eddie, and I. Coffey. *Church Next: Quantum Changes in Christian Ministry*. Leicester: IVP, 2000.
———. and Ryan Bolger. *Emerging Churches*. Grand Rapids: Baker, 2005.
Giddens, Anthony. "Living in a Post-Traditional Society." In *Reflexive Modernization: Politics, Tradition and Aesthetics in the Modern Social Order*, ed. U. Beck, A. Giddens and S. Lash, 56–109. Stanford: Stanford University Press, 1994.
———. *Modernity and Self Identity*. Stanford: Stanford University Press, 1991.
Gill, Robin. *A Vision for Growth*. London: SPCK, 1994.
———. *Churchgoing and Christian Ethics*. Cambridge: Cambridge University Press, 1999.
———. C.K. Hadaway, and P.L. Marler. "Is Religious Belief Declining in Britain?" *Journal of the Scientific Study of Religion* Vol. 37, No. 3 (1998) 507–16.
Gilling, B. "Convinced Christians Convincing Convinced Christians? A Study of Attenders at a Luis Palau Meeting." In *Rescue the Perishing: Comparative Perspectives on Evangelism and Revivalism. Waikato Studies in Religion*, ed. D. Pratt, 77–93. Vol. 1. Auckland: College Communications, 1989.

Global Christianity: A Report on the Size and Distribution of the World's Christian Population. Available at http://www.pewforum.org/Christian?Global-Christianity-exec.aspx. December 19, 2011.

"God is Alive." *MacLean's Magazine* (April 12, 1993) 32–50.

Goodhew, David, ed. *Church Growth in Britain, 1980 to the Present Day.* Farnham: Ashgate, 2012.

Greeley, Andrew. "The Persistence of Religion." *Cross Currents* Vol. 45, No. 1 (1995) 24–41.

Hadaway, C.K. *Church Growth Principles: Separating Fact from Fiction.* Nashville: Broadman Press, 1991.

———. and P.L. Marler. "All in the Family: Religious Mobility in America." *Review of Religious Research* Vol. 35, No. 2 (1993) 97–116.

———. P.L. Marler, and M. Chaves. "What the Polls Don't Show: A Closer Look at U.S. Church Attendance." *American Sociological Review* Vol. 58 (1993): 741–52.

Hammond, Philip E. *Religion and Personal Autonomy.* Columbia: University of South Carolina Press, 1992.

Hanciles, Jehu. *Beyond Christendom: Globalization, African Migration and the Transformation of the West.* Maryknoll: Orbis, 2008.

Harvey, Claire. "Free-range Soul Searching Replacing Organised Religion in NZ." *New Zealand Herald*, December 31, 2006.

Hastings, A. *A History of English Christianity, 1929–1985.* London: Collins, 1986.

Hastings, Ross. *Missional God, Missional Church: Hope for Re-evangelizing the West.* Downers Grove: IVP, 2012.

Hay, D., and K. Hunt. *Understanding the Spirituality of People who don't go to Church.* Cambridge: Cambridge University Press, 2000.

Heelas, P. "Introduction: Detraditionalization and its Rivals." In *Detraditionalization: Critical Reflections on Authority and Identity,* ed. P. Heelas, S. Lash and P. Morris, 1–20. Cambridge: Blackwell, 1996.

———. "The Spiritual Revolution: From 'Religion' to 'Spirituality.'" In *Religion in the Modern World: Traditions and Transformations,* ed. L. Woodhead, et. al, 357–77. London: Routledge, 2000.

———. *The New Age Movement.* Oxford: Blackwell, 1996.

Hertel, B.R. "Work, Family and Faith: Recent Trends." In *Work, Family and Religion in Contemporary Society,* ed. Nancy T. Ammermann and W.C. Roof, 81–121. New York: Routledge, 1995.

Hervieu-Léger, Daniéle. *Religion as a Chain of Memory.* Cambridge: Polity, 2000.

———. "The Twofold Limit of the Notion of Secularization." In *Peter Berger and the Study of Religion,* ed. Paul Heelas, David Marin, and Linda Woodhead 112–26. London: Routledge, 2001.

Hiebert, P. *Anthropological Reflections on Missiological Issues.* Grand Rapids: Baker Books, 1994.

Higgs, Robert J. *God in the Stadium: Sports and Religion in America.* Lexington: University of Kentucky Press, 1995.

Hill, Geoffrey. *Illuminating Shadows: The Mythic Power of Film.* London: Shambala, 1992.

Hill, Michael, and W. Zwaga. "Civil and Civic Engineering: A National Religions Consensus." *New Zealand Sociology* Vol. 2, No. 1 (1987) 25–35.

Hillard, D. "The Religious Crisis of the 1960s: The Experience of the Australian Churches." *The Journal of Religious History* Vol. 21, No. 2 (June, 1997) 210–23.
Hoge, David A., and Dean R. Roozen. *Understanding Church Growth and Decline.* Cleveland: Pilgrim Press, 1979.
———. Benton Johnson, and Donald A. Luidens. *Vanishing Boundaries: The Religion of Mainline Protestant Baby Boomers.* Louisville: Westminster John Knox, 1994.
Horrell, David. "'Race,' 'Nation,' 'People': Ethnic Identity-Construction in 1 Peter 2:9." *New Testament Studies* No. 58 (2011) 123–43.
Hout, M., and C.S. Fischer. "Why More Americans Have No Religious Preference: Politics and Generations." *American Sociological Review* Vol. 67, No. 2 (April, 2002) 15–190.
Hughes, P., et al. *Believe it or Not: Australian Spirituality in the 1990s.* Surrey Hills: CRA, 1995.
Hungsberger, B. "Apostasy: A Social Learning Perspective." *Review of Religious Research* Vol. 25, No. 1 (1983) 21–38.
Hunt, Stephen, Malcolm Hamilton, and Tony Walter, eds. "Tongues, Toronto, and the Millennium." In *Charismatic Christianity: Sociological Perspectives,* 1–19. Basingstoke: Palgrave MacMillan, 1997.
Hutchinson, W., and C. Wilson. *Let the People Rejoice: Billy Graham's 1959 New Zealand Crusade.* Wellington: Crusader Bookroom Society, 1959.
Inbody, Tyron. *The Faith of the Christian Church: An Introduction to Theology.* Grand Rapids: Eerdmans, 2005.
Inglehart, R. *Modernization and Postmodernization: Cultural, Economic and Political Change in 43 Societies.* Princeton: Princeton University Press, 1997.
International Social Science Survey Programme. Department of Marketing, Massey University, 1991, 1998, 2008.
Jackson, Bob. *Hope for the Church: Contemporary Strategies for Church Growth.* London: Church Publishing House, 2002.
Jackson, H. *Churches and People in Australia and New Zealand 1860–1930.* Wellington: Allen & Unwin, 1987.
Jacobs, D.R. "Contextualization in Mission." In *Toward the Twenty First Century in Christian Mission,* ed. J.M. Phillips and R.T. Coote, 235–44. Grand Rapids: Eerdmans, 1993.
Jamieson, Alan. *A Churchless Faith.* Wellington: Philip Garside Publishing, 2000.
Johnston, Robert. *Reel Spirituality.* Grand Rapids: Baker, 2000.
Johnstone, P. *Operation World: A Day to Day Guide to Praying for the World.* Kent: SIL Books, 1978.
Joseph, Tokerau. "Cracked Coconuts: An Exploration of Why Young Cook Islanders are Leaving Cook Island Congregations of the Presbyterian Church of Aotearoa New Zealand." MTh thesis, University of Otago, 2005.
Kaldor, Peter, et al. *Build My Church: Trends and Possibilities for Australian Churches.* Adelaide: Openbook Publishers, 1999.
———. *Winds of Change: The Experience of Church in a Changing Australia.* New York: Lancer, 1994.
———. J. Bellamy, and B. Hughes. "A Time of Opportunity." *Australian Ministry Digest* (July-September, 1999) 18–19.
———. et al. *Shaping a Future.* Adelaide: Open Book, 1998.
Kelly, Dean. *Why Conservative Churches are Growing.* New York: Harper & Row, 1972.

Kenneson, Philip D., and James Street. *Selling Out the Church: The Dangers of Church Marketing.* Eugene: Wipf & Stock, 2003.

Keysar, A., E. Mayer, and B. Kosmin. "No Religion: A Profile of America's Unchurched." *Public Perspective* (January/February, 2003) 40–44.

Kitchen, J. *The Postmodern Parish.* Herndon: Alban Institute, 2003.

Kreider, Alan. *The Change of Conversion and the Origin of Christendom.* London: Trinity Press International, 1999.

Küng, Hans. *The Church.* New York, NY: Image Books, 1967.

———. *Theology for the Third Millennium: An Ecumenical View.* New York: Doubleday, 1998.

Laidlaw, Chris. *Somebody Stole My Game.* Auckland: Hachette New Zealand Ltd., 2010.

Lindsay, D. Michael, and George Gallup Jr. *Surveying the Religious Landscape.* Dalton: Morehouse Group, 1999.

Lineham, Peter. "Three Types of Churches." In *Thinking Outside the Square: Church in Middle Earth*, ed. R. Bodde and H. Kempster, 199–224. Auckland: St. Columba's Press & Journeyings, 2003.

———. "Tongues Must Cease: The Brethren and the Charismatic Movement in New Zealand." *CBRF Journal* (December 1982) 7–51.

———. "World Cup Shows Rugby is our 'Surrogate Religion.'" Available at www.massey.ac.nz/massey-news/article. September 29, 2011.

Lofland, J., and Rodney Stark. "Becoming a World Saver: A Theory of Conversion to a Deviant Perspective." *American Sociological Review* Vol. 30 (1965) 862–75.

Luckmann, Thomas. *The Invisible Religion.* London: MacMillan, 1967.

Lyall, David. *Integrity of Pastoral Care.* London: SPCK, 2001.

Lyden, Joseph. *Film as Religion: Myths, Morals and Rituals.* New York: NYU Press.

Lynch, Gordon. *Understanding Religion and Popular Culture.* Oxford: Blackwell, 2005.

Lyon, D. *Jesus in Disneyland.* Oxford: Polity Press, 2000.

MacDonald, G. Jeffrey. "From U.S. Churches that are Growing, a Sound of Drums." *The Christian Science Monitor* (January, 2007) 1–10.

———. *Thieves in the Temple: The Christian Church and the Selling of the American Soul.* New York: Basic Books, 2010.

MacKay, H. *Turning Point: Australians Choosing Their Future.* Sydney: MacMillan, 1999.

Macpherson, Cluny, and La'avasa Macpherson. "Evangelical Religion among Pacific Island Migrants: New Faiths or Brief Diversions." *Journal of Ritual Studies* Vol.15, No. 2 (2001) 27–37.

Mansill, M. "PYM Snapshot Data, 2005." Wellington: Presbyterian Church of Aotearoa New Zealand, 2005.

Marler, P.L., and David A. Roozen. "From Church Tradition to Consumer Choice: The Gallup Surveys of the Unchurched American." In *Church and Denominational Growth*, ed. David A. Roozen and C. Kirk Hadaway, 253–77. Nashville: Abingdon, 1993.

———. and C. Kirk Hadaway. "Testing the Attendance Gap in a Conservative Church." *Sociology of Religion* Vol. 60, No. 2 (1999) 175–86.

Martin, David. *The Breaking of the Image: A Sociology of Christian Theory and Practice.* Oxford: Basil Blackwell, 1980.

———. *The Religious and the Secular.* New York: Schocken Books, 1969.

———. "Towards Eliminating the Concept of Secularisation." In *The Penguin Survey of the Social Sciences*, ed. J. Gould, 169–82. Harmondsworth: Penguin, 1965.

———. and C. Ostwalt. *Screening the Sacred: Religion, Myth and Ideology in Popular American Film*. Boulder: Westview Press, 1995.

Martyn, J. Louis. *Galatians: The Anchor Bible*. New York: Doubleday, 1997.

Massey, James Earl. "Reconciliation: Two Biblical Studies." In *A Mighty Long Journey: Reflections on Racial Reconciliation*, ed. T. George and R. Smith, Jr., 199–222. Nashville: Broadman and Holman, 2000.

Matthews, P. "The Afterlife." *The New Zealand Listener*, December, 1999, 17.

McBain, Douglas. *Fire over the Waters: Renewal among Baptists and Others from the 1960s to the 1990s*. London: Darton, Longman & Todd, 1997.

McGavran, Donald. *Understanding Church Growth*. Grand Rapids: Eerdmans, 1970.

McKay, Hugh. *Turning Point: Australians Choosing Their Future*. Sydney: MacMillan, 1999.

McKnight, Scott. "Five Streams of the Emerging Church." *Christianity Today*. Available at http://www.christianitytoday.com/ct/article_print.html?id=40534. February, 2007.

McLaren, Brian. *Reinventing Your Church*. Grand Rapids: Zondervan, 1998.

McLaren, David. *Mission Implausible: Restoring Credibility to the Church*. Milton Keynes: Paternoster, 2004.

Mead, Loren. *Once and Future Church: Reinventing the Congregation for a New Mission Frontier*. Herndon: Alban Institute, 1991.

Meeks, Wayne. *The First Urban Christians: The Social World of the Apostle Paul*. New Haven: Yale University Press, 1986.

"Members We Can Do Without." *New Zealand Baptist*, May, 1967, 2.

Micklethwaite, John, and Adrian Wooldridge. *God Is Back: How the Global Revival of Religion is Changing the World*. New York: Penguin, 2009.

Migliore, Daniel. *Faith Seeking Understanding: An Introduction to Christian Theology*. Grand Rapids: Eerdmans, 1991.

Miller, Donald E. *Reinventing American Protestantism*. Berkeley: University of California Press, 1997.

Miller, Gordon. "Leadership Letter." *World Vision Auckland* 157 (July/August, 1999) 1–6.

Mol, Hans. "Church Attendance Survey." *Research Project No. 4*. Christchurch: Dept. of Sociology, University of Canterbury, 1962.

———. *The Fixed and the Fickle: Religion and Identity in New Zealand*. Waterloo: Wilfrid Laurier University Press, 1982.

Moltmann, Jürgen. *The Church in the Power of the Spirit: A Contribution to Messianic Ecclesiology*. New York: Harper & Row, 1993.

———. *The Spirit of Life: A Universal Affirmation*. Minneapolis: Fortress, 1992.

Morgenthaler, S. *Worship Evangelism*. Grand Rapids: Zondervan, 1995.

Morris, Desmond. *The Soccer Tribe*. London: Jonathon Cape, 1981.

Moyers, Bill. "Joseph Campbell and the Power of Myth." PBS documentary series, 1988; released by Mystic Fire Video, Inc., 1997.

———. and Joseph Campbell. *The Power of Myth*. Norwell: Anchor, 1991.

Moynagh, Michael. *Changing World, Changing Church: New Forms of Church, Out-of-the-Pew Thinking, Initiatives that Work*. London: Monarch Books, 2001.

———. *Church for Every Context: An Introduction to Theology and Practice.* London: SCM, 2012.
———. *Emergingchurch.intro.* Oxford: Monarch Books, 2004.
Naylor, T.H., and William L. Willimon. *Downsizing the U.S.A.* Grand Rapids: Eerdmans, 1997.
Newbigin, Lesslie. *A Word in Season.* Grand Rapids: Eerdmans, 1996.
———. "The Enduring Validity of Cross-Cultural Mission." *International Bulletin of Missionary Research* 12 (1988) 50–53.
———. *The Gospel in a Pluralist Society.* Grand Rapids: Eerdmans, 1989.
New Zealand Families Today. Wellington: Government Press, 2004.
"New Zealand's Most Trusted People." Available at http://www.readersdigest.co.nz/new-zealand-most-trusted-people-2013. 2013.
Ng, Thong. "A Focus on the Fastest Growing Baptist Churches in New Zealand." Thesis, NZ Baptist College, Auckland, 1984.
Niebuhr, H. Richard. *Christ and Culture.* New York: Harper Brothers, 1953.
Novak, Michael. *The Joy of Sports.* New York: Basic Books 1976.
Oates, Joyce Carol. "Lives of the Latter-day Saints." *Times Literary Supplement*, July 12, 1996, 9.
Ostwalt, C. *Secular Steeples: Popular Culture and the Religious Imagination.* Harrisburg: Trinity Press International, 2003.
Parks, Ted, and Tim Stafford. "The Shockingly Ordinary Purpose-Driven Life of Rick Warren," *Christianity Today.* Available at www.christianitytoday.com/tc/2003/006/4.16.html. November/December, 2003.
Parrott, R., and R.D. Perrin. "The New Denominations." *Christianity Today* (March 11, 1991) 29–33.
Percy, Martin. *Engaging with Contemporary Culture: Christianity, Theology and the Concrete Church.* Aldershot: Ashgate, 2005.
———. *Power and the Church: Ecclesiology in an Age of Transition.* London: Cassell, 1998.
———. *The Salt of the Earth: Religious Resilience in a Secular Age.* London: Sheffield Academic Press, 2001.
———. "Things are not as Bad as you Think: Religion in a Secular Age." *Ministry Today* 22 (October, 2002) 9–12.
Perrin, R.D., P. Kennedy, and D.E. Miller. "Examining the Sources of Conservative Church Growth: Where Are the New Evangelical Movements Getting their Numbers?" *Journal for the Scientific Study of Religion* Vol. 36, No. 1 (1997) 71–80.
Perry, Alan C., and Paul E. Webster. *The Religious Factor in New Zealand Society.* Palmerston North: Alpha Publications, 1989.
———. *What Difference Does It Make? Values and Faith in a Shifting Culture.* Palmerston North: Alpha Publications, 1992.
Phan, Peter C. "Social Sciences and Ecclesiology." In *Theology and the Social Sciences*, ed. Michael Barnes, 56–72. Maryknoll: Orbis, 2001.
Pilarzyk, T. "Conversion and Alternation Processes in the Youth Culture." *Pacific Sociological Review* 21 (1978) 379–405.
Pope John Paul II. *Redemptor Hominis.* Encyclical No. 21.2, March 4, 1979.
Posterski, D.C., and I. Baker. *Where's a Good Church?* Winfield: Wood Lake Books, 1993.

Powell, Ruth, and Kathy Jacka. "Moving Beyond Forty Years of Missing Generations." NCLS Occasional Paper 10. Sydney: NCLS Research, 2008.
Presbyterian Church of New Zealand, Reports of Committees to the General Assembly. Wellington: PCNZ, 1973, 1974.
Price, Joseph L. "An American Apotheosis: Sports as Popular Religion." In *Religion and Popular Culture in America*, ed. Bruce David Forbes and Jeffrey H. Mahan, 195–212. Berkeley: University of California Press, 2000.
———. "The Super Bowl as Religious Festival." In *Sport and Religion*, ed. S. J. Hoffman, 13–15. Champaign: Human Kinetics Books, 1992.
Proceedings of the General Assembly of the Presbyterian Church. Wellington: Presbyterian Church in New Zealand, 1960.
Provincial Commission on the Charismatic Renewal: Proceedings of the General Synod of the Church of the Province of New Zealand, Christchurch, 1976.
Putnam, Robert. *Bowling Alone: The Collapse and Revival of American Community.* New York: Touchstone, 2000.
Redding, Graham. Inaugural lecture, School of Ministry, Presbyterian Church of Aotearoa New Zealand, Knox College, February, 2005. Available at http://www.roxborogh.com /REFORMED/calvin.htm. February, 2005.
"Religious Congregations and Membership: 2000." Available at http://www.glenmary.org/grc /RCMS_2000/findings.htm. December, 2000.
Rhoads, David. *The Challenge of Diversity: The Witness of Paul and the Gospels.* Minneapolis: Fortress, 1996.
Richardson, J.T. "Conversion to New Religions: Secularization or Re-enchantment." In *The Sacred in a Secular Age*, ed. P. Hammond, 104–21. Berkeley: University of California Press, 1985.
Richey, R. "Denominations and Denominationalism: An American Morphology." In *Reimagining Denominationalism: Interpretive Essays*, ed. Robert Mullin and Robert Richey, 74–97. New York: Oxford University Press, 1994.
Roberts, Richard. "Theology and the Social Sciences." In *The Modern Theologians: An Introduction to Christian Theology in the Twentieth Century*, ed. David F. Ford, 370–88. Oxford: Blackwell, 1997.
Robertson, Murray. "Presidential Ramblings." *NZ Baptist* (October 2008) 5–6.
Robinson, Martin, and Dwight Smith. *Invading Secular Space.* London: Monarch Books, 2003.
Romanos, Joseph. *The Judas Game: The Betrayal of New Zealand Rugby.* Wellington: Darius Press, 2002.
Roof, Wade Clark. *A Generation of Seekers: The Spiritual Journeys of the Baby Boom Generation.* San Francisco: Harper Collins, 1993.
———. "God is in the Details: Reflections on Religion's Public Presence in the United States in the Mid-1990s." *Sociology of Religion* Vol. 57, No. 2 (1996) 149–62.
———. *Spiritual Marketplace: Baby Boomers and the Remaking of American Religion.* Princeton: Princeton University Press, 1999.
———. "Toward the Year 2000: Reconstructions of Religious Space." *The Annals of the American Academy of Political and Social Sciences* 527 (May, 1993) 155–70.
———. and W. McKinney. *American Mainline Religion: Its Changing Shape and Future.* New Brunswick: Rutgers University Press, 1987.

———. and D.R. Hoge. "Church Involvement in America: Social Factors Affecting Membership and Participation." *Review of Religious Research* Vol. 21, No. 4 (1980) 405–26.

———. Jackson W. Carroll, and David A. Roozen. *The Post-War Generation and Establishment Religion*. Boulder: Westview Press, 1998.

Roozen, David A., and C. Kirk Hadaway, eds. *Church and Denominational Growth*. Nashville: Abingdon, 1993.

Roxburgh, Alan. "Pastoral Role in the Missionary Congregation." In *Church between Gospel and Culture*, ed. R. Hunsberger and C. Van Gelder, 319–37. Grand Rapids: Eerdmans, 1996.

———. *The Missionary Congregation: Leadership and Liminality*. Harrisburg: Trinity Press International, 1997.

———. and M. Scott Boren. *Introducing the Missional Church: What it Is, Why It Matters, How to Become One*. Grand Rapids: Baker, 2009.

Schaller, Lyle. *From Geography to Affinity*. Nashville: Abingdon, 2003.

———. *Tattered Trust: Is there Hope for your Denomination?* Nashville: Abingdon, 1996.

Schwartz, Christian A. *Natural Church Development: A Guide to Eight Essential Qualities of Healthy Churches*. Carol Stream: Church Smart Resources, 1996.

———. *Paradigm Shift in the Church*. Carol Stream: Church Smart Resources, 1999.

Sherkat, Dean. "Counterculture or Continuity? Competing Influences on Baby Boomer Religious Orientations and Participation." *Social Forces* Vol. 76, No. 3 (March, 1998) 1087–115.

Smail, Tom. "The Renewal of the Anglican Church: A Personal Account." *Anglicans for Renewal* (Summer, 1996) 6.

Snodgrass, Klyne. *Ephesians: NIV Application Commentary*. Grand Rapids: Zondervan, 1996.

"Soul of Britain with Michael Buerk: What do People Believe Today?" Available at www.facingthechallenge.org/soul1.htm. June 4, 2000.

"Sports Clubs Struggling." *Christchurch Press*, August 6, 2004, A–4.

Stackhouse, Max. "Contextualization, Contextuality, and Contextualization." In *One Faith, Many Cultures: Inculturation, Indigenization, and Contextualization*, ed. R.O. Costas, 3–13. Maryknoll: Orbis, 1988.

Stark, Rodney, and Roger Finke. *Act of Faith: Explaining the Human Side of Religion*. Berkeley: University of California Press, 2000.

———. and L.R. Iannaccone. "A Supply-side Reinterpretation of the 'Secularization' of Europe." *Journal for the Scientific Study of Religion* Vol. 33, No. 3 (1994) 230–52.

"State of the Union: Part 2." *New Zealand Herald*, May 19, 2010.

Stenhouse, John, Brett Knowles, and Anthony Wood. *The Future of Christianity: Historical, Sociological, Political and Theological Perspectives from New Zealand*. Adelaide: ATF Press, 2004.

Stookey, Steve. "Post-denominationalism." *Baptist Press*. Available at http://jmm.aaa.net.au /articles/8255.htm. August 12, 1998.

Sweet, Leonard I. *Aquachurch*. Loveland: Group Publishing, 1999.

———. *SoulTsunami*. Grand Rapids: Zondervan, 1999.

Taylor, Charles. *A Secular Age*. Cambridge: Harvard University Press, 2007.

Taylor, Steve. "A Kiwi Emerging Church: Yeah, Right!" In *New Vision New Zealand: 2008*, 311–19. Auckland: Vision Network, 2008.

Thomas, R. *Counting People In: Changing the Way we Think about Membership and the Church*. London: SPCK, 2003.
Thompson, D. "Just how Alive are our Churches in New Zealand?" *Challenge Weekly* (July 16, 1982) 15–17.
Thumma, Scott L. "Methods for Congregational Study." In *Studying Congregations: A New Handbook*, ed. Nancy T. Ammermann, J.W. Carroll, C.S. Dudley, and W. McKinney, 196–239. Nashville: Abingdon, 1998.
Tiatia, Jemaima. *Caught Between Cultures: A New Zealand Born Pacific Islands Perspective*. Auckland: Christian Research Association, 1998.
Tillich, Paul. *The Shaking of the Foundations*. New York: Scribners, 1948.
Tiplady, Richard. *World of Difference: Global Mission at the Pic 'n' Mix Counter*. Carlisle: Paternoster, 2003.
Torrance, Thomas F. *Atonement: The Person and Work of Christ*. Downers Grove: IVP, 2009.
Traviasano, R. "Alternation and Conversion as Qualitatively Different Transformations." In *Social Psychology through Symbolic Interaction*, ed. G.P. Stone and H. Faberman, 237–48. New York: John Wiley & Sons, 1970.
Troeltsch, Ernst. *The Social Teachings of the Churches*. Translated by O. Wyon. 2 Vols. London: George Unwin Ltd., 1931.
"Turbulent Priests." *Christchurch Press*, December 17, 2002, A–8.
Turner, Steve. *The Gospel According to the Beatles*. Louisville: Westminster John Knox, 2006.
"Two Worlds of School Rugby: Five Schools Spending $400,000 on 1st XVs." *New Zealand Herald*, August 12, 2013.
Van Engen, Charles. *Mission on the Way*. Grand Rapids: Baker, 1996.
van Hoozer, Kevin. *Is there a Meaning in this Text?* Grand Rapids: Zondervan, 1998.
———. "On the Very Idea of a Theological System: An Essay in Aid of Triangulating Scripture, Church and World." In *Always Reforming*, ed. A.T.B. McGowan, 134–74. Downers Grove: IVP, 2006.
Veitch, James. "Christianity: Protestants since the 1960s." In *Religions of New Zealanders*, ed. P. Donovan, 88–101. 2nd ed. Palmerston North: Dunmore Press, 1996.
———. "1961–1990: Towards the Church for a New Era." In *Presbyterians in Aotearoa*, ed. Dennis McEldowney, 142–82. Wellington: Presbyterian Church of New Zealand, 1990.
Volf, Miroslav. *After Our Likeness: The Church as the Image of the Trinity*. Grand Rapids: Eerdmans, 1998.
Wagner, Peter. *Our Kind of People: The Ethical Dimensions of Church Growth in America*. Atlanta: John Knox Press, 1979.
Walker, Andrew. "Thoroughly Modern: Sociological Reflections on the Charismatic Movement from the End of the Twentieth Century." In *Charismatic Christianity: Sociological Perspectives*, ed. S. Hunt, M. Hamilton and T. Walter, 17–42. London: MacMillan, 1991.
Walls, Andrew. *The Missionary Movement in Christian History*. Edinburgh: T&T Clark, 1996.
Walter, Tony. "War Grave Pilgrimage." In *Pilgrimage in Popular Culture*, ed. I. Reader and T. Walter, 63–91. London: MacMillan, 1993.
Ward, Kevin. "Losing My Religion? An Examination of Church Decline, Growth and Change in New Zealand, 1960 to 1999." PhD thesis, University of Otago, 2003.

———. "Rugby and Church: Worlds in Conflict?" *Reality* 53 (October/November, 2002) 26–30.

Warner, Robert S. "Work in Progress toward a New Paradigm for the Sociological Study of Religion in the United States." *American Journal of Sociology* Vol. 98, No. 5 (1993) 1044–93.

Watkin, Clare. "Organizing the People of God: Social Science Theories of Organization in Ecclesiology." *Theological Studies* 52 (1991) 689–711.

Weber, Max. *The Sociology of Religion*. Boston: Beacon Press, 1963.

Webster, A. *Spiral of Values*. Hawera: Alpha Publications, 2001.

Welbourn, F.B., and B.A. Ogot. *A Place to Feel at Home*. London: Oxford University Press, 1966.

Wells, David F. *The Courage to Be Protestant: Truth-Lovers, Marketers and Emergents in the Postmodern World*. Grand Rapids: Eerdmans, 2008.

Wernblad, Annette. *The Passion of Martin Scorcese: A Critical Study of the Films*. Jefferson: McFarland, 2010.

West, Brad. *Down the Road: Exploring Backpackers and Independent Travel*. Reston: API Press, 2005.

Williams, Rowan. *Mission Shaped Church*. London: Church Publishing House, 2004.

Willmer, H. "The Collapse of Congregations." *Anvil* Vol. 18, No. 4 (2000) 249–57.

Winter, Gibson. *The Suburban Captivity of the Churches*. New York: Doubleday, 1961.

"Withering Belief." *The Christchurch Press*, April 20, 2007, A–8.

Woodhead, L. *Peter Berger and the Study of Religion*. London: Routledge, 2001.

———. and P. Heelas. *Religion in Modern Times: An Interpretive Anthology*. Oxford: Blackwell Publishers, 2000.

Worsfold, J.E. *A History of the Charismatic Movements in New Zealand*. Bradford: Puritan Press, 1974.

Wright, N.T. "Whence and Whither Pauline Studies in the Life of the Church?" In *Jesus, Paul and the People of God*, ed. N. Perrin and R.B. Hays, 115–60. Downers Grove: IVP, 2011.

Wright, R. *The Outsider*. New York: Harper and Row, 1953.

Wuthnow, Robert. *After Heaven*. Berkeley: University of California Press, 1998.

———. *After the Baby Boomers: How Twenty and Thirty Somethings are Shaping the Future of American Religion*. Princeton: Princeton University Press, 2007.

———. *All in Sync: How Music and Art are Revitalizing American Religion*. Berkeley: University of California Press, 2003.

———. *Christianity in the 21st Century*. New York: Oxford University Press, 1993.

———. *Experimentation in American Religion*. Berkeley: University of California Press, 1978.

———. *Loose Connections: Joining Together in America's Fragmented Communities*. Cambridge: Harvard University Press, 2002.

———. *Sharing the Journey*. New York: Free Press, 1994.

Yoder, John Howard. *Essays Ecumenical and Ecclesiological*. Scottdale: Herald Press, 1998.

Young, L.A., ed. *Rational Choice Theory and Religion: Summary and Assessment*. New York: Routledge, 1997.

www.ingramcontent.com/pod-product-compliance
Lightning Source LLC
Chambersburg PA
CBHW070338230426
43663CB00011B/2371